השכל

Mussar Haskel

COURAGE TO CHANGE

Ethical discourses written by
the students of Yeshiva Toras Chaim
based on shmuessen given by their Rabbeim

Yeshiva Toras Chaim Toras Emes
www.ytcteam.org
ISBN: 978-0-615-66741-6

Interior layout by Avrohom Eliezer Friedman

Cover design by Ethan Berner
Phone: 301-785-4836
Email: info@ethanberner.com

MUSSAR HASKEL: COURAGE TO CHANGE

What is Marvin remembered for?

His love of Torah. Dedication to family. Passion for education. Entrepreneurial spirit. Positive approach to difficult situations. Kindness towards others. Talent for storytelling. Genuine enthusiasm for life. Enjoyment of classical music. *And those were just the qualities people knew about.*

He was one of the first people to see the inaugural issue of *Mussar Haskel* in 1995 on *Parashas* Chayei Sarah. His enthusiasm, radiance, and passion for the project – and its inherent mission to publicize Torah, the yeshiva, and integrity – were contagious.

Torah infused him with life. When his body was riddled with cancer and he was still attending shul, he notably remarked how the holiness of Torah would permeate his body and temporarily relieve his pain.

He battled cancer with exemplary courage – never to challenge Hashem's decree – but to continue living life to fulfill *mitzvos.*

RABBI A. HENACH LEIBOWITZ

67-18 GROTON STREET

FOREST HILLS, N.Y. 11375

Rabbinical Seminary of America
Dean

ראש הישיבה
ישיבת רבנו ישראל מאיר הכהן
בעל ,,חפץ חיים'' זצ"ל

מה מאוד שמחתי לראות תלמידי ישיבת תורת חיים
דמיאמי רכשו לבם דבר טוב לכתוב ולסדר בעריכה יפה
שיחות מוסריות מיוסד ע"פ מה ששמעו מדי שבוע בשבוע
בכותלי בית מדרש, מרבותם, שהם תלמידי ולהפיצם
לזכות את הרבים.

מה מאד נחוץ בדורנו אנו לעורר הלבבות בעניני תורה
ומוסר ע"פ עמקי דברי חז"ל ולהאיר חשכת הגלות במאור
תורתינו ובמיוחד לאלה השואפים לעלי' רוחנית.

השיחות הללו המופיעות בספר זה מיועדות במיוחד לאלה
המוכנים להשקיע עיון מרץ וזמן להתבונן בהן ולהכניסם
בלב פנימה.

מפאת טרדותי הסובבים אותי לא יכולתי לעיין בדבריהם
כדבעי ולתת הסכמה עלי', אבל ברכתי נתונה להם שתזכו
לזכות את הרבים שיהא שם שמים מתאהב ומתקדש ע"י
לקרב לבבות איש אל אחיו ולאביהם שבשמים.

[handwritten text]

אלתר חנוך העניך
באאמו"ר הגר"חד זצוק"ל הכהן לייבאוויטש

This approbation was written for and originally
printed in the first edition of Courage to Change
published in 1998.

YESHIVA
TORAS CHAIM
TORAS EMES

We greet with great joy and pride, the newly revised edition of Courage to Change. Written originally by our students Chaim Hirsch and Dovid Mandel, and edited by Dr. Allan Jacob, the first edition of Courage to Change, which is based on the weekly Mussar Shmuessen given by the Toras Chaim Rabbeim, was printed in 1998. Since that time, many things have changed. Yeshiva Toras Chaim Dr. Abe Chames High School has grown from a young school with a small student body, to one of the largest and most highly regarded Yeshivas outside the New York metropolitan area. Likewise, our former students have grown from young and inexperienced teenagers into Rabbeim and community leaders. As such, the need was felt for a newly revised and larger Courage to Change - one which would reflect the growth and maturity of our Yeshiva. Coordinated once again by Chaim Hirsch, this newly-revised edition will inspire, enlighten and motivate you to make the necessary changes to bring meaning and Kedusha into your lives.

It is very appropriate that this edition, as well as the original edition, is dedicated to the memory of Dr. Marvin Hirsch, of blessed memory. During his lifetime, Dr. Hirsch demonstrated many of the Mussar concepts found in these Seforim. Although he left us at a relatively early age, his legacy of chesed and courage continues to inspire, and his good deeds will endure forever.

May HaKadosh Boruch Hu bless all those who worked tirelessly to bring this Sefer to fruition, with bracha and hatzlacha in everything they do.

Rabbi Binyomin
Luban
Rosh HaYeshiva

Rabbi Yisroel Y.
Niman
Rosh HaYeshiva

Rabbi Mordechai
Palgon
Rosh HaYeshiva

305.944.5344 WWW.YTCTEAM.ORG KLURMAN CAMPUS 1025 NE MIAMI GARDENS DRIVE NORTH MIAMI BEACH, FL 33179

Rabbi Dovid Leibowitz זצוק"ל
Founding Rosh HaYeshiva 1933-1941

Rabbi A. Henach Leibowitz זצוק"ל
Rosh HaYeshiva 1941-2008

Rabbi Dovid Harris
Rosh HaYeshiva

Rabbi Akiva Grunblatt
Rosh HaYeshiva

ישיבת רבנו ישראל מאיר הכהן זצוק"ל
בעל ה"חפץ חיים"

י"ב מנחם אב , יום ג' לפר' ואתחנן, תשע"ב לפ"ק

שמחנו לראות גליונות מאירים מספר "Courage to Change" כרך ב', אשר חיברו תלמידי ישיבת תורת חיים דמיאמי, שרחשו לבם דבר טוב להוציא לאור את שיחות המוסר שנמסרו בישיבה הק' הנ"ל מאת ראשי הישיבה וההנהלה

הספר נכתב בשפה המדוברת במדינתנו ובעהשי"ת תהי' לתועלת גדולה לכל המעניינים בו. ואין ספק שחיבור כזה נחוץ בדורנו, שלימוד המוסר צריך חיזוק ובפרט להבין בעומק חכמת המוסר.

למרות שמחמת טרדות הישיבה לא הי' לנו פנאי לעיין בו כדבעי מ"מ אנו מכירים היטב מנהיגי ישיבת תורת חיים דהם תלמידי חכמים מופלגים ובעלי מוסר, ואנו מברכים אותם מעומק לבבנו שימשיכו לזכות את הרבים, וימשיכו עוד להפיץ מעיינותיהם חוצה להגדיל תורה ולהאדירה.

הכו"ח לכבוד התורה ולומדי',

עקיבא אליהו גרונבלאט

דוד הריס

Table of Contents

Introduction

By Rabbi Bentzion Chait
Founding *Rosh HaYeshiva*

Yeshiva Toras Chaim was founded in 1984. It was very small and new, yet it grew and has had *hatzlachah* beyond anyone's wildest imagination. I have often wondered why and how this happened. There are many contributing factors. The most powerful one is that of *zechus avos* – ancestral merit.

Rabbeinu Yonah, in his commentary to *Pirkei Avos* (2:2), says, "And all that you do, Hashem will cause you to succeed in the merit of your fathers who assist you." When we act on behalf of others with sincerity, we are aided with incredible guidance. Forces behind the scenes assist and enable us to accomplish far more than we could ever accomplish on our own.

We have been blessed with a *Rebbe – Hagaon HaRav* Alter Chanoch Henach Leibowitz, *zt"l*, who was the quintessential *osek betzorchei tzibur* – leader involved in the needs of the community – and fully invested in *harbotzas haTorah* – the dissemination of Torah. He instilled the essential ingredients of Torah leadership into his *talmidim* through his intense focus on Mussar – character development. These *talmidim* are now the heads of Yeshiva Toras Chaim. They have evoked *zechus avos* by their love and devotion to their talmidim and to our cherished *Mesorah*.

In addition, we have been blessed with *talmidim* who continue in the glorious path of Torah leadership and intense focus on character development. One of these outstanding *talmidim* is one of the founders of the original *Mussar Haskel* and project manager for this *sefer*, R' Chaim Hirsch, the son of Dr. Marvin Hirsch, *a"h*. Inspired by the lofty *middos tovos* of his father and the leadership of his *rabbeim*, R' Chaim embodies a love for his heritage and a thirst for personal growth through *Mussar*. This special *sefer* is dedicated to perpetuate the memory of Dr. Marvin Hirsch, Raphael Mordechai ben Yitzchak, *a"h*. May R' Chaim and his family continue to engender the force of *zechus* avos and be successful in all that they do *l'Shem Shamayim*. May they continue to inspire others to sanctify Hashem's name through their community involvement.

I am very pleased to see that the legacy of Dr. Hirsch lives on.

Rabbi Bentzion Chait

Foreword &
Acknowledgements

A *mussar* discourse delivered by *Rabbeim*... adapted by students, undergoing extensive editing and discussion... distributed weekly to shuls throughout South Florida... faxed and emailed world-wide... is this a project for high school students?

In our Yeshiva, it is.

Known as *Mussar Haskel* at its inception, dedicated students collaborated to document, publish, and distribute weekly *Divrei* Torah adapted from the ethical discourses – *mussar shmuessen* – given by their *Rabbeim*. The process of writing, editing, publishing, and distributing can be overwhelming and requires a team.

But where did it all begin?

With a *Rebbe* who had a vision and high school students who had the passion to execute it.

Towards the end of the 1994-1995 school year, a *Rebbe* sat with one of his *talmidim*, discussing several potential projects for the following school year. One of those projects involved high school students documenting the shmuessen delivered by the *Rabbeim*, then disseminating these *Divrei* Torah to the local shuls in South Florida.

On *Parashas* Chayei Sarah of the following school year, the project officially began. Two students, Dovid Mandel and Chaim Hirsch, drafted the very first issue of what would soon become known as *Mussar Haskel*.

Within weeks, the team grew – writers, editors, graphic designers, and computer experts were assembled as the project excelled with exciting momentum. It represented the model form of a team project – *Rabbeim*, students, general studies teachers, and working professionals collaborating for the single goal of publicizing *Divrei* Torah in South Florida. These individuals who contributed over the course of many years are: Ari Averbuch, Yitzy Becker, Avraham Benguigui, Yacov Benzaquen, Mordechai Bernstein, Moshe Bernstein, Tuvia Brander, Shaya Caro, Eliezer Casper, Jonathan Dahari, Micah Engel, Yoni Escovitz, Avi Gantz, Mr. Michael Gilchrist, Gabi Gittleson, Eliyahu Glatt, Yehoshua Dov Glatt, Chaim Goldenberg, Yehuda Goldenberg, Shlomo Grabina, Meir Grunblatt, Yosef Herman, Chaim Hirsch, Yedidiya Hirschhorn, Zalmi Kahn, Mr. Ari Kirschenbaum, Avrohom Lampert, Avi Mandel, Dovid Mandel, Yirmi Paritzky, Noach Rabovsky, Yubie Richt, Aryeh Rosenbaum, Binyamin Rosenbaum, Sholom Rosenson, Avrohom Sebrow, Yekusiel Sebrow, Mr. Daniel Stahl, Yitzy Turk, Shmuel Wasser, and Moshe Aryeh Yachnes.

One of the most critical components to the early success of *Mussar Haskel* and consistently throughout the years was general editor Dr. Allan Jacob. From the infancy days of the project and for years to follow, Dr. Jacob gave the students his full cooperation, instilling confidence in them, and wholeheartedly supporting their efforts. He spent many hours of his limited time editing and re-editing the initial drafts, tailoring them for publication. Words alone cannot adequately express proper gratitude for his dedication and efforts.

The project reached an exciting milestone in the fall of 1998 with the publication of the original *Courage to Change*, a compilation and celebration of the first three years of *Mussar Haskel* essays. Countless people contributed to the effort, including underlying sponsors. These supporters included Mr. and Mrs. Joel Brauser, Dr. and Mrs. Alvin Cohen, Mr. and Mrs. Ron Engel, Mr. and Mrs. Joe Finkelstein, Mr. and Mrs. Herb Fishler, Mrs. Corinne Hirsch Blumenstein, Rabbi and Mrs. Chaim Mandel, Mr. and Mrs. Jeff Milrad, and Dr. and Mrs. David Tuchinsky. Their financial and moral support was instrumental in catapulting the project to a new and exciting level.

Over the span of 17 years since the commencement of *Mussar Haskel*, the foundation and core of the project were – and continue to be – the *Rabbeim*. Their wisdom, insight, and hashkafa craft the groundwork for the students and their futures. The *Rabbeim* whose shmuessen were adapted and are included in this *sefer* are: Rabbi Yehuda Alber, Rabbi Avrohom Anton, Rabbi Yehuda Bergida, Rabbi Bentzion Chait, Rabbi Yaakov Dreyfuss, Rabbi Hillel Dudovitz, Rabbi Yaakov Flamholtz, Rabbi Yaakov Fried, Rabbi Chaim Glazer, Rabbi Avi Goldman, Rabbi Noam Grossman, Rabbi Akiva Grunblatt, Rabbi Naftali Kalter, Rabbi Dovid Klaver, Rabbi Binyomin Luban, Rabbi Chaim Mandel, Rabbi Dovid May, Rabbi Yisroel Niman, Rabbi Mordechai Palgon, Rabbi Zev Pam, Rabbi Yehoshua Schloss, Rabbi Shlomo Schwartz, and Rabbi Dovid Sharfman.

In compiling this *sefer* – consisting of select essays originally published between 1995 and 2012 – it became apparent that while there were an abundance of essays written during the school year *parashiyos* (e.g., *Sefer Bereishis*, *Sefer Shemos*, and *Sefer Vayikra*), there were several *parashiyos* absent due to the summer vacation. To fill this void, many of the Bais Medrash Zichron Ezra students contributed by drafting select shmuessen from *Chidushei HaLev*, written by our Rosh HaYeshiva, Rabbi

Binyomin Luban, on *Sefer* Bamidbar and *Sefer* Devarim. Spearheaded and managed by Beis Medrash student Yehoshua D. Grodko, these contributing students are: Avi Arnold, Daniel Epstein, Yoni Ghalili, Yehoshua D. Grodko, Mordechai Gruenstein, Tzvi Hertzberg, Ezriel Hoenig, Ashi Kasirer, Nadav Uriel Levine, Yisroel Mahgerefteh, and Shlomo Zalman Tropper. Their dedication, efforts, and assistance were critical in completing the *sefer* to include the summer *parashiyos*.

Several additional people invested countless hours into making the current book a success – the project would have stalled without their herculean efforts. Seena Eisenman graciously used her editing skills to refine numerous essays, Ilana Falick brilliantly added titles and filled the role as copy editor, Avrohom Eliezer and Leah Friedman were proficient in various project management logistics, Daniel Stahl and Samantha Hirsch were instrumental in refining the finished product with polished editing, Shira Sipper and Ruchie Schwartz spent countless hours managing the *parasha* dedications, and Ethan Berner used his talent and graphic art skills to design the front and back cover.

Mussar Haskel, and more specifically, this robust edition of *Courage to Change*, represents a signature landmark in the Yeshiva's growth. Not your typical *Divrei* Torah *sefer* on the weekly *parasha*, this book is the token symbol of hard work, collaboration, and teamwork among *Rabbeim*, students, and professionals. Coordinating a project of this magnitude over the course of many years with a constantly changing student roster is challenging and rare. We are privileged and fortunate that it is a reality in our Yeshiva. We hope you find the words of Torah in the coming pages refreshing, inspiring, and thought provoking. It is with this sentiment that we hope our continued emphasis on *mussar* imbues the highest ethical and character standards into our students, maximizing their potential as proud leaders of the next generation.

We graciously thank and pay tribute
to our generous sponsors who have each
dedicated one *Sefer* of the five *Chumashim:*

SEFER BEREISHIS
Berner, Hirsch, Lynn & Stoller Families

SEFER SHEMOS
Levine, Sipper, and Zisquit Families

SEFER VAYIKRA
Sobol Family

SEFER BAMIDBAR
Grodko Family

SEFER DEVARIM
Milrad Family

YOMIM TOVIM
Chames Family

SEFER BEREISHIS

Dedicated in memory of

Ruth and Harold Lynn
Raizel bas Moshe, a"h, and
Hershel ben Avraham HaLevi, a"h

Together, they created a life based on
love, laughter, and happiness.

Together, they created a marriage based on
respect, support, and *shalom bais*.

Together, they created seven children and taught them
the importance of integrity and strength of character.

Everything they did, they did together and they did it *b'simcha*.

Their love for each other enabled them to open their hearts so
fully to others, thereby teaching their children the importance
of acceptance and peace.

They touched the lives of all who were fortunate enough to
have known them and their legacy lives on in the hearts of all
who loved them.

Parashas Bereishis

In honor of

Josh

Jason

Alex

Tamar

I. Understanding Creation

The Torah tells us that Kayin and Hevel chose two different professions: Kayin chose to grow food and Hevel chose to raise sheep. The *Sforno* explains that Hevel wanted to raise sheep because he saw that it required greater wisdom than growing grains and vegetables.

We learn from the *Sforno* the importance of growing in wisdom. Hevel could have had many reasons for choosing his profession. However, he wanted to do something that would help him grow in his understanding of the world, which would ultimately bring him closer to Hashem. He recognized that it took great wisdom to know exactly how to breed and care for healthy sheep. Attaining that wisdom was a worthwhile goal and therefore he chose to raise sheep.

We see from Hevel that the Torah places value on seeking knowledge and wisdom for its own sake. Hevel did not need to know the science of sheep farming; he could have chosen a different profession. Surely there was enough room in the world for both Kayin and Hevel to farm the land and grow crops. However, the *Sforno* teaches us that Hevel decided to raise sheep in order to learn more and grow in wisdom.

All true wisdom comes from Hashem. If we understand the world Hashem created, we grow in our understanding of His wisdom. Additionally, we get a deeper understanding of Hashem's love and compassion for all His creations. Growing in wisdom will allow us to come closer to Hashem and appreciate His infinite compassion and kindness.

Parashas Noach

In loving memory of
Stanley DeCoveny OB"M

Mr. DeCoveny was dedicated to Jewish education, and always inspired in others the **"Courage to Change."** Mazal Tov to all of the dedicated Yeshiva Toras Chaim students on this magnificent Mussar Haskel!

Mr. & Mrs. Kenny Stowe and Family

I. It's the Thought That Counts

The complete and proper fulfillment of a *mitzvah* is determined by much more than simply performing the actions of the *mitzvah*. These actions may not be enough.

We should always ask ourselves what more is needed to enhance our level of accomplishment and serve Hashem in our utmost capacity. *Parasha*s Bereishis and *Parasha*s Noach suggest two specific ways to answer this question.

In *Parasha*s Bereishis, on the third day of Creation, Hashem first commanded (Bereishis 1:11), "Let the earth sprout forth vegetation: grass bringing forth seed," and then specifically commanded to the trees, "trees of fruit yielding fruit each after its kind." The command to the grass was not clearly spelled out as opposed to the command to the trees in which Hashem specified that each tree propagate "after its kind" – i.e., according to its own species, thereby prohibiting inter-breeding of tree species. However, in the next *posuk* it says, "and the earth brought forth vegetation: grass yielding seed after its kind." Hashem had not commanded the grass to grow according to its own species, yet it followed this rule anyway. *Rashi*, based on a *Gemorah* (Chullin 60a), explains that the grass had heard Hashem commanding the trees to limit their growth to their own kind, so the grass deduced that it too must grow only within its own species. The Torah is teaching us that when Hashem commands us to do something, we are not only obligated to perform the *mitzvah* as stated, but also required to apply any pertinent rules which may not have been specifically commanded to us. (These determinations must be made according to the strict methodology of the oral tradition, Torah *Shebe'al Peh* and *Da'as* Torah.)

In this week's *parasha*, *Parashas* Noach, there is an even greater lesson on how to perform *mitzvos* properly. The *Gemorah* (Sanhedrin 108b) relates an incident which involved Noach and the *urshina* bird in the *teiva* – ark. Noach's task of taking care of all the animals was extremely difficult. He had to feed them all at different times of the night and day because of their different eating habits and was constantly working to satisfy their needs. Noach noticed that the *urshina* bird had never bothered him for food and asked it why it never complained. It responded that it did not want to bother him and had satisfied itself on the leftovers of the other animals. Because of its extreme consideration towards him, Noach blessed the bird with immortality. (This bird, called the "Phoenix" in English, is known in mythology to rise from its ashes and live forever).

Later on in the *parasha*, after the *teiva* had settled on the mountains of Ararat, Noach sent out the dove to seek out and report back if there was dry land. When the dove returned with an olive branch, the *posuk* states, (Bereishis 8:11) "The dove came back to him in the evening – and behold, an olive leaf it had ripped with its mouth." Noach was ecstatic at the prospect of finally leaving the *teiva*. However, Noach did not give the dove any special *brocha* for having accomplished its mission. Rav Nosson Tzvi Finkel, *zt"l*, the *Alter* of Slobodka, analyzes and questions Noach's behavior. The *urshina* bird, which had performed an act of kindness, was blessed with immortality. On the other hand, the dove, which brought even greater happiness to Noach, was not blessed with anything! Why didn't Noach also bless the dove with immortality?

The *Alter* answers this question based on a *Midrash*. Since the dove had ripped off the olive branch, thereby destroying this tiny fragment of tree life, Noach's happiness was slightly diminished. True, the dove had fulfilled its mission, but the beauty of the deed was diminished in a small way. It was slightly flawed. Therefore, it did not inspire Noach to offer such a great blessing.

We all have a natural tendency to feel that when performing a *mitzvah*, everyone and everything else can be ignored because of our involvement in the holiest of pursuits. The Torah is teaching us that this is not true. One could be fulfilling every detail of Hashem's commandment but if his action has an even mildly negative impact, the beauty of the *mitzvah* is reduced. Doing a *mitzvah* is simply not a license to ignore its potentially negative impact on others.

We should be aware of both of these considerations when deciding how to perform a *mitzvah*: what is the complete and total way to fulfill this *mitzvah*, and what potentially negative impact our actions may have on others.

II. Taking Responsibility

People shoulder many financial, social, and family responsibilities that they have willingly or begrudgingly placed upon themselves. We are presented with responsibilities that are cast upon us uninvited during the course of our lives. Most people prefer to avoid this type of responsibility. However, the Torah teaches us how to act when faced with unexpected and even unwelcome responsibilities.

The generation of Noach was corrupt, and Hashem declared that there should be a flood to punish the people. After the waters receded, Noach, who had been spared, planted a vineyard and made wine. However, he overindulged and became deeply intoxicated. In his drunken state, he lay in his tent inappropriately exposed. His grandson Canaan, Cham's son, came by and saw his grandfather in this embarrassing circumstance. He went and told his father Cham, who told his brothers, Shem and Yefes, who came and covered him with great reverence and respect. After Noach awoke from his drunkenness and found out what had occurred, he cursed Canaan, the son of

Cham, proclaiming that Canaan would be a slave to his brothers forever.

The *Da'as Zekeinim MiBaalei HaTosafos* wonder why Noach cursed Canaan. What did Noach see in Canaan's actions that warranted a curse?

They answer that Noach saw a lack of responsibility in the way Canaan handled the situation. Canaan, who was the first to arrive on the scene and saw that something had to be done, was accountable to resolve this problem himself. Instead of accepting this responsibility upon himself, he passed the task onto others. In effect, Canaan had made his father and uncles his slaves by having them take care of his obligation. Therefore, Noach gave him the most fitting curse – that he should be a slave to his brothers forever.

People are under the misconception that they do not have to assume a responsibility that is not voluntarily undertaken. The Torah defines responsibility differently. When one comes upon a situation requiring action, it is his personal obligation to try to resolve the matter at hand if possible. When other people are in need, we are responsible to respond to their problems to the extent we are capable.

III. The Standard of Living

After building the *teiva* – ark – Noach waited for Hashem's instruction to enter it. As the *posuk* (7:1) says, "And Hashem said to Noach, 'Come into the *teiva*, you and your family.'" After the flood, Noach again waited until he was instructed to leave the *teiva* with his family and all the animals. It then (8:15-17) says, "Hashem spoke to Noach saying, 'Leave the *teiva* – you, along with your wife, your sons, and your son's wives. Take out with you every living creature from all flesh: birds, livestock, and all land animals that walk the earth.'" The *Midrash Rabbah* explains that Noach did not have to wait for Hashem's permission to leave the *teiva*. Rather, Noach decided on his own that the rules of *derech eretz* – respect – dictate that he wait until Hashem had commanded him. Noach's entry into the *teiva* had been on Hashem's directive, and therefore he felt he had to wait for Hashem's permission to leave.

Noach and his family endured tremendous hardships to properly service the animals on the *teiva* – to the extent that he never slept in order to pay close and constant attention to the welfare of the animals. The natural reaction when the rains abated would have been to run off the *teiva*, yet Noach restrained himself because he felt such an action would be a violation of *derech eretz*. Noach certainly had many valid reasons to leave immediately. Surely a small breach of *derech eretz* in such unusual circumstances would be acceptable, yet Noach held firm to his commitment that the rules for proper behavior are not negotiable, despite the extreme situation.

A great lesson can be gleaned from this incident. Even when there may be valid justifications, one must maintain the highest form of *derech eretz*. Many situations arise that can make us feel that we do not have to act in accordance with the standards of proper conduct because of mitigating circumstances. We must be especially careful not to relax our standards when feeling external pressure to act improperly, just as Noach resisted the urge to depart from the *teiva*.

Parashas Lech Lecho

L'zechar Nishmas

HaRav Binyomin Yehuda Pesach
ben R' Shmuel Eliyahu

Seth and Esther Entin

I. Inner Analysis

In this week's *parasha*, Lech Lecho, the Torah narrates the war waged by the alliance of the four kings against the five kings. Although Avrohom and his nephew and disciple, Lot, were not originally involved in this war, Lot was captured along with the other residents of Sodom and held captive by the army of the four kings. Avrohom, Lot's closest relative, took it upon himself to rescue Lot, thereby fulfilling the great *mitzvah* of redeeming a captive. According to the simple explanation of the verses,

Avrohom took a volunteer army of 318 of his men and attacked the army of the four kings. Despite the magnitude of the imbalance – a militia of 318 men versus a world-dominating army – Avrohom was miraculously victorious.

The *posuk* says that in preparation for battle, (Bereishis 14:14) "*Vayorek es chanichov* – He [Avrohom] armed his trained servants." *Chazal*, in Tractate Nedarim, explain that the verse is telling us that Avrohom, who was extremely wealthy, enriched these men with large amounts of gold and silver before the battle. The principal reason for these gifts was because Avrohom, knowing that in every war the winner keeps the spoils, did not want his men to become distracted after the battle by taking spoils and possibly overlook rescuing Lot. He was concerned that the men might forget their primary mission. By making them wealthy beforehand, he ensured that they would stay focused on saving Lot and only afterward would turn to the spoils.

Was Avrohom's fear reasonable? How could he think that these brave volunteers would forget to save Lot? If they were so interested in money, they certainly would have valued their lives even more and would never even have gone on this mission. Their willingness to risk their lives in total dedication to the *mitzvah* of saving Lot clearly demonstrated that they were not interested in money and would never be distracted by the spoils. Why was Avrohom even worried about this possibility?

A deep look at human nature reveals the answer. Very often we start a project clearly focused on our goal and highly motivated to achieve success. However, the *yetzer horah* – evil inclination – can very easily distract us with extraneous temptations, causing us to forget our original motivations. Avrohom's 318 men knew that their attempt to defeat a huge army required miraculous intervention by Hashem. Such intervention could only be counted on if the men's intentions were totally for the sake of Heaven. Any personal motives felt by the men would not have allowed Divine intervention. Avrohom was concerned that his volunteers would become briefly distracted by spoils long enough to cause them to lose their original focus. This small break in concentration and commitment could have profound effects on how these volunteers would perform and could lead to the failure of their mission.

It is essential that we prevent ourselves from becoming distracted from our personal goals (assuming we have defined them as the Torah insists we do) by taking time to simply think about them and ask ourselves if we are on course. When we look back at the commitments made on Yom Kippur, we observe that we may have become diverted from these goals. We must examine and analyze once again, and then again, what our commitments are. This process of *cheshbon hanefesh* – self-examination – will help us retain focus on our goals and remain on our original path.

II. The Reason for Ridicule

Throughout history and even up to the present time, the Jew has been subject to mockery and ridicule. The comments and sneers we have experienced have, at times, caused us to feel a sense of frustration. However, when viewed from another perspective, we can use these experiences to motivate us to follow in the Torah's path.

Avrohom *Ovinu* was the first person to recognize and teach others about Hashem and induce them to follow His ways. Nearly every person in the world believed in and worshipped idols. The *Midrash* says that Avrohom was constantly persecuted and ridiculed because of his beliefs and was even thrown into a fiery furnace by

Nimrod because he refused to bow down to graven images. Despite Avrohom's miraculous salvation, people did not cease mocking him.

Why did the people and their powerful leaders feel that they had to mock Avrohom? Why didn't they attribute his beliefs to the insane babblings of an eccentric and just ignore Avrohom? The world is full of bizarre philosophies! What motivated them to be so antagonistic?

Avrohom's beliefs made it uncomfortable for others to be around him because they understood, in the deep recesses of their hearts, that he was correct, and Hashem was the only true God. Despite this full comprehension, people were not prepared to act on these feelings. Therefore, Avrohom was a thorn in their side, a constant reminder of their erroneous ways. He evoked within them a sense of guilt for not believing in Hashem. Had they really believed that Avrohom was a lunatic, they would have ignored him, and even when mocking him, they would not have been as hostile! Their hostility demonstrates that they were uncomfortable about rejecting the truth. He was criticized not only by the political leaders, such as Nimrod, but even the average citizen on the street, whose position and power were not threatened by Avrohom. They all understood the truth but were not ready to accept it. Since they knew that he was right, they had to do something to remove their discomfort and therefore resorted to mockery and ridicule.

Avrohom's experience is a profound lesson for us. He ignored the endless ridicule and continued following and promoting the path of Hashem. Often, when we promote our beliefs to others, we become the victims of ridicule – sometimes even from our own people. We may be harassed, demeaned, or even degraded. Their motivation for insulting us is that we make them uncomfortable because we are doing the right thing. It may hurt and bother us, but we should take solace in the fact that they are the troubled ones. This was how Avrohom acted towards those who ridiculed him – he showed them love, affection, and kindness. In response to the hostile actions of others, we must react with love and kindness to them out of recognition of the inherent greatness in every person.

III. Enough is Enough

Avrohom and his nephew Lot, having accumulated great wealth during their stay in Egypt, returned to the land of Canaan. Shortly thereafter, the shepherds of Avrohom and the shepherds of Lot began arguing about where to graze their sheep, and to avoid a further deterioration in their relationship, Avrohom and Lot decided to separate. Lot, having been given first choice as to where to go by Avrohom, chose to live in the lush, green lands of Sodom, despite its decadent atmosphere.

In describing Lot's move, the *posuk* says, "*Vayisa Lot mikedem* – And Lot traveled from the east." The *posuk* seems to indicate that Lot traveled from their encampment in the east to the west, yet it is clear from later verses that Lot actually had traveled to the east and not to the west. Why did the Torah choose the word *mikedem* – east? The *Midrash Rabbah* explains that here *mikedem* refers to *mikadmon*, meaning that Lot distanced himself from the Creator of the world. By leaving Avrohom and going to Sodom, Lot was rejecting his belief in Hashem and a spiritually based lifestyle.

Lot had seen countless acts of kindness, righteousness, and piety in the house of Avrohom *Ovinu*. In fact, he was even quite used to seeing angels and miracles, as is later evident from Lot's calm reaction while hosting angels during their visit to rescue him before the destruction of Sodom. How could Lot fall to such a low level as to reject Hashem? While living a life with such closeness to Hashem and dwelling with a *tzadik* of Avrohom *Ovinu*'s stature, shouldn't living with Avrohom have made a lasting impression on him? Yet we see that his *yetzer horah* – evil inclination – was successful in convincing him to leave Avrohom and the path of Torah for a hedonistic life in Sodom!

This incident demonstrates the awesome power of the *yetzer horah*. Lot was unable to withstand the pressure of the *yetzer horah* even though he was living with one of the greatest and most influential men who ever lived. If he could be ensnared by his evil inclination under those optimal conditions, we are certainly susceptible to temptation. Therefore, we must be constantly aware of the threat that the *yetzer horah* poses to us and reinforce our resistance to the *yetzer horah*, using every possible means of defense. We cannot afford the luxury of feeling that we have done enough, as the *yetzer horah* is relentless and ever more creative in its goal of leading us to failure.

Parashas Vayeira

Dedicated in honor of

Rabbi Elchonon Goldenberg

for being such a great role model and Rebbe to our son, Noah, this year.

Aaron and Valerie Kurlansky

I. Jump to Action

In our performance of *mitzvos*, we invest varying degrees of effort. The same *mitzvah* performed by different people can have a different spiritual outcome and importance depending on the effort and attention to subtle details. This week's *parasha* reveals to us how Hashem records every detail of our actions.

Parashas Vayeira begins with Avrohom sitting outside his tent on the third day after his circumcision in great pain. Hashem did not want to burden him with guests and travelers and therefore intensified the heat of the sun to inhibit travel. Realizing that the absence of guests had caused Avrohom emotional pain, He sent three angels, in the form of weary travelers, to pass by the road near Avrohom's tent, to give him the opportunity to perform the *mitzvah* of hospitality. Avrohom, unaware of Hashem's plans, ran out to greet them and invited them to rest while he prepared a lavish feast. He proceeded to rush about eagerly preparing a beautiful meal of meat, bread, and cakes.

The *Sforno* points out that one can see how precious the *mitzvah* of hospitality was from the way the Torah specifically tells us that Avrohom "rushed" to greet his guests. He greeted them with great enthusiasm because he wanted to fulfill the *mitzvah* with maximum intensity, despite his pain and the heat of the day. He then served a lavish platter of exotic foods. This is how Avrohom acted every day to every traveler. Had Avrohom not run to greet them, his actions would still have been considered great. Yet the Torah does not ignore this added effort that further sanctified the act. Every added detail is recorded by the Torah. This teaches us that every nuance in our performance of *mitzvos* is noted and recognized by Hashem.

We should strive to be like Avrohom in regard to fulfilling *mitzvos*. Very often we may feel that the small details of our deeds are lost or camouflaged in the big picture, yet Hashem takes every single action and deed into account. This realization should motivate us to be very concerned and aware of each and every action we perform.

II. Mind Games

In this week's *parasha, Parashas* Vayeira, Hashem directs Avrohom to offer his son Yitzchok as a sacrifice. The Satan tried to dissuade Avrohom from fulfilling Hashem's command. At first, the Satan told Avrohom, "Old man, have you lost your mind? After 100 years you finally bore a child, and now you are going to give him up?!" Avrohom, ignoring the argument, responded that Hashem had commanded him to carry out this task and he was going to do it, no matter what the cost. The Satan then tried to persuade Avrohom with a different line of reasoning, "Even if you pass this test, what will you gain from it? Tomorrow and the next day you will have even more tests and failure at one point is inevitable. Why not give up now, while your son is still alive?" Avrohom once again answered the Satan by saying that he would fulfill that which Hashem had commanded.

When we analyze the Satan's second argument, it seems very perplexing. Hashem had commanded Avrohom to sacrifice his son to demonstrate to the world Avrohom's devotion and sincerity. Avrohom was so committed to fulfilling this command that he brought his own firewood for the altar upon which he would sacrifice Yitzchok to remove any excuse not to do Hashem's directive. Why did the Satan think that he could convince Avrohom not to listen to Hashem with his second argument? To what emotion was he appealing?

Satan was trying to cajole Avrohom into looking at the "big picture" rather than focusing on one challenge at a time. He tried to cloud Avrohom's thinking by telling him that although he may pass this test, future tests will be harder and he will surely fail them all. Therefore, why exert the effort on this test? The Satan had a very good argument and Avrohom understood it. Avrohom understood the power of the Satan's argument and knew it could not be directly refuted. Rather than respond directly to the argument, he blocked out the Satan and focused on the task at hand. He concentrated on the immediate problem at hand and focused on each test as it came, trying to pass them individually. Even if he were to fail later, earlier accomplishments would still have been achieved.

From Avrohom *Ovinu*'s reaction to the Satan, we can learn that when faced with a major problem or challenge, we should focus our attention and efforts to pass the test, rather than looking at the future tasks awaiting us. Otherwise, we will be overwhelmed and give up. If we follow in the footsteps of Avrohom, we will succeed in passing each test Hashem directs at us and not become intimidated by potential obstacles in the future.

III. A Powerful Presence

When the time had come for Yitzchok to marry, Avrohom sent his servant Eliezer to Aram Naharayim – Avrohom's homeland – to find a wife suitable for Yitzchok. When Eliezer arrived, he encountered Rivka – Yitzchok's cousin – drawing water from a well. Since Rivka was able to fetch water alone, without incident at a young age, *Chazal* conclude that the community in which her family lived was not a violent one. A similar picture of life in Aram Naharayim appears later in the story of Yaakov and Rachel.

However, in *Parashas* Shemos, a different kind of society is depicted. After Moshe *Rabbeinu* fled from Pharaoh, he stopped at a well in Midyan and met Yisro's seven daughters, who had come to the well to water their father's sheep. This well was not as safe as the previous two; the Torah relates that other shepherds tried to chase away Yisro's daughters, but Moshe protected them.

What was the difference between the well that Eliezer and Yaakov had visited, which was tranquil and safe, and the well that Moshe visited? What does the Torah mean to teach us by highlighting the difference between these two societies?

Chazal tell us that the character of the well at Aram Naharayim was influenced by the fact that Avrohom *Ovinu* had once lived there. Although Avrohom eventually moved on, his time among them left a lasting impression upon the residents of this region. The reason why the people at these wells treated each other civilly was because Avrohom, a man who epitomized *chesed* – kindness – had once lived there. This did not apply to Midyan. Since Avrohom had never lived there, his ideas and behavior could never have made an impact on its residents. Consequently, the people of Midyan treated each other abusively and disrespectfully.

Avrohom *Ovinu* was not the most popular person of his time. Although he had many followers, most of the world remained pagan. He was mainly alone in his belief that there was but one God. Nonetheless, his refined personality left a permanent impression on the places in which he had lived.

The Torah is showing us how much of an impact a person genuinely steeped in the ideals of Torah and *chesed* can have on a society, even if its other members do not accept his religious beliefs. While Avrohom was unsuccessful in convincing everyone to stop worshipping idols, he did impress them enough to motivate them to act in a respectful manner towards each other.

Every Jew possesses the power to redefine, through his actions and convictions, the values of the society in which he lives. We are all obligated to achieve a degree of refinement that will elevate those around us. Furthermore, we must strive to spend time in the presence of Torah personalities, so that we will be influenced and inspired by their conduct.

IV. Holy Is As Holy Does

This week's *parasha* exhorts us, *"Kedoshim tih'yu –* be holy." How does one achieve holiness? Does he have to deprive himself of all worldly pleasures to do so? Must he cut himself off from friends and relatives? *Rashi* tells us that wherever you find barriers against immorality, you will find holiness. It seems that guarding oneself against immorality is a significant step towards bringing *kedusha* into one's life.

We find an illustration of this concept in *Parashas* Vayeira. After Avimelch returned Sarah to Avrohom *Ovinu*, Avimelech asked Avrohom why he misinformed the guards that Sarah was his sister. Avrohom responded that he saw no fear of God in Avimelech's kingdom, and therefore was concerned he might be killed so that another man could take Sarah. *Rashi* explains that Avrohom's perception regarding Avimelech's subjects came from the question he was asked as he entered the city. Avrohom was asked what relationship he had with Sarah. As a traveler, the appropriate questions to ask would have been regarding whether or not he is hungry, or does he need assistance with lodging. The fact that the guards asked about Sarah showed Avrohom that their fear of God was lacking.

We see from here an important concept. Avrohom was able to ascertain a nation's relationship to God based upon their sensitivity to immorality. A nation close to God would have had protections against immorality, and the culture would have been one that eschewed inquiring about a traveler's female companion. The fact that they asked about Sarah not only spoke to their vigilance in regards to immorality, but also to their relationship to God in general.

Let us bring holiness into our lives by guarding against immorality. By doing so, not only are we protecting our virtue; we are enhancing our relationship with Hashem himself, *"Kedoshim tih'yu ki kadosh ani."*

Parashas Chayei Sarah

I. Closing the Deal

In *Parashas* Chayei Sarah, the Torah describes in great detail the negotiations leading to Avrohom's purchase of a burial plot for Sarah. Avrohom was interested in the *me'oras haMachpela* – the cave of Machpela – and approached the *Bnei Cheis*, the leaders of the region. He asked them to intercede on his behalf with Efron the Hittite, the owner of the cave. The *Bnei Cheis*, honored to have Avrohom in their city, agreed. After appropriate introductions, the *Bnei Cheis* dropped out of the negotiations and Avrohom proceeded to deal directly with Efron. Efron, who had actually been sitting there all along, answered Avrohom that he would gladly give the field as a gift. Avrohom rejected this offer and insisted on paying a price. Efron then suggested the enormous sum of 400 shekels (about one million ordinary shekels) for the cave and the land surrounding it. Avrohom agreed to pay Efron the money and buried Sarah.

The *Midrash Rabbah*, observing that the words "*Bnei Cheis*" are mentioned ten times during these conversations, in a seemingly unnecessary repetition, explains that because the *Bnei Cheis* helped Avrohom, it was as if they had fulfilled the Ten Commandments. The *Midrash* proclaims that whenever someone helps a great Torah scholar with a purchase, it is as if he has fulfilled all of the Ten Commandments. This mystifying *Midrash* requires explanation. At most, the *Bnei Cheis* acted as brokers and more likely should be perceived as mere bystanders who witnessed the event, perhaps to prevent either side from backing out of the deal. For this role, should they be considered to have had fulfilled all of the Ten Commandments? Even if we say that because of their "help" Avrohom now had more time to learn Torah and do *chesed*, does this justify equating this act of kindness to the fulfillment of the Ten Commandments?

The question emanates from a misconception of how to determine success and achievement. Many people believe that achievement is goal determined. In sports, who wins the trophy? The best team, the most valuable player; in the Olympics, it is the highest jump, the farthest throw, the longest distance. We tend to focus exclusively on the winners; everyone else is a loser. We generally ignore those who contribute to the success of others, yet we will blame all those even remotely involved in a failure. This is not how Hashem views our actions. Of course, one who excels in his own learning or in his fulfillment of *mitzvos* receives great rewards, but even the one who merely assists in that endeavor, helps finalize a deal, or is only a witness to ensure that a great man such as Avrohom should not have to be concerned with anyone laying claim that the sale was not done properly – he is also considered as having fulfilled the Ten Commandments.

Were we to realize how Hashem views our contributions, we would run to do even a small favor for someone knowing full well that Hashem never considers such involvement as small or insignificant.

II. Wordplay

Is the manner in which we speak to our family, friends, peers, and business associates important? Is our style of speech and ordering of words merely a form of communication, or does it contain a deeper meaning about who we are? If we used negative language, would that reveal our true character?

In this week's *parasha*, Eliezer, Avrohom's faithful servant, travels to Choron's family in Aram to find a wife for Yitzchok. Eliezer meets Rivka, Yitzchok's intended bride, and Lovon, her brother. In response to Eliezer's request to allow Rivka to return with him to Avrohom's house to become Yitzchok's wife, the *posuk* states (24:50) "And Lovon and Besuel answered and said, 'The matter comes from Hashem; we are unable to speak to you, bad or good.'" *Rabbeinu Bechaya* says that we can see two indications of Lovon's evil nature from this *posuk*: Lovon's having spoken before his father, showing disrespect, and Lovon's placing the word "bad" before "good," showing inner wickedness.

Lovon, one of the Torah's most evil personalities, was a murderer (he killed his father), trickster, crook, idol worshipper, liar, and a generally immoral person. The Pesach Haggadah tells us that Lovon was more evil than even the wicked Pharaoh from the times of Moshe. Pharaoh wanted to kill only the Jewish males and Lovon wanted to annihilate all Jews, by later trying to kill Yaakov. Why did *Rabbeinu Bechaya* choose to highlight the order of Lovon's words, a seemingly trivial point?

Rabbeinu Bechaya is teaching us a very valuable lesson. The choice and order of our words indicate far more than the actual meaning of words. When we speak, we open a window to our inner selves for others to see. Lovon's statement revealed his true inner character. The fact that he spoke before his father and said "*ra* – bad" before "good" indicated that evil was foremost in his mind. Consequently, by highlighting the manner in which Lovon spoke, *Rabbeinu Bechaya* illustrates that words give us insight about the person who stated them.

The Talmud relates an episode of Rebbi and his students who approached the carcass of a dog while walking down the street together. The students immediately began to complain about the terrible stench of the carcass. Rebbi turned to them and said "Look how white the teeth are!" The *Chovos HaLevavos* explains that we can learn from Rebbi that in our own speech it is important to highlight the good even in a bad situation. Rebbi was revealing his true nature, as a positive individual, in highlighting the good in this apparently ugly sight. One who tries to use positive expressions in a negative situation can be clearly identified as a positive individual. Since we broadcast our character through our speech, we must be careful with how we speak, as our character will be measured by our choice of words and how we emphasize them.

III. Paramount Priorities

Eliezer, Avrohom *Ovinu*'s trusted servant, upon arriving at the well outside Aram Naharayim on his mission to find a wife for Yitzchok, devised a test to identify the right girl. He would ask the girls at the well for a drink and the girl who offered him and his camels water would be the correct choice. He prayed to Hashem that his test would succeed and, moments later, Rivka approached the well and fulfilled all of Eliezer's conditions. After his introduction to Rivka's family, Eliezer told them how quickly his prayer to Hashem had been answered and asked that they let him promptly leave with Rivka. Rivka's brother, Lovon, and father, Besuel, responded enthusiastically: "This is from Hashem! We cannot say anything to you, good or bad." They were compelled to consent to the match because they understood that it was Hashem's will.

As Eliezer prepared to leave Aram Naharayim the next day, Rivka's mother and brother proposed to delay her departure. They wanted to prepare her thoroughly for the journey and subsequent wedding. Eliezer insisted on leaving immediately and the decision was left to Rivka, who agreed with Eliezer. Why did Rivka disagree with her family, who seemed to have her best interests in mind?

Rivka's family felt that the travel arrangements and subsequent marriage must be in complete comfort and elegance. Until their high standards were attained, they felt it improper for Rivka to leave. Eliezer and Rivka also may have wanted these enhancements but realized that the importance of immediately fulfilling Hashem's will outweighed all other secondary considerations. They were eager to sacrifice comfort and luxury to fulfill Hashem's will sooner.

The reaction of Rivka's family demonstrates that they had never unconditionally accepted their obligations to Hashem. This caused them to try to delay performing His will until their conditions were met. Eliezer and Rivka set the fulfillment of Hashem's will above all else and saw beyond these obstacles.

Each of us must examine our level of commitment to Hashem's *mitzvos* and strive to recognize their paramount importance. Only then can we be sure that small obstacles will not interfere with our responsibility to fulfill the will of Hashem properly.

Parashas Toldos

L'zechar Nishmas

R' Reuven Michoel
ben R' Yitzchok

Seth and Esther Entin

I. Exercising Control

At the end of *Parashas* Toldos, Yaakov receives a second *brocha* from Yitzchok, who also admonishes Yaakov to never marry a Canaanite woman. Yaakov then leaves his home to travel to a distant land to find a non-Canaanite wife. According to the *Sforno*, Eisov knew of this parting *brocha* and of his father's long standing antagonism to Canaanite women. Nevertheless, Eisov had earlier married such a woman! Eisov did not fully understand that the women from Canaan were not appropriate until he saw that Yaakov was sent away to be married. Only after these events did Eisov marry a woman who was not from Canaan. If Eisov had already known that the women of Canaan were evil, having earlier heard Yitzchok tell Yaakov not to marry them, why was an impact made on him only *after* he saw Yaakov leave?

The *Sforno* answers that Eisov never fully accepted that the women of Canaan were bad until he saw Yaakov act. Only then did he actually believe this. It is true that Eisov may have been aware of this attitude and even understood it completely, but it did not make an impact on him until he actually saw Yaakov leave.

We see from the *Sforno* that there is a tremendous difference between knowledge of a fact and acting on this knowledge. Even though Eisov had achieved great levels of *kibbud ov voeim* – respecting one's father and mother – it was still necessary for him to see Yaakov leave before he actually felt that the women of Canaan were an inappropriate choice.

There is a gap between awareness of a fact and acting based on this knowledge; a gap that can be overcome by observing another person who has successfully bridged it. For example, we all know that it is generally better not to respond to someone who is insulting us, but this knowledge is often inadequate for us to reach such a level of self control. Yet, when we see a friend not responding to an insult it makes a greater impact on us.

Even after Eisov had seen that Yaakov was sent away to get married and accepted on himself to no longer marry these women, he still remained married to his Canaanite wives! If seeing Yaakov leave made such a powerful impact on him that he finally felt that the Canaanite women were bad, why didn't he divorce them?

The *Ramban* answers that even though Eisov wanted to divorce them, his desires to keep them were too overwhelming! His desires were so strong that even after he had actually seen Yaakov leave and knew that it was wrong to keep them, he still could not counter his desires. This contradictory behavior demonstrates a very human quality. One may know and even feel what is right, but still be defeated by his desires. Therefore, we must (1) affirm within ourselves what is correct and (2) exercise control of our desires. Only through this combination of efforts will we be *zocheh* to serve Hashem properly.

II. A Positive Sign

In *Parashas* Toldos the *posuk* states (25:27), "And the young boys grew up." *Rashi* comments that this refers to when Yaakov and Eisov turned thirteen and their different paths in life were recognizable; as the next *posuk* says, "Eisov was a shrewd man, a man of the field, and Yaakov was a scholarly man who dwelled in tents," meaning that Eisov became a trickster and hunter while Yaakov spent his time studying Torah.

Avrohom *Ovinu* was one hundred and sixty years old when his grandchildren were born. When each became a *bar mitzvah* and took his divergent path, Avrohom was one hundred and seventy three years old. He died at the age of one hundred and seventy five. How can this be? We are told (25:8) that Avrohom died "*b'seivah tovah* – of a good old age." The *Midrash* says that Hashem had to end Avrohom's life early by five years so he should not see his grandson Eisov committing immoral acts. If these young men were already known for their particular deeds, Yaakov for his righteousness and Eisov for his wickedness, at age thirteen, then Avrohom was alive for two entire years witnessing the terrible acts that Eisov was performing!

The *Da'as Zekeinim* and *Sifsei Chachomim* both give the same answer. For two years prior to his grandfather's death, Eisov did his evil acts in private, even though everyone knew what he was doing. Eisov showed that he recognized the need to hide these acts from others. This minimized the pain that Avrohom felt. However, when Avrohom was one hundred and seventy five and Eisov had turned fifteen, Eisov ceased doing his evil acts privately. Hashem said that Avrohom must not be allowed to see this because it would be too painful. It must be pointed out that Eisov did the very same acts before and after he was fifteen. Only one factor had changed – the manner in which those acts were performed.

From this we see the importance of the manner in which an evil deed is done. Performing it openly and in public indicates a brazenness and a lack of character that has no redeeming or mitigating factors. When we do evil openly, we reveal a spiritual barometer indicating that corruption is so deeply embedded in our person that it is unlikely to be altered. On the other hand, when we do the most horrible things but are aware and concerned enough to do them privately, even though they are just as bad, this indicates that there are positive qualities in us and the privacy and discretion that are shown are positive signs.

III. Once More With Feeling

The Torah describes Yaakov's crossing into the land of Canaan from Aram in an apparently inaccurate manner. "And he got up on that night, and he took his two wives, his two concubines, and his eleven children, and he crossed the Yabok River." Actually, Yaakov had a twelfth child, his daughter Dina. *Rashi* comments that the reason the Torah did not count Dina was that Yaakov had sealed her in a box, so Eisov would not find her and want to marry her. *Rashi* adds that Yaakov was later punished for this act because Dina could have had a profound influence on Eisov to repent.

It is difficult to understand why Yaakov should have been punished for wanting to protect Dina. Yaakov did what any father should do to protect his daughter from an evil person. No father would expose his daughter to someone like Eisov. Why was Yaakov held accountable for this action?

The *Alter* of Slobodka, Rav Nosson Tzvi Finkel, explains that although Yaakov's action was not improper, his feelings at the time of this action were found wanting. As he was closing the lid of the box, he should have felt badly for having to keep Dina away from Eisov, thereby reducing Eisov's chances of repentance. He should have felt pain about his brother's condition and regret about what he had to do. *Rashi*'s analysis of Yaakov's actions and their consequences teaches us an important lesson. It is true that one must distance himself from any unnecessary exposure to a person who has rejected a Torah lifestyle or has hostility to those who serve Hashem. Nevertheless, one should feel regret that his brother has fallen so low and sadness that he cannot spend the time and effort to help him. The temptation to feel only relief at having successfully avoided such a person should be resisted, as it is self-centered. One must also feel sorry for this person. The balance of both feelings will enable us to properly influence others and still protect ourselves from being adversely influenced by them.

IV. Blinded by Desire

This week's *parasha*, Toldos, recounts the incident in which Eisov sold his birthright to his younger brother, Yaakov. After a tiring day of hunting, Eisov returned home famished and saw the pot of lentil soup that Yaakov had cooked. To satisfy his hunger, Eisov decided to relinquish his birthright in return for the lentils.

The *Ramban* is perplexed by Eisov's decision. Didn't Eisov realize the historical importance and uniqueness of the birthright? How could he give it up for a mere pot of soup?

The *Ramban* explains that Eisov did, indeed, realize the value of the birthright. However, he made a simple business calculation. A hunter by profession, Eisov realized that his life was constantly in danger, and it was quite possible that he would be killed before his father's death. If this were to happen, he would never receive any of the benefits of the birthright. Although he understood its significance, Eisov deemed the birthright worthless because he might never have lived to enjoy it. This is what Eisov meant when he said to Yaakov, "Behold, I am going to die, so of what use is the birthright to me?"

However, another question arises. The birthright was an extremely valuable possession. Why was Eisov willing to give up the birthright based on the mere possibility that he might die before his father? With such important matters at stake, how could Eisov ignore the chance that he might outlive Yitzchok? In fact, *Chazal* tell us that not only did Eisov outlive Yitzchok, he even outlived Yaakov!

To clarify this, the *Ramban* explains that it is the nature of a foolish and immature person to focus only on immediate benefits to himself. Eisov's present desire to satisfy his appetite caused him to focus only on the bowl of lentils in front of him and dismiss the potential consequences of forfeiting the birthright. Although Eisov was a very intelligent individual, he could not control his craving for food. His thought process therefore became distorted, causing him to think irrationally.

The *Ramban*'s analysis of Eisov's motivation teaches us a very important lesson. A person who allows himself to be influenced and guided by personal desires rather than Torah values can easily become blinded by the need for immediate gratification, even if he is brilliant. Frequently, his whims render him unable to comprehend the long-term, foolish results of his actions and cause his vision to be very short sighted.

All of us must strive to maintain a balanced perspective when we are forced to decide between two possible courses of action. In order to ensure that we will make the proper decisions, we must make the fulfillment of Torah ideals the object of our endeavors, and then cautiously evaluate the situation.

Parashas Vayeitzei

I. Justice for All

Yaakov, while on the road to Choron, gathered rocks around him and lay down to sleep. *Rashi* says that the rocks started "fighting" with each other to earn the privilege of being under the head of Yaakov as he slept. What aspect of Yaakov's greatness merited that the rocks should fight over him?

In order for us to answer this question, let us look at how Yaakov acted with regard to others. When Yaakov arrived at Choron, he came upon a well with shepherds standing by it and greeted them saying, "How are you, my brothers?" Yaakov did not know these shepherds at all! Yet, he called them his brothers in an effort to make them feel happy and lift their spirits. This demonstrates the extent to which Yaakov *Ovinu* was concerned for other people.

There is a story told about Rav Yaakov Kamenetsky, that after his passing, a nun was observed crying over his death. Many people wondered about this, and when she was asked why she was crying she answered them that Rabbi Kamenetsky was the only one who wished her a "good morning" at the start of the day. This story shows us that Rav Yaakov Kamenetsky tried to make every human being feel special and honored.

In continuing the story of Yaakov, the Torah relates that Yaakov admonished the shepherds by telling them, "The day is still long; it isn't time to bring in the flock! Give the sheep water and go graze them!" Why would Yaakov, who traveled to Choron to search for a wife, stop and talk to the shepherds when he was involved in looking for a wife? Not only would this not help his mission, but it might hurt it! Furthermore, why was Yaakov, who was not the shepherds' boss, involved in matters that were not even his business?!

The *Sforno* states that it was disgusting in the eyes of Yaakov to see the shepherds, who were getting paid to do a job, just sitting around and talking. Therefore, Yaakov felt that it was necessary to interrupt his search for a wife in order to tell the shepherds to get back to work. Yaakov, who saw the shepherds doing something improper, was driven to stand up for the truth. He felt that justice was not happening and it bothered him. He interrupted his important mission to make the shepherds understand that what they were doing was wrong, even though it might hurt him, and even if it was not really his affair.

Knowing all this, we can better understand why the rocks were fighting as to which one should be under the holy head of Yaakov *Ovinu*. The whole world respected him because of the way he acted with people. He treated shepherds as if they were his brothers, and wanted to help them follow the correct path of justice. We should aim to emulate Yaakov *Ovinu*'s manner of treating and respecting people, as well as his passionate concern for justice.

II. Hidden Kindness

Gifts are a sign of affection, love, and concern, and a more substantial gift makes us feel happier and more thankful to the giver. Sometimes we overlook the smaller, more constant gifts given to us. This week's Haftorah provides us with an insight as to how we should feel with regard to these less impressive but regular favors that we receive.

The Prophet Hoshea admonishes the Jewish people for engaging in idol worship, an act that demonstrates ingratitude to Hashem for everything He did during the Exodus. For this act of ungratefulness, the Jews are seen as deserving destruction. At the very least, the Jews should properly show appreciation to Hashem by following His commandments. Not only is Hoshea's message of great relevance to us, but the way he chose to express this message teaches us an important lesson.

Hoshea, in his prophecy, states (13:5), "I knew you in the desert, in the land of thirst." The *Metzudos Dovid* points out that "I knew you in the desert" refers to Hashem's continuous concern for our day-to-day physical and spiritual needs while traveling forty years in the desert. He provided sustenance for us under all conditions continuously rather than supplying us intermittently. Hoshea chose to highlight to the Jews the way the kindness of Hashem was offered in a constant and regular manner.

The great miracles themselves demand that we obey, serve, and express thanks to Hashem. He gave us the Well of Miriam, the Clouds of Glory, the tasteful food of *manna*, and many other great gifts. The gifts themselves would be adequate reason for our gratitude. Yet the *Metzudos Dovid* chose to emphasize how they were given – through Hashem's continuous Divine intervention. The manner in which these gifts were given to us also warrants our compliance with His commandments. Hashem's love for us is seen by His steady guidance, not only by His impressive miracles.

We see that a constant favor can have more of an impact on us than a single, albeit impressive gift. We rarely receive great gifts, but people do care for us in small ways every day. For these acts of kindness, they deserve more credit than we would give for a single outstanding deed. Many people in our circle of family and friends care for us every day. They show us love and concern in a financial, emotional, or spiritual way. While these expressions of concern may not seem impressive, they are consistent. We must appreciate these people for their generosity and adequately express our gratitude toward them.

III. Profit Margin

Yaakov decided to settle into a peaceful "retirement" at the age of 108 after a very difficult life full of stress, disappointment, and aggravation. His encounters with his mortal enemy, Eisov, his spiritual enemy, Lovon, and the event with his daughter Dina, all contributed to his eagerness to relax a bit. Yaakov felt that he had experienced enough trying events for one lifetime, but

Hashem had different plans for Yaakov. Shortly thereafter, the brothers sold Yosef into slavery and told Yaakov that Yosef had been killed. Yaakov's life was shattered and remained so for twenty-two years.

The *Midrash* explains this course of events. Even though *tzadikim* may yearn for personal tranquility, Hashem feels that since the reward in the next world for all their *mitzvos* is so great, they should not expect a comfortable existence in this world. This *Midrash* seems to fall short in its explanation. Why not give the *tzadik* a reward in both worlds?

The *Alter* of Kelm pointed out that Yaakov's retirement plan was to spend day and night learning Torah and doing *mitzvos*. After so many years of hardship, what was so wrong with wanting to spend his last years in such holy pursuits? The *Alter* explains that although it is true that Yaakov had a difficult life, his dedication to Hashem during these times earned him incomprehensibly great rewards in the next world, making the troubles in this world seem negligible. Yaakov's continued service to Hashem, despite the trauma of losing Yosef, lead to even more reward in the next world. Any reward Yaakov would receive for serving Hashem during easy times would be enhanced by performing this service under difficult circumstances. Additionally, the spiritual growth he would achieve by overcoming this difficult challenge would surpass the growth caused by doing a *mitzvah* under less difficult circumstances.

All of us experience difficult challenges and make personal sacrifices in order to serve Hashem properly. We know that we gain from the experience, but is the benefit worth the cost? The Torah teaches us that when undergoing hardships we have to look at the commensurate spiritual growth and reward we will earn when we withstand those hardships and challenges.

IV. Rewarding Struggles

Early in this week's *parasha*, Hashem appears to Yaakov *Ovinu* in a dream and identifies Himself as the "God of Avrohom" and the "God of Yitzchok." *Rashi* tells us that Hashem typically would not have referred to Himself as the "God of Yitzchok" while Yitzchok was still living. Even if one is very pious, Hashem does not associate His name with him while he is alive because he may deviate from his righteous ways and show himself unworthy of the connection between his name and that of Hashem. Should that person remain righteous until his death, then Hashem will attach His name to him. Although Yitzchok was alive at this time, the term "the God of Yitzchok" was appropriate because Yitzchok was blind and confined to his house. He, therefore, had no evil inclination or potential for sin and was considered like a dead person.

At the end of the *parasha*, Yaakov tells Lovon that without the help of Hashem – the "God of Avrohom" and the "One Whom Yitzchok fears" – he would have left the house of Lovon empty handed. Why doesn't Yaakov refer to Hashem as "the God of Yitzchok," as Hashem Himself had in Yaakov's dream?

Rashi explains that Yaakov was afraid to use this term because Hashem does not join His name with the name of a living person. This explanation, however, seems to contradict *Rashi*'s earlier explanation that Yitzchok was an exception to this rule. Why was Yaakov fearful of saying "the God of Yitzchok" if Hashem had already said it Himself?

The *Taz* explains that for Yaakov to say "the God of Yitzchok" would have been a breach in his obligation to honor his father. The greatness of a person is measured by the challenges he has overcome to rise to a higher level.

By connecting Hashem's name to his father's name, Yaakov would be implying that his father no longer had an evil inclination to overcome and his saintly behavior would then be viewed as less of an accomplishment.

The *Taz*'s explanation is based on the obvious truth that to succeed by overcoming an evil inclination is a greater accomplishment than succeeding without difficulty. When one feels he is having difficulty in achieving a greater spiritual level, he may become dejected. If he realizes that the more difficult the challenge of conquering his evil inclination, the greater his reward, then his struggle will become easier.

V. Realizing Falsehood

The Torah tells us that when Yaakov *Ovinu* arrived in Choron, he chanced upon shepherds herding their sheep from the field. Yaakov first inquired from them about his location and whether Lovon lived nearby. The shepherds told him that he was in Choron, that Lovon indeed lived nearby and that his daughter, Rachel, was at that moment on her way to the well where Yaakov was. Yaakov then asked them why they were bringing the sheep in from the field so early in the day.

Yaakov came to Choron by the request of his father with a sacred duty to find a wife for himself from the family of Lovon. After an arduous trip, he is so near to his goal, Rachel is even in view, but instead of rushing to greet her, he pauses to ask the shepherds about their sheep. What was so important that it could distract Yaakov from his mission?

The *Sforno* comments that Yaakov's third question emanated from a perception that the shepherds were cheating their employers. To cheat and steal were so anathematic to Yaakov, that despite the importance of his mission, he couldn't bear to witness it and be silent.

In today's world, we are surrounded by *sheker* – falsehood. At times, it is so easy to "turn the other way" when we see dishonesty around us. We may even think to ourselves, "I would get involved, but it will take up too much of my precious time. After all, it's not as if I'm doing anything wrong." We see from Yaakov that we must stand up for what is right. It is our duty to strengthen ourselves and be sure that we are never complacent when confronted with dishonesty.

Parashas Vayishlach

I. Overcoming Jealousy

After the death of Yaakov's wife Rachel, Reuven, Leah's son, moved his father's couch from Bilhoh's tent to his mother's tent. He did this because he wanted to encourage his father to be with his mother, Leah. The Torah shows its disapproval of this act by recording it in harsh terms, "*Vayeilech Reuven vayishkav es Bilhoh* – And Reuven went and lay with Bilhoh." Ultimately, Reuven was punished by having some of his firstborn rights taken away from him and given to Yosef. In light of this, it is difficult to understand a *Rashi* in last week's *parasha*.

Leah's first son was Reuven. The word "Reuven" can be split into two words, "*re'u* – see" and "*ven* – son." *Rashi* tells us that when Leah named him, it was as if she were telling people to "look at my son" and see the difference between him and Yitzchok's son, Eisov. Eisov gave away his own firstborn rights to his brother, Yaakov, voluntarily, and yet afterward was jealous of Yaakov. In contrast, Leah saw, with her *ruach hakodesh*, that when Reuven would be punished in the future by having the rights of the firstborn taken away from him against his will (because he would move the couch of his father), and given to Yosef, he would show absolutely no jealousy of Yosef. To the contrary, when Yosef was thrown into the pit, Reuven was the only one of the brothers who tried to save Yosef.

His name therefore reflects how nobly he would behave when punished for a future sin. Yet, this choice of name by his mother warrants explanation. Even though his name reflected a positive personality trait, it also alludes to a terrible sin! Why did Leah do this?

In order to answer this, we need to understand the power of jealousy. Yeshaya the Prophet tells us that during the Messianic era, the world will be very peaceful, and nobody will take advantage of anyone else. Everyone will have full faith in Hashem. That being so, we should be able to assume that there will be no jealousy because people will realize that whatever they have is enough. However, the *posuk*, according to *Rashi*, then explicitly says that Moshiach ben Dovid and Moshiach ben Yosef will not be jealous of each other. This *posuk* seems to be telling us something obvious. If the entire world will have a great trust in Hashem, surely the two Moshiachs will have enough trust to overcome their jealousy of each other! Why does this need to be added explicitly?

We can suggest that even though one intellectually knows that jealousy is wrong, the emotion of jealousy is very hard to conquer. This challenge persists even if one has developed complete faith in Hashem. Therefore, it was necessary for the *posuk* to tell us that the Moshiach will not have the trait of jealousy.

Jealousy can be an extremely dangerous force, and when one overcomes jealousy, the impact can be powerful. Reuven's sin was almost completely overshadowed by his tremendous willpower in overcoming jealousy. This level of achievement was even greater than all of his other great character traits and defined his basic nature. His mother chose to name him Reuven to praise him for conquering jealousy, an achievement that far outweighed the allusion to his sin. May we be *zocheh* to emulate the ways of Reuven and reach the level where we truly accept the fact that Hashem gives every person exactly what he needs.

II. A Little Something Extra

Parashas Vayishlach begins by describing Yaakov's preparations in anticipation of his encounter with Eisov. While they were still in the house of their father Yitzchok, Yaakov had received the firstborn *brocha* instead of Eisov. Even though Yaakov had rightfully acquired the firstborn rights from Eisov, Eisov regretted the transaction and developed a bitter hatred towards Yaakov. Now, as Yaakov was returning from Lovon's house with his wives and children, Eisov was planning to wage war against Yaakov. The *posuk* states (32:4)

"Yaakov sent messengers ahead of him to his brother Eisov." Many commentators wonder why Yaakov sent advance messengers. The *Ralbag* explains that Yaakov sent the messengers to give Eisov an intimate and personal account of what had happened to Yaakov since the brothers had last seen each other. The messengers were instructed to tell Eisov about certain personal aspects of Yaakov's life that would only be told to a person who was considered to be very close to Yaakov. The *Ralbag* continues to explain that Yaakov hoped that Eisov would feel touched by this gesture and cease the hatred he displayed towards Yaakov.

Eisov was on the verge of waging war to kill his own brother and had already decided to destroy Yaakov. Why did Yaakov feel that sharing personal feelings would cause Eisov to diminish his hatred? How could Yaakov even consider that Eisov would calm down just because Yaakov would reveal aspects of his life to Eisov? Why would Eisov change his mind just because of close feelings displayed to him?

Yaakov understood that if he were to relate personal and intimate aspects of his life to Eisov, that would be enough to cause Eisov to reconsider how Yaakov felt towards him. It would show a sense of caring and personal friendship between them that would make Eisov aware of how much Yaakov really cared for him. Therefore, Yaakov sent messengers to relate to Eisov his personal experiences. This would show how close Yaakov felt to Eisov and would, it was hoped, diffuse the hatred that Eisov felt. The *Ralbag* says that we see from Yaakov's actions that if one wants to diffuse the hatred existing between himself and an enemy, he should do something personal that shows a sign of closeness between them. In doing so, the hatred that one feels towards another is released. Even with a mere acquaintance, a personal touch can do wonders to enhance a relationship. All of us are in many different relationships in life and the way to strengthen these relationships is by showing our family and friends how deeply we are concerned about them.

III. Follow My Lead

A leader who influences and teaches others to follow in a certain path need not have a large following. We are all leaders of our family, community, or society. This week's *parasha* portrays an incident which gives us an insight into the significance of leadership.

Yaakov *Ovinu*, after crossing the Yabbok river, on his return to Israel from a prolonged stay in Padan Aram, realized that a few minor items had been left behind and crossed back to retrieve them. He was then attacked by an unidentified assailant and became engaged in a vicious struggle. The *Midrash* tells us that this person was the Angel of Eisov, Yaakov's evil brother, who was trying to annihilate Yaakov. They wrestled all night with no one gaining an advantage until finally the angel was able to injure Yaakov but not enough to defeat him. The fight ended at sunrise when the angel had to ascend back to the heavens to sing praises to Hashem.

What possible significance could this mugging have to the Jewish people? The *Sforno* (32:26) explains that the physical struggle that ensued is a metaphor for the spiritual struggle between the children of Yaakov and Eisov. The angel was unable to defeat Yaakov because Yaakov was constantly thinking about Hashem and His greatness, and this focus protected him from the wrath of the angel. To overpower Yaakov, the angel distracted Yaakov for a split second by revealing to Yaakov the future sins of Jewish leaders in later generations. Yaakov became agitated over this vision and lost his concentration for a moment, allowing the angel to injure him slightly.

The angel could have shown Yaakov many other terrible events that have occurred in our history such as the destruction of the first and second *Batei Mikdosh*, the persecution of the Jews in times of the Spanish Inquisition, or even the tragedy of the Holocaust! What was so uniquely devastating to Yaakov about the leaders' sins?

As long as the Jews have good leaders, they will ultimately follow in the Torah's path because they have the appropriate leaders to guide them. The greatest cause for concern for Yaakov was the leaders' stumbling since that would result in the Jews having no proper authority to guide them.

Flaws in leadership have dire consequences. When a leader acts improperly, the follower will most surely become corrupt. Being that we are leaders to our family and friends, we must remember the importance of this role and assume the proper responsibility and behavior.

IV. Appreciating Hardship

At the historic meeting between Pharaoh and Yaakov, Pharaoh was surprised at how old Yaakov appeared and immediately inquired, "How old are you?" Yaakov, who was only one hundred and thirty years old, responded that his life was short and bitter, meaning that he was actually younger than he appeared, but looked much older because of the problems he had experienced with Eisov and Lovon, his wife Rachel's early death, his daughter Dina's having been captured, and Yosef having been taken away from him for twenty-two years.

A *Midrash* tells us that each word in Yaakov's response caused him to lose a year of his life. Why should Yaakov be punished for answering Pharaoh's question honestly? Even though Hashem had eventually saved him from Eisov and Lovon, returned Dina from Shechem, and allowed him to see Yosef alive and well, he had still suffered through these painful events! If he was only telling the truth, without any exaggeration, why were precious years taken from his life?

Apparently, it was deemed inappropriate for a man of Yaakov's stature to say that his life was short and bitter. Although it seems that he was only answering the question posed to him, he should have answered it without editorial comment and simply said that he looked older because of his many troubles. Instead he characterized his *entire* life as harsh and bitter, showing a small but significant lack of appreciation for all the good Hashem had done for him. This seemingly small lack of gratitude in someone of Yaakov's stature was serious enough to cause him to lose thirty-three years of his life.

The hardships and challenges we experience in our daily lives should not influence our general outlook on life by causing us to deem it harsh and difficult. Every moment in this world can be used to serve Hashem and is therefore extremely precious. We must take advantage of the opportunities that we have to serve Hashem and view life as meaningful, productive, and in a generally positive light.

V. Appreciating Advice

Dovid *HaMelech*, at the end of his life, advised his son Shlomo, "*V'chazakta v'hayisa l'ish* – You should be strengthened and merit to be a man!" (*Melachim* 1 2:1) The *Meforshim* explain that this meant that Shlomo should be *sho'el eitza* – seek the advice of others.

It is mind boggling that Dovid *HaMelech* should need to give this type of suggestion – to seek the advice of others – to his brilliant son, Shlomo! Certainly, there could be a more meaningful last will and testament for Shlomo *HaMelech*, the wisest of all men!

The answer can be gleaned from this week's *parasha*. The *posuk* states, (34:25) *"V'yikchu shnei bnei Yaakov Shimon v'Levi* – The two sons of Yaakov [Shimon and Levi] killed all the males in the city of Shechem for violating their sister, Dina."

The *Midrash Rabbah* (80:10) states that from the extra word in the *posuk*, *"shnei* – two," we learn that Shimon and Levi did not consult each other as they should have prior to carrying out this attack on the male population in Shechem.

If they both came to the same decision on their own, what real benefit could they have had in seeking each other's counsel? They would surely have reached the same ultimate conclusion to kill all the males in the city!

The answer teaches us an important lesson and a fundamental insight into human dynamics. Remarkably, had Shimon and Levi consulted each other first, they may have exited that conversation with a totally different conclusion than to kill the people of Shechem. Despite the fact that they each were inclined to attack, nevertheless, through open dialogue and the benefit of hearing someone else's opinion, their eyes may have been opened to a new perspective and viewpoint.

We are faced with numerous decisions and calls to action. Do we merely find people, even our spouses, who happen to agree with our positions? Or do we engage in open-minded conversation and debate, asking for advice, searching, perhaps, for a new perspective or different angle on the matter?

This is why Dovid *HaMelech* bequeathed this advice to Shlomo. We can only be guaranteed to make correct decisions when we are *sho'el eitza*. Let's revisit some of our "foregone conclusions" and reanalyze their basis through healthy dialogue by meaningfully being *sho'el eitza*!

Parashas Vayeisheiv

In honor of our esteemed Roshei Yeshiva

Rabbi Binyomin Luban
Rabbi Yisroel Yitzchok Niman
Rabbi Mordechai Palgon

Jonathan and Abby Rubin

I. A Labor of Laziness

Yosef's relationship with his brothers was very strained. Yosef had told his brothers about two dreams he had predicting he would rule over them, and they reacted with jealousy and hostility towards him. Yosef knew this, yet when Yaakov *Ovinu* told Yosef to check up on his brothers while they were shepherding in Shechem, Yosef replied, "*Hineni* – Here I am." Yosef's response cannot be taken literally as he was already in Yaakov's presence talking with him! The *Ibn Ezra* explains that what Yosef meant by answering his father "*hineni*" was, "I will do as you say." The *Avi Ezer* elaborates on this interpretation. The Torah is telling us that Yosef was being zealous and did not act like a lazy messenger who, when told to do something, asks: "When should I do it? Where do you want me to go? Which road do I use to travel there?"

Why does the Torah consider these questions indicative of a lazy messenger? How else will the messenger know what to do? Certainly a good messenger must get full instructions!

Even though these types of questions may be important, often they emanate from a lack of motivation or simple laziness. Yosef's usage of the word "*hineni*" tells us that he was ready to fulfill his father's command right away, even before he knew how he would do it. Yosef had a very good excuse not to go – he was afraid that his brothers might kill him. Nevertheless, he did not ask the questions of a lazy messenger. He controlled his *yetzer horah* – evil inclination – and said, "I am here, ready to do as you say, without questioning."

We often make up "reasonable" excuses why we should avoid doing certain things. "How can I do this? I can't; I won't." Those reactions often are a product of our own laziness. We must honestly and diligently analyze what needs to be done and constantly question whether we are asking questions out of laziness.

Many of us believe that even if we are sometimes lazy, we will be able to overcome our laziness when the situation requires it. However, this is not true. Once a person is lazy, that *middoh* affects all aspects of his behavior.

When the *Bnei Yisroel* were in Egypt, Moshe *Rabbeinu* came upon an Egyptian taskmaster who was beating a Jew to death. Moshe took up the cause of his fellow Jew and killed the Egyptian. When word spread about the death of the Egyptian, he quickly fled from Egypt out of fear for his life. *Rabbeinu* Yonah points out that this act of fleeing hastily was an act of *zerizus* – zeal. Only someone who is a *zoriz* would be able to flee so quickly. Why is this true? Anyone whose life was in danger would run away as soon as possible! So why is Moshe *Rabbeinu*'s quick escape labeled as an act of *zerizus*?

A lazy person will not be able to act like a *zoriz*, even in times of imminent danger. Even though he truly wants at that moment to be a *zoriz*, he will not be able to act in a way that is contrary to his nature. If Moshe had not been a *zoriz* in other matters, he would not have been able to act with *zerizus* and leave Egypt so quickly, even though his life was in danger.

We can see two insights about the *middoh* of laziness from Yosef and Moshe. Yosef's response teaches us that our questions and excuses may at times reflect underlying laziness that we may not even be aware of. Moshe's ability to act quickly teaches us that we must overcome laziness in every situation in order to act appropriately in an urgent situation.

II. Contemplative Gratitude

Parashas Vayeisheiv describes the breakdown of the relationship between Yosef and his brothers that ultimately led to outright hatred. This terrible course of events was partially caused by Yosef himself who spoke *loshon horah* about his brothers to Yaakov, their father, and also by Yaakov's display of favoritism towards Yosef by giving him the special cloak. The situation ultimately deteriorated to the point that the brothers convened a formal court and decided that Yosef was attempting to cause Yaakov to curse them and exclude them from the tribes. This act qualified Yosef as a *rodeif* – one who is pursuing another – and therefore, *halachically* subject to the death penalty. Reuven, intending to return later to save Yosef, objected and suggested that rather than kill Yosef, they should throw him into a pit.

The *posuk* states (37:22) "And Reuven heard and saved him from their hands." What did Reuven hear? The *Midrash Rabbah* (*Bereishis Rabbah* 84:15) explains that "hearing" is to be interpreted as realizing or becoming aware of an important issue. Reuven remembered an event that had taken place many years earlier. After Rachel, Yaakov's wife, died, Yaakov moved his marital couch from her tent into his concubine Bilhoh's tent. Reuven (incorrectly) felt that Yaakov had erred in judgment by placing his marital couch in a secondary wife's tent and he therefore brazenly moved Yaakov's couch back into his mother's tent. When Yaakov became extremely upset at Reuven for intruding on his personal, private life, Reuven felt such guilt about his actions, that he assumed he was no longer included as one of the Tribes of Israel. Years later, Yosef repeated one of his two dreams. A sun, moon, and eleven stars were bowing down to Yosef. These eleven stars represented all eleven brothers. Yosef had included Reuven in this count! Reuven felt great relief to hear Yosef include him as one of the brothers. At the tribunal convened by the brothers, Reuven recalled this feeling of relief and continued to feel a sense of gratitude towards Yosef for providing this relief. This led him to prevent the brothers from killing Yosef.

Yosef had not intended to assure Reuven that he was still one of the tribes and relieve Reuven of his worries. Yosef was merely relaying his dream. Why did Reuven feel that he owed Yosef anything? Why should Yosef's inadvertent "favor" years earlier stop Reuven from killing Yosef?

We can understand this *Midrash* by expanding our understanding of what creates an obligation of gratitude. Reuven took notice of the inadvertent good that he benefited from. Even though Yosef only played a passive role in reassuring Reuven, it was enough for Reuven to feel a debt of gratitude towards him. Reuven focused on the "favor" done for him and was prevented from allowing the brothers to kill Yosef.

We need to take time to recognize, contemplate, and appreciate the good that is done for us – even if it may seem at times minor or inadvertent. We may already be aware of good that is done for us, but if we take the time to contemplate it more deeply, we will develop a stronger appreciation. This can radically alter our perspective of events and people.

III. Jealous Judgment

Jealousy is a trait that can affect a person's behavior and judgment insidiously and cause a person to commit serious *aveiros* – transgressions. This week's *parasha* shows us the extreme degree to which jealousy can impair judgment. The feud between Yosef and his brothers arose when Yaakov gave Yosef a beautiful coat and was further aggravated when Yosef publicized a dream foretelling how his brothers would bow down to him. Shortly thereafter, Yaakov asked Yosef to check on his brothers who were in the fields of Shechem pasturing the sheep. When the brothers saw Yosef approaching from afar, they convened a meeting to pass judgment on him and, after pondering the situation, concluded that Yosef, by trying to make the brothers appear unworthy in Yaakov's eyes, would cause Yaakov to bless Yosef exclusively. The brothers would lack the blessings from their father and thereby be cut off from this world and the next world. The brothers ruled that Yosef was a *rodeif* – one who is pursuing another – and therefore must be killed. The *Gemorah* (*Shabbos* 10b), going beyond the simple understanding of the verses, explains that jealousy was the cause of the brothers' hatred toward Yosef and their decision to kill him. The *Gemorah* is revealing to us the subconscious motives behind this act. Undoubtedly, the brothers would never have acted upon their conclusion had they been aware that jealousy was playing a role in their decision. We must conclude that either the brothers were not even aware of their jealousy towards Yosef or felt that they could separate their personal feelings from their "objective" judgment.

We see that jealousy, a trait that the brothers may not have even detected in themselves, caused their judgment to become impaired without their being aware of the impairment. They most certainly would have claimed they were being objective in their judgment. Jealousy has the power to distort the way one views a situation and can cause one to act in a very negative manner. Moreover, very often one does not even recognize that he is jealous. Even if we try to be honest with ourselves, and claim that we can separate our feelings from our judgment, this episode demonstrates that it is impossible to be objective when one has a personal stake in a decision. If the sons of Yaakov, the founders of the *Shivtei Kah* – the Twelve Tribes – could not succeed in separating their personal involvement from their thought processes, certainly we will be subject to this interaction. We must be ever cognizant of this dangerous trait, remembering that it can potentially change our attitudes and damage our relationships.

IV. Fleeing from Temptation

This week's *parasha*, Vayeisheiv, recounts the incident involving Yosef and his master Potifar's wife, who was determined to seduce Yosef to have relations with her. Yosef rebuffed every effort, explaining: "How could I do this great evil and sin to my God?" Finally, when she and Yosef were alone in the house, she grabbed his clothing and insisted that he have relations with her. Yosef immediately ran from her, leaving his outer garment in her hand, as the *posuk* says: "He left his garment in her hand, and he fled and went outside." The next *posuk* states: "And it was when she saw he had left his garment in her hand, and he fled outside that she called to the people of the household and said to them, 'See, he brought us a Hebrew man to mock us!'" Why does the first *posuk* state that Yosef "fled and went outside," but the next *posuk* only says that he "fled outside?"

The *Sforno* answers that the first *posuk* was written from Yosef's perspective and the second *posuk* was written from *Aishes* Potifar's perspective. Yosef ran out of her room, but calmly and slowly walked out of the house, in order to appear inconspicuous and avoid being questioned. Therefore, the first *posuk* says that he both "fled and went outside." Since Potifar's wife only saw Yosef flee from her room, she assumed he had continued running out of the house. Therefore, the second *posuk* only says, "and he fled," omitting the words "and he went." Potifar's wife mistakenly thought that Yosef had run from the house, thereby causing a commotion, which would lead people to investigate the incident and suspect her. She therefore fabricated a story to cover her tracks.

However, another question surfaces. If Yosef felt that walking calmly and slowly out of the house would avoid suspicion, why didn't he leave Mrs. Potifar's room in the same way? Didn't he realize that by fleeing her room, Potifar's wife could mistakenly conclude that he had acted in a panic causing her to make a false accusation? Yosef's deliberate actions of running from her room but walking from the house put his life in danger. Why didn't he also walk away slowly and calmly from her room, assuring that she would remain silent?

The *Sforno* answers that even though Yosef realized that walking slowly out of Mrs. Potifar's room was in his best interest, and fleeing from her could lead to imprisonment or even death, he was afraid that if he stayed a few seconds longer he might succumb to her.

From Yosef's actions, we learn how far one must go to remove oneself from situations of potential sin in which his *yetzer horah* might overpower him. Even at the expense of endangering oneself, one must avoid or withdraw from situations which could result in spiritual harm. Although one may be committed to acting properly, there is no assurance that the *yetzer horah* will not be victorious at the last moment.

Parashas Mikeitz

I. Calming a Conflict

The beginning of *Parashas* Mikeitz relates the strange sequence of events that catapult Yosef *Hatzadik* to the royal palace as ruler of Egypt. In this capacity, Yosef was able to implement a national plan to save Mitzrayim from the imminent peril of a famine. Other countries, such as Canaan, were left unprepared for this crisis. The famine ultimately forced Yosef's brothers to travel to Mitzrayim to seek food. When the brothers appeared before Yosef, who was directly in charge of the storehouses, they did not recognize him, but Yosef, recognizing his brothers, arrested them and accused them of being spies. Yosef detained Shimon in Egypt and decreed that the remaining brothers be sent home with a mission of bringing back Binyomin for Yosef to see, thereby proving their story.

Upon hearing Yosef's decree, the brothers said to each other that the unfolding events were a punishment for selling Yosef. Reuven then told his brothers (42:2), "Behold I told you, do not sin with the child and you did not listen..."

The *Sforno* explains that the brothers still assumed that they had been correct in their judgment that Yosef was a *rodeif*. They presumed that Yosef was indeed trying to induce Yaakov, their father, to curse them, thereby assuring their death in this world or in the World to Come. The brothers had come to recognize, however, that when Yosef pleaded for mercy, they should have heeded his request. Reuven had always disagreed with the brothers and felt, incorrectly, that they had interpreted Yosef's actions as a premeditated plot to harm them. The actions in question, Reuven argued, were like those of a child: spontaneous and without any hidden agenda.

The *Sforno*'s explanation of Reuven's argument is most difficult. Firstly, Yosef was no longer a child when those events occurred. He was seventeen years old and already an accomplished Torah scholar. *Chazal* tell us that Yaakov taught all the Torah he learned in *Yeshivas Shem V'ever* to Yosef. Yosef having resisted the *nisayon* of *Aishes* Potifar – Potifar's wife – demonstrates he had much *Yiras Shomayim*. *Rabbeinu* Yonah writes that the ability to foresee the consequences of one's actions is a necessary ingredient of *Yiras Shomayim*. Surely we can conclude that Yosef, who had acquired much *Yiras Shomayim*, would not act as a child and behave haphazardly. It is, therefore, hard to understand Reuven's defense of Yosef to his brothers, yet we see that with all of Yosef's intellectual prowess, his actions in some way still reflected his young age. He did not always give as much thought to his actions, as he might have done had he been older. Therefore, Reuven argued that Yosef's actions do not constitute a premeditated plot.

Children, young adults, or even mature people may cause us harm or discomfort and we may often conclude that it was a deliberate act performed with malice. As we have seen from Reuven's argument, it is quite possible to mistakenly ascribe a deeper intent to a person who otherwise has none. This can escalate an innocuous situation into an interpersonal conflict thereby generating much unnecessary ill will for the parties involved. If we were ever cognizant of this idea, we would find that many of our reactions in such situations would be muted. By constantly reminding ourselves of this obvious but elusive fact, we can enrich our lives and avoid conflict.

II. A Daily Dose of Inspiration

In this week's *parasha*, Pharaoh had a series of strange dreams. All of his officers attempted to interpret his dreams, but Pharaoh was not satisfied with any of their explanations. The Cup-bearer remembered that, while he was in jail, Yosef had interpreted his dream correctly and consequently told Pharaoh of Yosef and his abilities. Pharaoh summoned Yosef and told him the dreams. Yosef, by miracle of the Divine will, was able to interpret them to Pharaoh's liking. Pharaoh appointed him viceroy in charge of preparing Egypt for the future famine. The *posuk* (41:41) says, "And Pharaoh said to Yosef, 'See that I have placed you in charge of the entire land of Egypt!'" The *Sforno* comments that Pharaoh wanted Yosef to accomplish this vital task and was motivating him to do an excellent job.

Did Yosef need motivation? He knew that failure meant returning to prison. In mentioning to Pharaoh that a wise man would be needed to store, guard, and ration food for the coming famine, Yosef subtly hinted that he thought himself to be capable of rising to the challenge. Pharaoh gave Yosef the job he very much desired. Having received the coveted position and knowing the consequences of failure, Yosef would certainly work with great diligence. Was Pharaoh's additional motivation accomplishing anything? Pharaoh understood the value of encouragement. Despite Yosef's great self-interest and incentive, Pharaoh knew that a few extra words of encouragement would potentially further motivate Yosef to greater success by heightening his focus on his assignment.

We see from here how additional encouragement can motivate an individual to accomplish tremendous deeds. No matter the situation or task, a bit of motivation can have a great effect even on those who do not appear to be in need of encouragement. We may often think that we are already motivated, focused, and prepared to encounter many goals in our lives. If someone as great as Yosef required additional motivation, then surely we, who are not as great, must remember to constantly seek these additional inspirations for ourselves. This can be accomplished by studying the ethical works of *mussar* daily, which will help us find sources of motivation, causing us to become better focused on accomplishing our many goals.

Parashas Vayigash

In memory of our zeida
Sam Kalchman

*Rabbi Tzvi and Karen Nightingale
and Family*

I. Small But Significant

Parashas Vayigash relates the climax of the saga of Yosef and his brothers. Yosef finally reveals his identity to them and inquires about the welfare of his father, Yaakov. Once Yosef learns that his father is well, he orders the brothers to return quickly to *Eretz Yisroel* to tell his father that he is alive and the viceroy of Egypt, as the *posuk* states, "Hurry and go up to my father..." (45:9). The *Sforno* explains that Yosef was trying to spare his father any additional pain that Yaakov was feeling about Yosef's loss. Yosef wanted his father to hear that he was alive and well and put an end to the grief that his father had been suffering as quickly as possible. Later, when Yosef was telling the brothers to bring his father to Mitzrayim, the verse states (45:13), "Therefore, tell my father of all my glory in Egypt and all that you saw; but you must hurry, and bring my father down here." Here the *Sforno* comments that Yosef did not want to delay the satisfaction that Yaakov would feel by actually seeing him.

The second *Sforno* is difficult to understand. Yaakov had spent many years without Yosef. When he finds out that Yosef was alive, all his pain and grief will have been dissipated. It is true that Yaakov would be happier by actually being able to see Yosef, but would this additional happiness justify the brothers rushing back to Egypt? The whole family had much to do. They had to pack up all of their belongings and travel to Egypt. Why did Yosef feel that a delay of a day or two would make an important difference, particularly Yaakov's transformation from a state of misery to a state of ecstasy upon hearing the good news?

Yosef understood that even a small amount of happiness is significant. Delaying the reunion between him and his father would in fact make a great difference to him and Yaakov, even if it might seem to others to be negligible. Hastening the reunion would bring Yaakov that much more *simcha* and therefore was important to Yosef. Consequently, he urged the brothers to do everything in their power to hasten the joyous reunion.

Small acts of kindness towards another seem to be the focus of Yosef's intention and are considered significant because they show how much a person cares. Even if it is a simple "hello" in the morning, it can uplift another person. Sometimes we become involved in a big event and tend to minimize the seemingly insignificant acts of kindness that need to be displayed. These small acts of kindness can make a great difference.

II. Ending Embarrassment

How far should we go to avoid hurting another person's feelings? Must we sacrifice personal gain or even subject ourselves to possible harm just to avoid causing another person embarrassment?

Two events in this week's *parasha* answer this question. The brothers appear for the third time before Yosef *Hatzadik*, the viceroy of Egypt, and Yosef has decided that the time is right to reveal his identity. Yosef had not seen his brothers for twenty-two years, and now that the proper time had arrived to reveal his identity to his brothers, he was bursting with emotion and excitement. Only after excusing the Egyptian officers and ministers from the room to avoid causing his brothers' embarrassment did Yosef exclaim, "I am Yosef, whom you sold as a slave" (*Rashi* 45:1). How could Yosef bear waiting the extra moment or two it took for the Egyptians to leave? He could have justified not sending out the Egyptians since they would eventually hear that the brothers had sold Yosef into slavery. The brothers only had themselves to blame for any public embarrassment they may suffer. According to the *Midrash Rabbah* (Bereishis 93:9), by sending out his bodyguards, Yosef was also taking a great personal risk because his brothers might have killed him! Yosef's greatness is demonstrated by his sensitivity to this extra embarrassment, even under great emotional stress. Yosef did not want to add more pain to an already painful situation.

Another incident occurs in the *parasha* that delivers a similar message. When Yosef settled his brothers in Goshen, he required every Egyptian to relocate to a different section of the land. *Rashi* (47:21) explains that Yosef did this so that the Egyptians should feel like "exiles" and not call his brothers "exiles." Even though Yosef presumably had a justification for causing hardship to the Egyptians and their families, wasn't this action too extreme? Certainly the embarrassment would be minimal as they were the viceroy's brothers! Apparently, the difficulty of relocating the entire Egyptian nation was worth sparing his family the slight embarrassment of being called "exiles."

In the Baranovitch Yeshiva, the *shamash* who lit the heating furnace every morning was absent and the *mashgiach*, Reb Yisroel Yaakov, went to light the fire. As the *mashgiach* bent over the fire, a student, thinking he would play a joke on the *"shamash,"* went over to Reb Yisroel Yaakov and nudged him, pushing him farther into the hot furnace. The *mashgiach* knew that if he turned around, the student would realize whom he had pushed into the fire and would be very embarrassed! The *mashgiach* therefore stayed in the same position, causing his beard to become singed by the fire, until the student left. The hallmark of a great person is his great sensitivity to others as evidenced by the extremes he will go to avoid embarrassing them.

III. Emotional Control

The beginning of this week's *parasha* describes Yehuda's desperate plea before Yosef on behalf of his youngest brother. Yehuda explained to Yosef that their aged father, Yaakov, was deeply attached to Binyomin; he would suffer incredibly and die if Binyomin did not return. According to *Chazal*, Yehuda's words contained an implicit threat: if Yosef did not release Binyomin, Yehuda and his brothers, who were all men of great physical prowess, would free Binyomin by force, killing Yosef and Pharaoh if necessary. The *Midrash* explains that Yosef had intended to carry out the charade even further to allow his brothers the opportunity to repent completely for his sale. When he heard of the anguish that it would cause to his father Yaakov, he decided to reveal himself. However, before Yosef revealed himself, he dismissed all of his attendants and servants from the room. *Rashi* explains that Yosef's intent was to avoid embarrassing his brothers in the presence of the Egyptians. Finally, Yosef wept aloud, and told his brothers who he really was.

Yosef's actions are surprising. The *pesukim* stress Yosef's pressing emotional need to reveal himself to his brothers. After being separated from his beloved father and brothers for twenty-two years, given the opportunity to reunite, we would expect Yosef to blurt out the truth, ignoring the presence of any bystanders. Furthermore, Yosef's fear that Yehuda and his brothers might kill him before his identity was established would tend to discourage Yosef from secluding himself with his brothers and delaying his announcement. Nevertheless, Yosef was able to restrain himself until he had seen to it that his brothers would not be humiliated by his revelation.

This description of Yosef's conduct teaches us the degree of self-control that the Torah expects a Jew to exhibit even while experiencing extreme emotions. Yosef *Hatzadik*'s emotions were totally guided and subjugated to the requirements of *halacha*.

Another example of Yosef's unique self-discipline occurs later in the *parasha*, when Yosef finally went to greet his father after twenty-two years of separation. The *posuk* says that he "appeared before his father." Both Yosef and Yaakov had longed for each other's company throughout the period of separation. Undoubtedly, Yosef was deeply looking forward to the prospect of meeting his father after so many years. However, the *posuk* emphasizes that Yosef appeared before his father, rather than seeing his father, because Yosef's only goal was to ensure that his reunification with his father was as enjoyable and meaningful as possible for Yaakov. Once again, Yosef has set aside his personal, emotional considerations to maximize his father's pleasure, as required by the *mitzvah* of *kibud ov* – honoring one's father.

Yosef's exemplary self-control can serve as a model for us in our own lives. We must remember that on many occasions, Yosef *Hatzadik* demonstrated supreme self-discipline under nearly impossible circumstances. By emulating Yosef's unconditional commitment to *halacha*, as well as his sensitivity to the feelings of others, we can incorporate Torah wisdom into every moment of our lives.

Parashas Vayechi

I. The Root of the Problem

After Yosef revealed his identity to his brothers, they were understandably apprehensive about how Yosef would deal with them, as they had sold Yosef as a slave after almost killing him. Now, he was the absolute ruler of the Egyptian empire. Yosef recognized what was troubling his brothers and tried to calm them by declaring his sincere forgiveness. He even went so far as to equate his love for them to his love for his full brother, Binyomin, who had no part in the sale of Yosef.

Following Yaakov *Ovinu*'s death years later in *Parashas* Vayechi, we again find the brothers concerned that Yosef would plan revenge. The *Da'as Zekeinim* (Bereishis 50:16) explains that as Yaakov's funeral procession passed the pit into which Yosef had been cast into by his brothers, he paused and recited the blessing that is said upon visiting a site where one has been miraculously saved. The memory of this tragic event was alive in Yosef's mind and without Yaakov alive to keep the peace, the brothers feared Yosef would kill them. *Rashi* (ibid. v. 19) tells us that this time, Yosef used a new and somewhat perplexing argument to reassure his brothers – "If I kill you, I will look bad," he said. "People will say I took my brothers, supported them, and then turned on them and had them executed. Furthermore, all ten of you tried to kill me and failed to do so; how then will I be able to kill all of you?"

Yosef had already told his brothers several times that they were forgiven and had sustained them as royal guests for seventeen years. Why were they suddenly afraid for their lives and why did Yosef use such a cold, pragmatic argument that does not seem to express forgiveness or a feeling of love for his brothers.

The reaction of Yosef's brothers upon seeing Yosef standing at the pit illustrates an important aspect of human psychology. The vivid image of a serious traumatic event invoked a powerful emotional response. Even though the brothers knew Yosef had forgiven them, the sight of him praying by the pit generated such strong anxiety that they feared the worst, albeit irrationally.

Yosef understood the nature of their reaction and responded appropriately. To tell his brothers that he had forgiven them would have been insufficient. They already knew that and were still anxious. Rather, Yosef directly addressed their fear of his revenge with logical arguments to prove that it was groundless. The power of these arguments assuaged their worries enough to allow their intellect to take over and once again conclude that Yosef meant them no harm.

This lesson is essential in dealing with any situation in which we have to reassure others. Simply telling someone that everything is all right or that you forgive him is not enough to overcome a feeling of anxiety. One must look for the underlying roots of the problem and try to deal with them as well. From Yosef *Hatzadik* we learn to look deeper for the source of a friend's anxiety and develop strategies that allow us to reassure them properly.

II. Timing Is Everything

In *Parashas* Vayechi, as Yaakov approaches the end of his days, Yosef is summoned to his bedside and commanded to bury him with his ancestors in *Me'oras Hamachpela* – the cave of the patriarchs. Yaakov, in a seemingly unrelated speech, tells Yosef about the death and burial of Rachel, who was Yaakov's wife and Yosef's mother. The *posuk* states (48:7), "...when I came from Paran, Rachel died on me in the land of Canaan on the road...and I buried her there on the road..." Yosef had known for years that his mother had been buried on the roadside and not in *Me'oras Hamachpela*, but he had never been told why. Yaakov was now revealing to Yosef the reason Rachel had not been buried at *Me'oras Hamachpela*.

Rashi comments that Yaakov knew that Yosef had some misgivings about Yaakov not providing Rachel a more honorable burial in the proper place. Yaakov related a prophecy that when the Jews would later go into exile during the times of Nebuzaradan, Nebuchadnezzar's general, the Jews would pass the grave of Rachel, who would ask in a tearful prayer to Hashem that mercy be shown to us and we be returned from exile. Rachel's burial site would serve in a special capacity as a catalyst for the redemption. Yaakov's revelation was intended to put to rest Yosef's misgivings about Rachel not having been buried in *Me'oras Hamachpela,* as she had been buried in a very important location. This knowledge would assuage any negative feelings Yosef may have had towards Yaakov, since he now understood that his father's actions had a divine and essential purpose.

The *Sifsei Chachomim* questions why Yaakov did not explain the prophecy to Yosef many years earlier. Why did Yaakov wait until the last possible moment, when he was on his deathbed, to relieve Yosef's concerns? Yosef probably had felt unsettled for many years that his mother had been buried along the roadside. Why did Yaakov wait so long?

The *Sifsei Chachomim* answers that Yaakov knew that the revelation of a future exile and persecution would itself cause Yosef new pain and he wanted to spare Yosef this additional pain. Yaakov was balancing two conflicting questions – should he tell Yosef the reason his mother was buried along the roadside and remove Yosef's misgivings about Yaakov, or should he spare Yosef the pain of the prophecy. Yaakov decided that it was not right to put Yosef in a painful situation any earlier than necessary. This was an act of sensitivity in which Yaakov was careful not to cause Yosef any emotional pain prematurely. As Yaakov approached death, he felt that it was now necessary to tell Yosef; otherwise Yosef would never know this vital information. Yaakov most certainly was motivated to tell this to Yosef earlier and remove the questions Yosef might have about Yaakov's actions. Yet we see Yaakov ignored this personal motivation to adhere to the strictness in the laws of interpersonal relations – the requirement of extreme sensitivity to another person. We, too, must learn to measure our emotions against the standards of these "laws" in order to ultimately do what is proper.

III. Simply *Chesed*

When the Jews left Egypt, to travel to *Eretz Yisroel*, they bypassed the shorter route through territory inhabited by a Canaanite sect because Hashem wanted to spare this sect the disruption of having their land used as a passage. They deserved this protection because their ancestors had lived on the route taken by Yaakov's burial procession. What had these Canaanites done to deserve this protection? This week's *parasha*, *Parashas* Vayechi, relates that a large procession including Yosef, the Viceroy of Egypt, and his brothers accompanied Yaakov in his final journey from Egypt to *Eretz* Canaan for burial. When the procession arrived in Goren HaAtod, a city on the bank of the Jordan, the local Canaanites took note of the large funeral procession. The *Yalkut Shimoni* explains that the local population did no more than merely point to the funeral procession and acknowledge its significance. They simply noticed that a funeral was taking place, took a moment to think about it and stated that Egypt has suffered a great loss. Yet, this simple act showed respect for Yaakov, and Hashem credited this act of *chesed* towards a deceased man and made the Jews take a different route to *Eretz Yisroel*.

What had the Canaanites really done to deserve this special protection two centuries later? Anyone would have noticed that a large funeral was taking place in their land. Why was this seemingly insignificant act of acknowledging the loss important enough to merit their being saved from having the Jews come through their land? The answer is that a seemingly insignificant act of *chesed* towards Yaakov was actually very significant, as indicated by their reward.

We can learn from here the importance of doing any act of *chesed* and the reward we will receive. If the Canaanites could merely lift a finger and be so heavily rewarded, how much more so will we be rewarded for performing a difficult *chesed*. If we appreciate the importance and the reward for doing any *chesed*, we will find it easier to act in such a manner.

IV. Compromising Values

We often underestimate the influence our surroundings can have on us. There is a tendency to say to oneself, "I can handle the pressure I feel from those around me. I am strong enough to overcome it." The Torah teaches that one's environment indeed can have a significant impact on his behavior.

In this week's *parasha*, the Torah enumerates the eleven sons of Yaakov *Ovinu* who came down to Egypt and then says, "*V'Yosef haya b'Mitzrayim* – Yosef was in Egypt." *Rashi* explains this is praise for Yosef. He retained the same level of purity and righteousness that he acquired in his father's house throughout his difficult sojourn amidst the decadence of Egyptian culture.

It is indeed noteworthy that the Torah chooses this as praise for Yosef. Shouldn't one expect that Yosef, the "*ben zekunim*," who, *Rashi* himself learns that at the tender age of seventeen, had acquired all of his saintly father Yaakov's Torah, would preserve his *kedusha* despite whatever those around him were involved in? Rather, we see that even a great *tzadik* such as Yosef could be influenced by his surroundings.

We also see that Yosef persevered. He was able to retain his father's Torah and keep himself from being affected by those around him. It was indeed possible for him to be exposed to this foreign culture and, undoubtedly through great effort, maintain his purity and righteousness.

The lesson for us is two-fold. Firstly, we must be aware of the dangers that are posed by the values of those around us. We are quite susceptible to being tempted to compromise our Torah values, even if in a small way. Secondly, we see that it is possible to overcome the influence of society and not dilute our values. Let us make it a priority to minimize our association with those who would have a negative influence on us, and redouble our efforts to maintain our *kedusha*.

SEFER SHEMOS

Dedicated in memory of our beloved mother:

Jeanette Levine, a"h
Chaya Yachet Elka bas R' Yisroel Yitzchak, a"h
1958-2009

Our mother exemplified personal growth through Torah, and in so doing, served as a role model for her family, community and so many others. Although we fondly remember her as the *eishes chayil* and *ba'alas bitachon* she was, we also recognize that it was only through her constant efforts to improve that she achieved this. It is, therefore, quite appropriate that she be remembered in the pages of this distinguished *sefer, Courage to Change.*

It is further fitting that this *sefer* bear her name and memory because she was a dedicated employee and avid supporter of the Toras Emes/Toras Chaim institutions. She had a deep love and appreciation for the *yeshiva* and its ideals, and she expressed that love through her words and actions.

May the *divrei* Torah and *mussar* contained in these pages serve to inspire its readers, and in that merit, may it be a *zechus* for her *neshama.*

Josh and Gitty Levine
and family

Marc and Talia Levine
and family

Ari and Shira Sipper
and family

Jonah and Reena Zisquit

Parashas Shemos

I. Hope for the Hopeless

Is success only an occasional outcome and failure a natural part of the life experience? What can we do to ensure our own success?

The story of Moshe's birth has much to teach us about how to succeed in life. Pharaoh had decreed that all newborn boys should be thrown into the Nile River. Although the Egyptians knew Yocheved was expecting a baby, she delivered a few months early and as they did not expect her delivery for another three months, she was able to hide Moshe in the house. As the ninth month ended, this arrangement became impossible and Yocheved came up with a plan to save Moshe. Praying to Hashem for the best, she placed him in a waterproof basket and set the basket in the Nile River. A few moments later Moshe was found by Pharaoh's daughter, Basya, who took him home and raised him in Pharaoh's house.

The Torah explains why Yocheved hid Moshe. The *posuk* says (2:2), "And she gave birth to a son, and she saw that he was good, so she hid him for three months." The *Ramban* asks a very obvious question: Any mother would go to extreme lengths to save her child and certainly would at least try to hide him. Why does the Torah emphasize that "he was good" as if to explain Yocheved's actions? *Chazal* tell us that the whole house lit up when Moshe was born. The *Ramban* explains that the Torah uses "he was good" to express that Yocheved saw in this light a sign of something unique and special about Moshe, far beyond what a mother would usually see in her baby. Therefore, she thought of ways to save him after the three months had passed.

The *Ramban* has not answered his own question! The *posuk* tells us that Yocheved saw something special about Moshe and saved him, implying that had Yocheved not seen something special about Moshe – she would not have saved him? Yet we know that any mother would want to save her child even without seeing something special in her baby!

The *Ramban* must be telling us that the situation was so dangerous that other mothers were not trying to save their babies from Pharaoh's decree – they had all given up hope. They were not even thinking about how to get around the decree because they perceived the situation as hopeless. Had Yocheved not seen something special in Moshe, she probably would have also given up hope that Moshe was able to be saved. Even the best of people, such as Yocheved, can give up hope. Therefore, Hashem had to send a special sign to motivate Yocheved to try to save Moshe.

Certainly, if one gives up, one will fail. Therefore, when we feel that all hope is lost, we must give ourselves an extra push and try again. Then we may even succeed. An unpredictable turn of events or unforeseen force may change the outcome. This is more than simply an inspirational or motivational tool. It is a fact. Often the difference between success and failure is determined at the last moment – before totally losing hope. *Chazal* teach us that Hashem never presents us with a challenge unless we are able to overcome it, albeit with great effort. We choose how much effort to invest into every problem. Had Yocheved not seen the special sign attending Moshe's birth, she would probably have given up and not saved him. Yet, her act of abandonment would have been uncalled for. People stop trying because they feel the situation is hopeless and accept defeat. If we knew that it is possible to succeed, we would try harder rather than give up. We should never lose hope in any situation and in the merit of this conviction, may we succeed in all of our endeavors.

II. Giving Thanks

We all recognize the importance of expressing a sense of gratitude – *hakoras hatov* – towards people who have helped us. It is equally important to understand the outcome of failing to show *hakoras hatov* to our fellow man. Can the result of a lack of *hakoras hatov* have extreme consequences? How dangerous can this act of ingratitude really be?

In *Parashas* Shemos, the *posuk* says (1:8), "And a new king arose over Egypt who did not know Yosef." In *Rashi*'s second interpretation, he was the same king

Pharaoh whose dreams had been interpreted by Yosef years earlier, thereby saving Egypt from famine. According to the second interpretation, the original Pharaoh changed his attitude towards the Jews and issued harsh decrees.

The *Yalkut Shimoni* explains that years earlier, Yosef had saved Egypt by developing a sophisticated system to store the excess harvested grain during the seven years of plenty, making it available during the ensuing seven years of famine. In gratitude, the Jews were given official status as an aristocratic class and the Egyptians were prohibited from commercial or social interaction with them. After Yosef died, Pharaoh's advisors insisted that the status be revoked, thereby allowing the Egyptians to do business and intermarry with the Jews – but Pharaoh rejected their request. His decision emanated from a deep sense of gratitude – *hakoras hatov* – recognition of the good that Yosef performed for them. The Egyptians continued to press Pharaoh and ultimately forced a suspension of Pharaoh's monarchy. Three months later, Pharaoh relented and was reinstated as king in return for his consent to let his people mingle with the Jews.

The *Yalkut Shimoni*, explaining the last part of this *posuk* that states, "who did not know Yosef," offers that Pharaoh, motivated by self-interest, chose to ignore all the good that Yosef had done for him and Egypt. Pharaoh's recognition of what Yosef had done for him had vanished. A parable is given to explain how Hashem felt towards Pharaoh at this time. When an assassin murdered the king's friend, the king ruled that this assassin should be killed – not only because he had committed a capital crime but also because the king felt that the assassin could be capable of killing the king as well! The king thought, "Once the assassin is killing important people, maybe I will be next!" Hashem felt the same way towards Pharaoh.

If Pharaoh were prepared to deny the immense good that Yosef had done for him, eventually he would come to completely deny the good that Hashem does for him. The course of subsequent events involving Pharaoh and Moshe clearly demonstrates that Pharaoh did indeed deny any good that Hashem had ever performed for him.

The ingratitude of ignoring Yosef's contribution by allowing the Jews to be demoted seems relatively minor in contrast to Pharaoh's later behavior. However, both acts show an attitude of ingratitude – the first small act ultimately evolved into a total denial of Hashem!

If one allows himself to harbor even a small amount of ingratitude, eventually he will deny Hashem, the ultimate source of good. A bad trait that a person tolerates within himself is a malignancy that grows to produce serious problems. We must heighten our awareness of the good that is displayed to us and constantly show our recognition and gratitude.

III. Miracle of Miracles

Throughout history, Hashem has bestowed upon the Jewish people many special miracles. Our nation's very survival is nothing short of miraculous and yet sometimes we are forgetful or not even cognizant of this phenomenon and the obligations and responsibility created by our unique historical heritage.

This week's *parasha* introduces us to Moshe *Rabbeinu*, the greatest leader in the history of the Jewish nation. At the time of Moshe's birth, Pharaoh had decreed that all Jewish baby boys were to be drowned in the Nile River. When Moshe was born, his mother, in a seemingly futile attempt to prevent him from being taken by the Egyptian authorities, placed him in a basket and sent him floating down the Nile River. Basya, Pharaoh's daughter, who was standing at the riverbank, saw the baby floating down the river and she stretched out her hand, which miraculously extended to a supernatural length allowing her to grasp the basket and pull it ashore. Basya adopted the young child as her own son and gave him the name, Moshe, because, as she said, "Because from the water I withdrew (Moshe) him."

Many years later, after Moshe left Egypt, he was tending the sheep of Yisro, his father-in-law. One day, as Moshe led the flock to the edge of the desert, his attention was distracted by a burning bush that was not being consumed by the fire. As Moshe walked over to the bush to investigate, Hashem called out, "Moshe, Moshe" to attract his attention. Hashem then revealed to Moshe that it was his obligation to ultimately redeem the Jewish people from their Egyptian bondage.

We find in the *Midrash Rabbah* that Moshe had ten additional names: Yered, Avigdor, Chaver, Avi Socho, Yekusiel, Avi Zanuach, Toviya, Sh'maya, Ben Nesanel, and Levi. Nevertheless, when Hashem spoke to him, He addressed him as Moshe, his Egyptian name! Why didn't Hashem call to Moshe using any of his "Jewish" names?

Hashem used the name that evoked the memory of a miraculous event in Moshe's life: being saved from Pharaoh's decree. Hashem was reminding him that a miracle had been performed to save his life. This awareness would help Moshe understand why it was his responsibility to fulfill this mission.

Miracles have been performed for the Jewish nation throughout the generations that have been just as amazing as those performed for Moshe *Rabbeinu*. Just as Moshe realized that his existence was extraordinary, and therefore he had an obligation to serve Hashem, we too must recognize we have a similar obligation. Our historical reward is unique among nations. We have been saved many times and are consequently responsible for learning and acting upon Hashem's Torah and *mitzvos*. Specifically, existence of the *Bnei* Torah – ones who study and delve into Torah – in today's world can only be viewed as a miracle. This further enhances their obligation to sustain and teach Torah. Each Jewish man, woman, and child has personally been given this obligation. It is incumbent upon each of us to conduct our lives in accordance with the Torah, in recognition of all the miracles performed specifically for us.

IV. Material Entrapments

The *Ramban* in his *Igeres*, extols the benefits of humility, *"She'he tovah mikol hamiddos tovos* – It is the best of all virtuous character traits,"* and warns of the dangers of haughtiness. A person who lacks modesty and humility can remain impervious to even the most compelling motivating factors to do *teshuva*. Many factors can influence a person's pride, not the least of which is one's surroundings.

We see an example of how one's environment can affect his humility in our *parasha*. After Pharaoh is subjected to the plague of *dam* – blood, we are told that he returned to his palace and his heart did not heed the message of the plague. *Rabbeinu Bechaya*, at the beginning of *Parashas* Bo, comments on the fact that the Torah tells us Pharaoh first returned to his palace, and only then did he ignore the plague. *Rabbeinu Bechaya* attributes Pharaoh's ability to tune out the call to repent due to the pride and arrogance he felt upon entering his palatial home.

When one analyzes this, it is truly astonishing. All of Egypt was in turmoil; there was no water to drink. The

Midrash tells us that even the walls of Pharaoh's palace were dripping blood! Pharaoh, however, when surrounded by his royal trappings, was impervious to the message of the devastating plague.

We see how far one's being in comfortable, materialistic surroundings can dampen the effects of a call to *teshuva*. Let us recognize that when we are in our own "castles" and feeling quite comfortable with our worldly successes, there is a danger that we too could come to ignore the call to *teshuva*.

Parashas Voeira

I. A Light in the Darkness

Moshe and Aharon were the greatest leaders in world history. At an advanced age, they began an undertaking of universal significance under the direction of Hashem. We should not deceive ourselves to think that they were mere instruments in the hands of Hashem – and perhaps had Hashem chosen any one of us, we too could have succeeded. Moshe and Aharon were not chosen to become great leaders but were chosen because they already were great leaders. How did they achieve this level of greatness, thereby meriting that Hashem should appoint them the leaders of *Klal Yisroel*?

In *Parashas* Voeira, the *pesukim* (6:29-27) first point out that Moshe and Aharon were the people that came and spoke to the *Bnei Yisroel*, and then later, the *posuk* repeats that Moshe and Aharon were the people who also spoke to Pharaoh. Why would the Torah mention this apparently similar fact twice?

The *Sforno* emphasizes that the Torah is teaching two distinctly different points. The Torah first tells us that Moshe and Aharon had the proper status to carry Hashem's message to the *Bnei Yisroel* and be heard by them. Then the Torah adds that Moshe and Aharon were also of such status that they could speak to Pharaoh and that Pharaoh would listen to them. Their status demanded that they receive a royal audience and moreover that Pharaoh pay attention to them!

What does the *Sforno* mean when he says that Moshe and Aharon had the status to be heard? Isn't that a direct outcome of the fact that they were the greatest people of that generation?

The *Sforno* might be telling us that Moshe and Aharon's status was enhanced because they believed in themselves, and because of this greater status, Pharaoh heard them. Without this confidence and belief that they could succeed, they might not have gained Pharaoh's attention and might have failed in their mission.

This *Sforno* highlights a fundamental concept: If a person does not believe he can accomplish a certain mission, he will fail. However, if one has faith in one's ability to succeed, then the chances of success are increased. This internal attitude will be evident to those who see him, thereby enhancing his status in the eyes of others. One must believe in his heart that he can accomplish something. Even under adverse circumstances, one can accomplish as long as he believes in himself, because he will put forth the needed effort to succeed.

The *Ibn Ezra* adds a further dimension to our understanding of Moshe as a leader. Moshe had been brought up in a secular society. Certainly, a Torah environment and family would have been more appropriate for the future leader of the Jewish people! The *Ibn Ezra* answers that because Moshe was treated like a prince in the house of Pharaoh and given great honors, he developed a great sense of self-esteem. This gave Moshe the courage to tell one Jew to stop hitting another Jew and later to kill a *Mitzri* beating a Jew. Similarly, Moshe's defending Yisro's daughters at the well in Midian indicated a sense of dignity and self-esteem. He had developed the character traits necessary to influence others. Moshe's sense of self-esteem led him to believe that he could make a difference.

One man can make an impact on society, even a society that is decadent. The impact of leadership can only be felt if the leader feels that he is able to influence those around him. If a person has no self-confidence, he will not be able to overcome the challenge needed to succeed. However, if we recognize our potential and realize that we can accomplish our mission, we will succeed. Just as a star shines in the dark, we can make an impact on the people around us in a dark society.

II. The Image in Us

In *Parashas* Voeira, Hashem commands Moshe to warn Pharaoh that plagues will befall him and his country if he does not free the Jewish people from slavery. After the sixth plague, boils, Hashem tells Moshe to tell Pharaoh, "The only reason I let you (Pharaoh) survive was to show you My strength, and so that My name will be declared all over the world." Hashem was explaining why He, Who is capable of performing awesome and mighty miracles, did not simply destroy the Egyptians and free the Jewish people! The *Sforno* says that Hashem is giving two reasons why He performed these miracles and did not directly bring the Jews out of Egypt. First, Hashem says that the plagues were "to show [Pharaoh] My strength" so that he would recognize Hashem and realize that the plagues were a warning that he was doing something wrong and he would repent. Also, Hashem wanted His name to be spoken of throughout the generations. This means that people would discuss the awesome and great miracles that Hashem performed, thereby disseminating His Name, causing a *kiddush* Hashem.

We can easily understand that Hashem would want to create a *kiddush* Hashem amongst people. The devastating plagues that befell Egypt, the most powerful nation in the world, and miracles performed for the Jews, would make His Name known universally and for many generations to come. These wondrous acts of Hashem would be a central topic of discussion because they defied nature – water turning into blood, hail made of fire and water, etc. People will be amazed at Hashem's power and might and recognize His greatness. However, the first reason as explained by the *Sforno*, to motivate Pharaoh to do *teshuva*, requires further elucidation. Why would Hashem be so concerned that an evil person be given a chance to be forgiven for his bad ways? Had not Pharaoh forced the Jews to perform backbreaking labor, appointed Jewish taskmasters to beat their own brethren, and bathed in the blood of Jewish babies? Is it justified to delay the redemption to grant Pharaoh the opportunity to do *teshuva*? Is this an adequate reason for Hashem to perform so many miracles?

We see from here that Hashem cares for each and every individual. If He was willing to delay the redemption of the Jews just so that one person – Pharaoh – would be able to do *teshuva*, it must be that Hashem really is concerned – even for one who is on the lowest level of evil behavior. This shows us *godlus ho'odom* – that even though one is a *rasha*, and we can legitimately hate him for that, we still must recognize the fact that he is a human being (and was created *betzelem Elokim* – in God's image), and that fact alone gives him a certain status of importance.

Chazal tell us, "*Ma hu rachum, af atoh rachum* – just as Hashem is merciful, so too you should be merciful.*" This is not referring to mercy alone, but to all the attributes of Hashem. *Chazal* are telling us that we must try to emulate the ways of Hashem. If He defied the "laws of nature" and performed great miracles, thereby holding back the Jews in Egypt, in order that one person should be motivated to repent, then Hashem is showing us that every single person has an inborn status of great significance, and we must recognize this and behave accordingly. We certainly may hate *resho'im* (provided one meets the Torah's definition for a *rasha*) but not to such a degree that the hatred impinges on our appreciation of his inherent status of a *tzelem Elokim*. We must feel this way towards everyone, not only our family and friends but even others, simply because they are a *tzelem Elokim*.

III. Too Right to be Wrong

Hashem provided the Egyptians an early warning of the pending plague of hail so that they would be able to shelter their livestock and other possessions. Hashem wanted only to destroy the vegetation and trees of the fields that the Egyptians had forced the Jews to work on. Not wanting to punish the Egyptians any more than necessary, Hashem warned them, expecting that they would bring in everything else. Ignoring Moshe's advice, the Egyptians left the animals outside, and they were destroyed. Their destruction could be viewed as an incidental consequence of having been left out in the hail. Yet, the *Midrash Rabbah* says that when Hashem saw that the Egyptians did not heed the warning, He made the hail even stronger to ensure that *everything* left outside would be demolished. The killing of the animals was not merely an incidental occurrence; it was a direct punishment from Hashem for ignoring His warning.

For which sin were the Egyptians punished? Surely they cannot be blamed for not having total belief in Hashem, as it is not reasonable to expect that they should be on such a level. Rather, they were punished for not even *considering* such a destructive event possible. They did not allow themselves to believe anything else other than, "We are right, and the hail will not come." If they had even entertained another possibility, they certainly would have brought in their livestock. In their obstinacy, they were unable to think for even a moment that they were wrong, despite the fact that six plagues had already struck, and certainly Hashem would keep his word with the seventh. They were punished for their blind stubbornness.

When people are involved in disputes, they are often unable to admit that they may be wrong. They believe that they would not be embarrassed to admit the truth, but because they are not thinking straight, they simply do not see the other side. Their emotions compel them to ignore the other party's arguments. The possibility that they may be incorrect *does not even enter* their minds.

Such an attitude can lead a person down the path of destruction. We must not also be blinded by our emotions that prevent us from thinking clearly and considering other explanations and perspectives. Simply being *aware* of this phenomenon can give us a better perspective of our own attitudes and positions.

Parashas Bo

I. Internal Controls

Most of us have experienced a loss of self-control during highly emotional or tense moments in our lives. In the aftermath, we usually commit to improve ourselves, yet the development of self-control requires much introspection and hard work over many years. This week's *parasha*, *Parashas* Bo, gives us a standard against which we can measure to what degree we must develop our self-control and in which situations it should be maintained.

After the ninth plague, darkness, Pharaoh agreed that the Jewish people would be allowed to travel into the desert to serve Hashem, but he insisted that the herds remain in Egypt. Moshe, refusing to even negotiate with Pharaoh, demanded that the herds accompany the people into the desert for sacrifices. Angry and disgusted, Pharaoh ordered Moshe to leave his palace immediately, never to return, under penalty of death, and Moshe agreed. This turn of events presented an unexpected problem for Hashem. Hashem had planned to warn Pharaoh in a few weeks of the final devastating plague that would herald the redemption and Exodus of the Jewish nation, but now Moshe would not be able to return to Pharaoh's palace and warn Pharaoh. Hashem, therefore, decided that His Presence should descend immediately into the impure environment of Pharaoh's palace to inform Moshe of the final plague and all other preparations that would be necessary for the Exodus. Hashem further instructed Moshe to warn Pharaoh that after this plague, Pharaoh and his servants would actually bow down to Moshe and beg him to leave with the Jews.

After receiving the prophecy from Hashem, Moshe began to describe for Pharaoh all the graphic details of the impending plague of the firstborns. When Moshe reached the point in the prophecy of Pharaoh and his servants bowing down, Moshe said, (Shemos 11:8) "Then all these slaves of yours will come down to me and bow to me..." Moshe said that only the servants will bow down to him – implying that this act of subservience would not include Pharaoh! *Rashi* explains that Moshe deliberately excluded Pharaoh from his declaration out of respect for Pharaoh's position as king. It would be disrespectful for a king to be told that he would have to bow down.

Within the context of the preceding events, this degree of self-control demonstrated by Moshe is remarkable. *Rashi* earlier mentions that Moshe was very upset at Pharaoh for having spoken to him angrily and telling him never to return to his palace. Nonetheless, even during such a tense and hostile moment, Moshe, who had nothing to fear, was able to show total control of his anger and emotions in maintaining his respect for a king. One could argue that Moshe should have informed Pharaoh that Pharaoh would bow down to Moshe in the future. Doing so would have enabled Pharaoh to be more cognizant of the word of Hashem, since Pharaoh would realize that what Moshe had said earlier was correct! However, Moshe realized that this accomplishment would be at the expense of showing disrespect to a king.

We all have the ability to perfect control over our emotions and feelings to such a point that we are able to maintain self-control not only in easy situations, but even under extreme pressure and in compelling circumstances. Very often, we find ourselves in situations where self-control is abandoned in reaction to the stress and tension we feel. We must train ourselves by constant deep reflection and hard work before the situations occur, so that our self-control will be a natural behavior. We will then be able to maintain self-control during these challenging situations.

II. Healing Hatred and Haughtiness

Character improvement, one of life's most important goals, begins with repairing any flaws that may cause us to sin against Hashem or man. The first step is to realize when one has erred, and the greatest obstacle to this is *gaiva* – haughtiness – because it perverts one's thinking and prevents one from recognizing his errors. *Parashas* Bo offers a revealing insight into this concept.

Hashem, through Moshe and Aharon, asked Pharaoh, (*Shemos* 10:3) *"Ad mosai meianto leianos miponoy* – How long will you refuse to submit to Me?" *Rashi* explains that by using the word *"leianos* – to submit," a derivative of the word *ani* – a poor person, Hashem was instructing Pharaoh to humble himself before Him and free the *Bnei Yisroel*. Hashem was telling Pharaoh that his haughtiness and unwillingness to admit his mistakes were preventing him from liberating the Jews. Why didn't Pharaoh, who was so concerned about his image and status, realize that by keeping the Jews enslaved, he was committing an act of self-destruction? Pharaoh should have foreseen the final result of the plagues and the tragedy at the Red Sea and let the Jews go free. We must conclude that Pharaoh's haughtiness rendered him incapable of admitting a mistake and anticipating the tragic outcome at *Yam Suf*.

The *Ohr Zaruah Siddur* explains that the first step in *teshuva* is to ask Hashem to help us remove our haughtiness, which prevents us from realizing our mistakes. The powerful glare of *gaiva* must not be underestimated as it can blind us to our most obvious mistakes. To see our own faults so we may improve them requires that we work hard to overcome any *gaiva* we possess.

At the beginning of *Parashas* Beshalach it says, *"Beshalach Paroh es ha'am vayehi* – And it was when Pharaoh sent out the people." The *Midrash Tanchuma* explains that the word "sent" is telling us that Pharaoh did not just send the Jews on their way, but escorted them out of Egypt. The *Midrash* continues: "And why did the Torah use this word [sent]? Because the mouth that said, 'I will not send them' changed and said, 'I will send them.'" What was Pharaoh's reward? The Torah says later in *Devarim* (23:8), "Do not despise the Egyptian."

This *Midrash* puzzles the *Lev Eliyahu*. First, what was so strange about Pharaoh's escorting the Jews out of Egypt that it merited being recorded for all future generations? After all, Egypt had just been struck with the ten plagues and countless first-born children had just been killed. Didn't Pharaoh escort them out to spare his nation from further suffering and death? Pharaoh's reward, the commandment to not despise an Egyptian and allow their converts to marry a Jew after three generations, implies that had Pharaoh not escorted the Jews out of Egypt, the Egyptians would have forever been denied the right to marry into the Jewish people. Why was a seemingly minor action rewarded so greatly?

The *Lev Eliyahu* explains that to change one's character is the most difficult undertaking. Even if Pharaoh's decision was motivated by self-survival, it was very difficult for him to reverse his position and allow the Jews to leave. He was therefore rewarded greatly. This *Midrash* highlights how difficult it is to change one's *middos* and the great reward one receives for success.

The *Gemorah* (*Bava Metziah* 32b), in a similar vein, discusses whether allowing an animal to suffer pain is a Torah or rabbinical prohibition. The *Gemorah* attempts to prove that it is rabbinical from the following case: "If your friend is unloading his overburdened animal and your enemy is loading up his animal, you are supposed to help your enemy." If causing pain to animals were a Torah prohibition, one would have been required to unload the friend's animal rather than load the enemy's. This proves causing pain to animals is a rabbinical prohibition! The *Gemorah* refutes this by suggesting that although allowing an animal to suffer pain is a Torah prohibition, perfecting one's character, in this case by overcoming hatred, supersedes it. The *Gemorah* is referring even to a case when hatred towards this person might be sanctioned by the Torah (because he violated certain well-known prohibitions, such as adultery), and still one is supposed to overcome that hatred rather than prevent an animal from suffering. We are told to disregard an animal's pain, even if it is only to help one overcome a small amount of his inner hatred for another Jew.

These *pesukim* from *Parashas* Bo, *Parashas* Beshalach, and the *Gemorah* in *Bava Metziah* serve to teach us vital lessons regarding character improvement. We learn from Hashem's instructions to Pharaoh how blinding our pride can be; when we act in an arrogant fashion, it is very difficult for us to recognize our faults. We see from Pharaoh's reward for escorting the Jews out of Egypt how difficult it is to admit one is wrong and overcome a bad *middoh*. Finally, the *Gemorah* shows us that the necessity to change our attitudes must be one of our top priorities. The foundation of personal growth begins with improving character, and, with these lessons in mind, we can better pursue this lifelong goal.

III. *Derech Eretz* Comes First

In the beginning of *Parashas* Bo, Moshe and Aharon warned Pharaoh about the plague of locusts that would befall Egypt if Pharaoh refused to allow *Bnei Yisroel* to leave. Moshe and Aharon then described to Pharaoh that mass destruction would result from the locusts that would cover the entire land and consume anything that had survived the hail. After conveying Hashem's warning to Pharaoh, Moshe and Aharon immediately left the palace.

Fearing Egypt would be completely obliterated, Pharaoh's servants suggested that he let *Bnei Yisroel* serve their God. At the servants' request, "Moshe and Aharon were returned to Pharaoh," and further negotiations resumed. However, Pharaoh remained unyielding and Moshe and Aharon were kicked out of the palace; "He threw them out from in front of Pharaoh."

On this incident, the *Riva*, one of the *Baalei Hatosafos*, asks that if Moshe and Aharon saw that Pharaoh was not willing to conform to their demands, why did they remain in his presence until the situation deteriorated to the point that they were disgracefully thrown out of the palace? Why didn't they leave the palace on their own a few moments earlier, in a more dignified manner rather than staying until Pharaoh had lost his temper?

The *Riva* answers that this meeting with Pharaoh was different than all the other meetings. All the other meetings with Pharaoh had been initiated by Moshe and Aharon, but this time Pharaoh had initiated the meeting by inviting Moshe and Aharon to the palace. Since they had been invited to speak to Pharaoh, leaving without his permission would have shown a lack of *derech eretz*.

However, another question arises. Although Moshe and Aharon didn't want to show a lack of *derech eretz* towards Pharaoh by leaving without permission, by staying they risked creating an even greater problem. If they, the leaders of *Klal Yisroel*, were thrown out of the palace, it would result in a tremendous *chillul* Hashem! Isn't avoiding this potential *chillul* Hashem more important than showing respect to Pharaoh?

HaRav Henoch Liebowitz, *ZT"L*, in the *sefer Chiddushei HaLev* on the Torah, answers that from Moshe's actions we see that, in fact, just the opposite is true. The leaders of the Jewish people acting disrespectfully towards Pharaoh would constitute an even bigger *chillul* Hashem than being sent out of his palace.

This is the reason why Moshe and Aharon chose not to leave the palace.

From the actions of Moshe and Aharon, we see how crucial it is to act with *derech eretz*. If Moshe and Aharon felt that it was so important to show proper respect to Pharaoh that they allowed the incident to result in a *chillul* Hashem, certainly we should be careful to show the proper respect and *derech eretz* to our fellow Jews. Although at times we may think we have a good reason not to do so, we must weigh our rationalizations very cautiously and realize that acting with *derech eretz* is the ultimate *kiddush* Hashem.

IV. Small Acts of Kindness

In the *Shema* we recite twice daily, we are commanded, *"V'ahavta es Hashem Elokecha* – Love Hashem, your God." One effective way to bring oneself to fulfill this command is to focus on all the good that Hashem bestows upon us. When we contemplate and realize all Hashem does for us, it naturally engenders feelings of love and appreciation. One might think that only very meaningful and significant benefits would have the effect of fostering these emotions, but we see from this week's *parasha* that it isn't so.

As *Bnei Yisroel* are on the verge of leaving Egypt, Moshe commands them to "Remember this day." Surely, a miracle such as this deserves to be remembered forever. However, in the next verse, Moshe remarks, "Today you are leaving in the spring," *Rashi* explains that Moshe was asking *Bnei Yisroel* to focus on the kindness Hashem was bestowing upon them by redeeming them at a time when the weather was good. In the summer, it is quite hot in Egypt, and in the winter, it tends to rain.

If, for example, after having spent 30 years in prison on a life sentence with no chance of parole, a prisoner were now pardoned by the President, that prisoner would be very thankful and full of joy! The emotional elation he would feel upon walking through the prison gate would scarcely be tempered by inclement weather. *Bnei Yisroel* were receiving the ultimate pardon after 210 years of subjugation. Their sentence was one of unspeakable horrors, back-breaking slavery and death. What additional gratitude could *Bnei Yisroel* possibly feel to Hashem?

We must say that *Bnei Yisroel*, by focusing on the relatively smaller kindness, could come to feel a level of appreciation for Hashem's *chesed* that could not be attained by contemplating the larger *chesed* alone. There is seemingly no limit to the amount of love and appreciation one can feel, and for every additional benefit one receives, he has the ability to increase his feelings of gratitude toward the giver.

We can foster a greater relationship with Hashem, by focusing on all He does for us, great and small. Let us realize that we can improve our relationships with those around us by reflecting on the kindness we receive from them. Even small acts of kindness done for another have the ability to engender warm feelings of gratitude.

Parashas Beshalach

I. Behind the Scenes

In *Parashas* Bo, Hashem instructed the Jewish people to slaughter a lamb and put its blood on their doorposts and lintel as a protection against the plague of the slaying of the firstborn. The very act of Jews slaughtering a lamb also served as a punishment to the Egyptians because they would have to see their deity, the lamb, being slaughtered in front of them.

Why did Hashem choose an act so antagonistic and hurtful to Egypt – the slaughtering of a lamb – as a vehicle to spare the Jews the punishment of the slaying of the firstborn?

The *Midrash* answers that during the enslavement of the Jews, the Egyptians made a point of going out into a field, catching a deer, bringing it home, slaughtering it, and cooking it – all the while forcing the Jews to watch the Egyptians cook and eat the delicious meat. The Jews felt tortured because they were hungry and could not partake of the meat.

The *Midrash*'s source for this answer is a *posuk* in this week's *parasha*. Upon arriving at the Midbar Sin, we are told (*Shemos* 16:3), "And the *Bnei Yisroel* said to them (Moshe and Aharon), 'We would rather have died at the will of Hashem while still in Egypt where we sat by the pot of meat, while we ate bread to be satiated, than die of hunger now in the desert.'" This implies, explains the *Midrash*, that the Jews only sat by and watched the pots of meat but were not allowed to partake of the food. Therefore, Hashem punished the Egyptians by causing them suffering and pain as they watched the Jewish people slaughter the Egyptians' beloved deity. (This also demonstrates how Hashem deals with man – measure for measure. Just as the Egyptians tortured the Jews with food, so too, the Jews caused pain to the Egyptians through food.)

In *Parashas* Beshalach, we find that after the Jews crossed the *Yam Suf* and traveled to Midbar Sin and ran out of food, they began to complain to Moshe, as quoted above. "We would rather have died through Hashem in Egypt as we sat by the pot of meat, while we ate bread to be satiated, because we have been brought by you to this desert to kill all of this congregation with famine!" The very same *posuk* used by the Jewish people to claim that there was abundant food and meat in Egypt is also cited by the *Midrash* as an example of the torture the Egyptians exerted upon the Jews! How could the *Midrash* feel that the *Bnei Yisroel* could overlook the fact that this event had caused them a tremendous amount of pain? They had been forced to sit and observe and were not given even a tiny piece of meat! They had been enslaved and beaten! Didn't the Jews remember these horrible times? How could they express fond memories of the meat in Egypt?

It is true that when the Jews were being tortured in Egypt, they did feel a tremendous amount of pain associated with the "pot of meat" episode. However, over time, the pain caused by this event became disassociated from the meat itself. They remembered the meat and other luxuries in the land of Egypt as well as the pain inflicted upon them by the Egyptians, but the two became disconnected in their minds. Even though intellectually they knew that they had suffered, their emotion was focused on the materialism of Egypt. Especially during a time of anxiety, due to the great hunger in Midbar Sin, they did not focus on the negative side of the experience – that they were not able to partake of that meal – only on the luxuries that they saw. It is human nature to be attracted to material pleasures and comforts. Therefore, the *Bnei Yisroel* concentrated on the delicious piece of meat and did not remember its association with the pain they had felt.

There was once a student who told his principal that he expected to become a professional hockey player when he grows up. However, the boy was skinny and short and would never succeed as an athlete. The principal wanted to know why he wanted to be a professional hockey player and the student replied that he could earn a lot of money and gain fame! The boy refused to realize that he would never make it because of his build and he only focused on the attractions of being a hockey player. How often do we wish that we were in somebody else's shoes – somebody wealthy, famous, or powerful. However, if we look behind the veneer of wealth and fame, we will see the troubles and pain such people often suffer. We must constantly train ourselves not to be misled by the superficial trappings, for they do not bring lasting results. Only the dedication to Torah and the perfection of one's *middos* can bring true happiness.

II. A Worthy Opponent

The miraculous devastation of Egypt, the world's greatest superpower, followed by the splitting of the sea and the drowning of the Egyptian army had given the Jewish people the reputation of invincibility in the eyes of the world. We were held to be extremely powerful, feared, and respected by all but one nation, the nation of Amalek. Taking it upon themselves to try to destroy this impression, they foolishly decided to directly attack the Jewish nation. Although they were handily defeated, the Torah commands us to never forget what Amalek did and to eradicate them from the face of the earth. This *mitzvah* is so important that it is taught in this *parasha* and repeated again in *Parashas* Ki Seitzei. What is so special about Amalek to warrant them having become eternal enemies deserving of genocide?

Rashi, in *Parashas* Ki Seitzei, answers with a parable of a hot-tub filled with boiling water. Any person who would immerse into the hot-tub would be burned. One person stupidly immersed into the scalding tub and sustained great injury. However, other people now began to think that he had cooled off the tub enough so that the next person might stand a better chance of enduring the challenge, even though the water was still steaming. The same is true about Amalek. Since the Jews were the most feared nation at that time, no one would dare provoke them. They are likened to the boiling tub. Amalek, by being the first nation to attack us, "cooled" us off in the world's view.

Every nation knew that whoever fought with us would be defeated, and the battle with Amalek had reinforced that point as they, too, were defeated. Why didn't this incident confirm the belief that we were invincible? Why should the other nations now feel more encouraged to try to attack us after witnessing Amalek's defeat?

Even though we defeated Amalek quickly and easily, we still sustained a "loss" from their attack. The other nations, which had previously not even entertained the thought of attacking us, now felt that we might be harmed and damaged if they used a better strategy. Amalek paved the way for other nations to attack us. We went from the realm of being a nation that was beyond attack to a nation that could be attacked. Before Amalek, others did not even consider the option of war. After Amalek, the issue was which is the best offensive strategy. We went from being invincible and "in our own league" to a "tough opponent" that might be defeated with the right strategy. Amalek is responsible for that profound shift in how the world perceived us.

Our attitudes about performing any action can be affected by seeing another do that action. Just as Amalek caused other nations to follow in their wicked path, so too an individual can influence his friend to commit an unthinkable sin by simply doing that sin. Many sins may seem implausible and unimaginable – beyond the realm of possibility. We simply cannot fathom them being done. However, once we hear that others have done them, the barrier of the unimaginable becomes broken. Before it was unthinkable – now it is simply wrong. We must place ourselves in the type of environment in which this first and most important barrier to transgressing the word of Hashem will never be removed.

III. Wise at Heart

We all recognize the great importance of doing a *mitzvah*. However, when the performance of a *mitzvah* requires the sacrifice of a material gain, we are tempted to overlook the importance of the *mitzvah* and choose to seek out that gain. Perhaps we tell ourselves that we already have many *mitzvos* or that other opportunities for *mitzvos* will surely present themselves.

Shlomo *Hamelech* tells us in *Mishlei*: "A wise heart will take *mitzvos*." The *Gemorah* applies this *posuk* to Moshe *Rabbeinu*, among others. During the Exodus from Egypt, while *Bnei Yisroel* were collecting valuables from the homes of the Egyptians, Moshe was recovering Yosef *Hatzadik's* coffin from the Nile River to bring it to *Eretz Yisroel*. For this reason, says the *Gemorah*, Moshe is called "wise at heart."

The praise given to Moshe for this act seems overstated. When an observant individual contemplates the proper course of action, he will certainly realize that the eventual reward for a *mitzvah* in the next world is far greater than any immediate physical or material gain. If this is so obvious, why is Moshe *Rabbeinu* called "wise at heart" for doing the *mitzvah* of retrieving Yosef's coffin instead of collecting booty? Would it not have been more appropriate to point out the failure of the people to act on what they knew to be true?

Yet, Moshe *Rabbeinu* is praised for making what appears to be an obvious choice. This demonstrates that making such a choice is actually quite difficult when faced with a distracting material temptation. Moshe *Rabbeinu*, however, thoroughly understood that every *mitzvah* is far more significant than a short-term material gain. This realization was so embedded in his heart that even when faced with a material sacrifice, he viewed the *mitzvah* of taking Yosef's coffin as far more valuable, earning for Moshe *Rabbeinu* the praise of being "wise at heart."

Many times we excuse ourselves from performing a *mitzvah* because we fail to properly value it. We might say to ourselves that we have already put much of our time to good use and that a little wasted time should be insignificant. However, if we consider the importance of every *mitzvah* and strive to be an individual who is "wise at heart," we will try harder to perform every *mitzvah* available.

IV. Coping with Challenge

Sometimes, when things start to go wrong, we tend to feel overwhelmed. Challenges seem to come upon us in groups, and threaten to crush us. However, there is an insight from this week's *parasha* that can give us a practical suggestion regarding how to manage mounting challenges.

The Torah tells us *Bnei Yisroel* left Egypt with a *yad ramah* – high hand. The *Rashbam* explains this to mean that upon the Exodus, *Bnei Yisroel* had no worries at all, until they realized that Pharaoh was chasing them. However once they saw Pharaoh in pursuit, the Torah says *Bnei Yisroel* complained, "Are there no graves in Egypt that you took us out here to the wilderness to die?" The *Rashbam* explains their complaint to mean that even if Pharaoh wasn't chasing them, there is no food or water in the wilderness and they are sure to die of thirst and starvation.

This is baffling. One would not expect Pharaoh's chase to affect their fear of thirst and starvation. The wilderness didn't change. If they had no fear of starvation before Pharaoh's threat, there is no logical reason for *Bnei Yisroel* to be fearful now that Pharaoh was chasing them.

We see, rather, that when times were good, *Bnei Yisroel* had the internal fortitude and faith to overcome the challenge of traveling in the wilderness without adequate food and water. However, when they faced an unrelated challenge – Pharaoh's chariots – their ability to cope was shaken. A challenge they had previously overcome confronted them again and now threatened to overwhelm them.

We need to recognize that we too, when presented with a new challenge, have an innate propensity to feel apprehensive and beleaguered with multiple trials that didn't concern us before the current crisis. When we start to feel weighed down by multiple challenges, let us ask ourselves: if each challenge had presented itself separately, could we have coped? Let us analyze our challenges individually, and with Hashem's help, we can find within ourselves the internal fortitude to persevere and prevail.

V. Maintaining Inspiration

It seems to be a frustrating cycle: someone or something in our lives inspires us to improve our performance of *mitzvos* and we respond by increasing our commitment to the Torah, only to lose steam after a short while. We slip back to our previous status quo, waiting for the next dose of inspiration to give us another short-lived boost. What can we do to maintain each "high" and achieve long-term growth? The *Ralbag* at the beginning of this week's *parasha* provides an insight that can help answer this question.

In order for the *Bnei Yisroel* to become the chosen nation of Hashem and receive the Torah, it was necessary that they leave Egypt. The *Ralbag* explains that it is for this reason that Hashem went to great lengths to ensure that *Bnei Yisroel* would not attempt to return to Egypt. The *Chumash* tells us that Hashem didn't lead *Bnei Yisroel* directly to *Eretz Yisroel* in order that they wouldn't head back to Egypt upon seeing the ravages of war.

Additionally, Hashem made sure that *Bnei Yisroel* took all their possessions with them, plus the finest of the Egyptians' possessions so that the prospect of returning to Egypt would never be worth it. Hashem had an objective to accomplish, so He did everything possible to bring about its realization.

The *Ralbag* applies this concept to the way we, too, should conduct ourselves. In any endeavor we undertake, it is critical to employ every effort (within human means) to achieve success. If a project or mission is important enough for us to invest our time and energy, it should be implemented in a calculated manner, doing everything within our ability to ensure success.

It seems that the *Ralbag* would advise us to respond to inspiration by taking small but meaningful steps. Each commitment we make should be thought through carefully, taking into account any obstacle that may potentially deter us. We should work hard and stay focused on our goal until we attain it. We will then enable ourselves to build on our success, reaching awesome heights in *Avodas* Hashem.

Parashas Yisro

In honor of
Rabbi Binyomin Luban

Robert Moskovitz

I. Coveting the Unattainable

The culmination of *Parashas* Yisro is *Matan* Torah, the giving of the *Aseres Hadibros* — the Ten Commandments — at *Har* Sinai to the entire Jewish people. The Divine Presence was clearly evident to the millions of Jews standing at the mountain. They saw and heard the presence of Hashem. This universally significant event is clearly the greatest event in human history, and because these commandments are fundamental principles that guide the life of every Jew, a close scrutiny and deep understanding of them are essential.

The final commandment states, "One may not covet another person's house, wife, maid, slave, ox, donkey, or anything else that belongs to your neighbor." The *Sforno* explains how a person can overcome the emotional feeling of envy and coveting. We should view the object that belongs to another as practically unattainable – it is impossible for us to acquire it. One who feels that something is beyond his grasp and impossible to acquire will not desire it. If we can convince ourselves it is not attainable, then we will not desire it. An example that illustrates this point is if a pauper sees a beautiful princess, he knows that he can never marry her. The vast social chasm between them makes marriage impossible, and it would therefore be irrational for him to think he could marry the princess. When he sees her, he will have no real desire for her. (This does not mean that he does not desire beautiful women, only this particular woman. Since he knows that he can never marry a princess, he will not even bother trying.) The *Sforno* says that the way to fulfill the commandment of not being desirous of certain things is to feel that these items are practically unattainable.

What does the *Sforno* mean that a person should view the possessions of his friend as unattainable? They are attainable! Couldn't we just offer to buy them from our friend, or force him to give it to us? Yet the *Sforno* is telling us that we can train ourselves to view what others have as unattainable! How is this possible?

Everything in this world comes from Hashem, and Hashem gives us exactly what we need – no more and no less. Desiring and taking something that is not ours is futile because every person's yearly entitlement is decided by Hashem on Rosh Hashanah. We receive our calculated portion and gain nothing by taking another person's belongings because Hashem did not allot them for us. Furthermore, nobody can take from us what Hashem has ordained for us to have. Once a person understands this, he knows that the possessions of others are impossible to obtain. Even if he succeeds in getting these items, he will lose something else.

Conversely, if a person does feel within himself a desire for something that belongs to another, this indicates that he must believe that it is within his reach. He is lacking in the *middos* of *emunah* and *bitochon* – faith and trust in Hashem. The way to train ourselves to view the possessions of others as unattainable is by realizing and internalizing the awareness that everything is carefully given to us by Hashem.

II. The Divine Level

Parashas Yisro relates the defining event in our history – *Matan* Torah – the revelation of Hashem Himself to the entire Jewish nation and the giving over of the Torah. The Torah describes in great detail the sequence of events leading up to *Matan* Torah with the accompanying thunder, lightning, and powerful shofar blasts. Our ancestors, witnessing this event, were profoundly affected, and the entire event left an indelible impact on our spiritual psyche – an impact that survives to this day. We are over three thousand years away from this revelation and find ourselves in a society that is the antithesis of a Torah society. It may be difficult for us to appreciate the Torah properly. How can we heighten our appreciation of the Torah?

Earlier, in *Sefer Shemos*, when the Jews were approaching the Exodus, the Jewish people were instructed to ask the Egyptians for their gold and silver, in fulfillment of Hashem's promise to Avrohom that the Jews would leave Egypt wealthy. The *posuk* states (11:2), "Speak now in the ears of the people, and let them ask every man of his fellow (*rei'eihu*)..." The word "*rei'eihu*" (translated as "fellow man") refers to the Egyptians and is explained to mean that the Jews were in the same class as the Egyptians, and therefore, both groups were referred to by the same generic term "*rei'eihu*." How could the Torah imply that the Jews were in the same class as the Egyptians? How can one possibly even think to place the Jews, who were slaves, with Egyptians who killed babies, in the same category? The Egyptians were a murderous, immoral, and evil society!

Rabbeinu Bechaya answers that the Torah was addressing the Jewish people prior to the giving of the Torah – when we could still be considered in the same generic category as the Egyptians. Once the Torah was given to us, the Torah would no longer refer to the Jews and non-Jews with a common expression such as "*rei'eihu*" since we were no longer in the same category as the rest of mankind.

Why does *Matan* Torah confer upon us a special status in comparison to all other peoples? There are two types of moral and ethical value systems – man-made and Divinely ordained. Every society, including the Egyptians, had a value system constructed to allow society to function. However, because these systems are man-made, they will inevitably collapse. Adherents to these systems will ultimately find themselves behaving improperly – albeit within the rules of their system. The Torah – a Divinely ordained value system – is perfect. It survives infinitely and dictates proper behavior in every situation. Without the Torah value system, there was nothing to prevent the Jews from descending to the same level as the Egyptians. However, once the Torah was given to them, it would no longer be possible for the Jews to fall to the level of the Egyptians. Adherents to the standards of the Torah are qualitatively distinct from other people. Other codes of laws merely create quantitative differences among peoples. The reason for this is that all of the other legal and ethical systems are man-made, containing flaws that will ultimately result in failure. However, the Torah is flawless, and therefore, it cannot fail. Since the Torah has this advantage of being perfect, adherence to it places the Jews in a distinct category. This is why the Jews are never classified again in the same category as non-Jews.

We see from here a very powerful tool to better motivate us to learn and appreciate the Torah. Since the Torah is perfect, it can help us achieve perfection. At the least, it can prevent us from descending to disgusting levels of behavior. This awareness will inspire us to learn and appreciate the Torah much more.

III. Renewable Energy

In this week's *parasha,* the Jews arrive at *Har* Sinai to accept the Torah. The *posuk* (19:17) tells us, "Moshe led the people out of the camp, toward the Divine Presence, and the entire nation stood under the mountain." The *Gemorah* (*Shabbos* 88a) explains that the *posuk* should be interpreted literally. Hashem lifted a mountain over *Bnei Yisroel* and threatened that if they did not accept the Torah, the hovering mountain would bury them. The *Gemorah* questions that since a commitment made under duress is unenforceable, this interpretation of the *posuk* could provide an excuse for not keeping the Torah. The *Gemorah* answers that *Bnei Yisroel* are precluded from using this excuse because immediately after the Purim miracle, we accepted the Torah willingly without being threatened. *Rashi* explains that this eagerness to re-accept the Torah was because of the love for the miracle that we had been granted. We were saved from the decree of

Haman and were therefore highly inspired to willingly accept the Torah again.

If the hidden miracles of Purim inspired us to accept the Torah, why didn't the ten plagues or the splitting of the sea inspire us at *Har* Sinai? Why did we need Hashem to force us to accept the Torah? Shouldn't the greatness of the Exodus have sufficiently inspired us to accept Hashem's words with open hearts and minds?

The answer seems to lie in the timing. The miracle of Purim and the re-acceptance of the Torah occurred contemporaneously. On the other hand, the ten plagues, splitting of the sea, and Exodus from Egypt preceded *Har* Sinai by several weeks. By the time *Bnei Yisroel* arrived at *Har* Sinai, the motivational value of the miraculous events had somewhat dissipated and therefore Hashem had to force us to accept the Torah.

We can glean from here that no matter how great the inspiration, with the passage of time, its motivational value is likely to diminish. Just as the inspiration of the miraculous wonders from the Exodus did not sufficiently last to provide adequate motivation at *Har* Sinai, so too, we must recognize that when we become inspired through events or sermons, the motivational value will only last if preserved by constant review. The only way to counteract the deleterious effects of time is by constant review, such as having a daily time set aside to learn Torah and study *mussar*. This daily schedule of learning will preserve and renew our motivation, allowing us to become sufficiently focused and properly dedicated to the service of Hashem.

IV. Time for Respect

The *Midrash* (*Vayikra Rabbah* 9) states, "*Derech eretz kadma laTorah* – Treating others with proper respect comes before Torah." From this week's *parasha*, we can gain deeper insight into this adage.

The *posuk* states (19:21), *"Reid, ha'ed b'am..."* Hashem told Moshe, "Go down from the mountain and warn the nation that they should not ascend or get near the mountain." Moshe responded (19:23), "No need to warn them. You have already warned them (not to ascend)." Subsequently, Hashem commands Moshe (19:24), "Go off the mountain and bring Aharon back up with you." After this, Hashem delivers the *Aseres Hadibros*.

The *Midrash Rabbah* annotates this entire strange dialogue between Moshe and Hashem (28:3). Hashem did not want Moshe on the mountain during the actual transmitting of the *Aseres Hadibros*. Having him there would create room for heretics to question the Divine authenticity of the Ten Commandments. After all, some might say that Moshe delivered them on his own.

At the same time, Hashem did not want to embarrass Moshe by telling him directly that he wasn't wanted on the mountain, so he hinted to him with an unnecessary instruction to descend and warn the people. Moshe did not "get it," and therefore responded, "You already warned the people!" At this point, Hashem contrived another "excuse," telling him, "Go down and bring Aharon back with you." When Moshe went down, the *Aseres Hadibros* were given.

When we analyze this scenario, an amazing lesson emerges. The stage was set for the most auspicious moment in history: Hashem's declaration of the *Aseres Hadibros*. Heralded by an awesome display of thunder, lightning, smoke, shofar blasts and fire, Hashem's presence descended upon *Har* Sinai. This was *the* moment that fulfilled the purpose of the entire creation of the world.

Yet, the entire moment is put on ice so that Hashem could minimize some hurt feelings of Moshe *Rabbeinu*. Moshe was the *anav mi'kol adam*, the most humble of men. Moshe was the leader of the Jewish People and Hashem's *eved ne'eman* – loyal servant. Certainly, under the circumstances, to prevent heresy and bolster *emunah baShem*, he would have gladly descended off the mountain. At worst, there could only have been a small trace of hurt feeling, so what was the problem?

We see from here the amazing *chashivus* – importance – that *derech eretz* has in the eyes of Hashem. Even a small, questionable hurt feeling is worth delaying the giving of the *Aseres Hadibros*. We often write off these small "indiscretions" as no big deal; they'll get over it. We especially justify hurting someone's feelings when we have lofty objectives, even for Torah causes. *Derech eretz* takes precedence because the Torah itself was delayed in its transmission to display proper *derech eretz*!

Parashas Mishpotim

I. Turning to *Tefillah*

Nearly everybody turns to Hashem for help in times of need. This is prayer. Many of us recognize that daily prayer is essential for our needs to be filled. This week's *parasha* contains the secret of successful prayer – prayer that gets results.

In this week's *parasha*, *Parashas* Mishpotim, the Torah commands us not to oppress a convert, widow, or orphan. The *posuk* says (22:22), "If you persecute him, for if he will cry out to Me, I shall surely listen to his cry." The meaning of the *posuk* is not clear. What is meant by the phrase "For if he will cry?" Does it mean that Hashem will answer the orphan because he was pained, or perhaps it is because the orphan prayed to Hashem? Which evokes the response from Hashem?

Rashi and the *Ramban* differ in their approaches. *Rashi* wonders why the *posuk* does not state the punishment that will be given to one who persecutes these people. He explains that the *posuk* is not trying to express to us a result but it is actually a direct threat; if you persecute him, you will get what you deserve because he will cry out to Hashem who will listen to him. According to *Rashi*, it is the pain of the orphan which causes the punishment of the oppressor. Hashem tells us that when He hears the convert, orphan, and widow's *tefillos* (which are their cries about the people persecuting them), He will punish the oppressor by taking things away from him. Hashem will take the oppressor's wealth and give it to them in response to their pain.

The *Ramban*, however, understands the *posuk* to be saying that all the convert, orphan, and widow have to do is cry out in *tefillah* to Hashem, and then Hashem will punish the oppressor and grant them what they need. The act of prayer itself will be the factor that incites Hashem's response.

The *Ramban* wonders why there is a special guarantee for the widow, orphan, or convert – a guarantee that their prayers will be answered. Why didn't Hashem give us a guarantee that our prayers will also be answered? The *Ramban* tells us that the convert, orphan, and widow generally have no one to whom they can turn to for help in times of stress. They have only a limited number of friends, and few family members to rely on. They rely primarily on Hashem for help. Their *tefillos* are completely focused, deep, and sincere, since they know that Hashem is their only true salvation. Therefore,

Hashem answers these extremely powerful *tefillos*. Even if they only cry out a little, Hashem feels sorry for them and answers their request. Their less intense cries can bring about a major change and improvement in their lives.

When we, who are not widows, orphans, or converts, sincerely ask Hashem for something and pray for it, we hope to get it. Often we don't. The reason for this is that we are lacking a true awareness of our complete dependence on Hashem, thereby weakening our prayers. In fact, Hashem does provide everything for us. Hashem will answer us when we realize that there is no other source of help besides Him. We must genuinely believe that we cannot rely on doctors, lawyers, financial planners, connections, or good friends. Rather, we must realize that Hashem has always provided everything for us and still does. Then our *tefillos* will be powerful and will be answered by Hashem – perhaps through these "messengers."

If this formula for successful prayer is true, then we should just acknowledge the fact that Hashem gave us everything and then all of our prayers would be answered, yet we see this is not so! Why can't we just put ourselves on the same level as the convert, widow, or orphan?

Perhaps it is because this effort is contrary to human nature. We know that deep inside, we do rely on our network of friends, and sometimes, even more so than on Hashem. When a problem arises, how often do we first ask them to help us and only later turn to Hashem? Even though at times we may ask Hashem for certain things, our main focus and expectation is on the work being done for us by others or even on our own effort. A simple commitment is not adequate to effect a deep internal change in attitude.

Our friends and helpers are only agents of Hashem, who perform His will. To make our *tefillos* successful, we have to feel that Hashem gave us everything – and without Hashem we would have nothing. Hashem will give us what we need if we recognize the fact that, in truth, we are no different than the convert, widow, or orphan – totally dependent on Hashem. This awareness is a lifelong mission requiring a tremendous amount of effort. If we can achieve such a level of belief, then our *tefillos* have a high probability of being answered.

II. Subconscious Sensitivity

If a person steals an object, he must return the object to the owner, and if the object is not available, he must refund its value. Under certain circumstances, he must repay the owner double its value as a penalty. However, the penalties of stealing certain livestock are even greater. The *posuk* (21:37) states, "If a person steals an ox or sheep and then slaughters or sells it, he must repay five oxen for an ox and four sheep for a sheep." Why is the sheep thief given a discount on his penalty and only pays fourfold instead of fivefold that the ox thief pays?

Rashi answers that the discount is in consideration of the humiliation the thief suffered. An ox can be led on the street easily, but a sheep must be carried on one's shoulder, thereby causing him some embarrassment. This embarrassment is based on his own feeling of humiliation even though nobody saw him steal the sheep. Hashem takes this humiliation into consideration because He cares very much for the honor of his creations, so He removes some of the penalty, even though the suffering was incurred while doing the sin.

Although *Rashi*'s explanation is most noble, does this really happen? When this thief returns home and has earned a sheep as a "reward" for his efforts, he does not feel the humiliation he has allegedly experienced. He is satisfied that he has achieved his goal of stealing a sheep. If this thief feels no disgrace or dishonor, why should the Torah be concerned about his nonexistent humiliation? Why should an embarrassment he doesn't feel be considered part of his payment and earn him a discount?

Hashem granted all of us a pure *neshoma* – soul – that resides within our bodies. Any emotional blemishes that occur during the soul's journey in this world create an impact on it. Since the soul is highly sensitive because of its purity, any slight negative action can trigger a damaging scar. This thief has stooped to such a low level that he disregards even his own self-respect. Even though he may not feel any conscious humiliation, his soul is subconsciously hurt. Hashem acknowledges this subconscious pain by reducing a fraction of his penalty. We may think that a lack of conscious pain means it does not exist. If we are not aware of it, there is no pain. We see in Hashem's treatment of the sheep thief that one is prone to even subconscious emotional trauma. Let us remember that when dealing with our family and friends, we must be highly sensitive to their feelings since the Torah teaches us that we must be sensitive to the subconscious hurt of others by being exceedingly careful in all that we do.

III. Loving Kindness

Consistency in actions and emotions is considered an enviable trait. Yet a *posuk* in this week's *parasha*, *Parashas* Mishpotim, seems to advise us otherwise. We are instructed that when one sees an animal struggling under its load – even if it belongs to a person he hates – the observer is obligated to help the animal. The *Targum*

Yonason explains which type of hatred the *posuk* is referring to. The *Gemorah* states that if a person observed a person commit an immoral act that all Jews know to be forbidden, and he therefore cannot judge him favorably, he *must* conclude that he is a *rasha* – transgressor. Since he alone knows about it, he may not tell others or even report the crime to *Beis Din*. However, he is permitted or even obligated to hate the *rasha*. The person who owns the struggling animal is this *rasha*. Nevertheless, the *Targum* says, he must temporarily cast off this hatred and go help the animal.

At first glance, the *Targum Yonason* is teaching us a profound insight into the laws of *chesed*. One must do *chesed* not only for someone for whom he has no legitimate reason to hate but even for someone whom he is allowed to hate.

The *Targum Yonason* adds that we must remove our hatred for this person when performing this *chesed*. Why is this emotional transformation needed? Why can't we just do the *chesed* while still bearing feelings of hatred for this person? The Torah is telling us that when doing a *chesed* for someone, it should not be a simple act of kindness, but should emanate from a desire to help this person – which stems from a true love for him. It is impossible to do a true *chesed* for someone at the same time that one feels hatred. Therefore, one must suppress the hatred temporarily to properly perform this *chesed* with a complete heart.

We often think that our emotions are entrenched within us and cannot be changed easily. Yet, we see that Hashem expects us to temporarily ignore a legitimate hatred for someone and convert it to a feeling of love in order to properly perform a *chesed*. If Hashem expects us to convert our feelings from hate to love in a split-second and after the *chesed* has been completed once again convert our feelings, then we must be capable of such emotional flexibility.

This verse has taught us three lessons in how to perform acts of *chesed*. First, we are required to do a *chesed* even for someone we don't like. Second, we must feel love for someone when doing a *chesed*. Finally, we have the ability to undergo radical emotional changes and must use this power to perform *chasodim* for all people properly.

IV. Soul Mates

This week's *parasha*, Mishpotim, forbids us to verbally abuse a convert. We were also strangers in Egypt and should be sensitive to the fragile nature of a convert and not cause them emotional pain. The *Rabbeinu Bechaya* asks that since the prohibition of not oppressing the convert is covered by the general prohibition of verbal abuse, why does the Torah feel the need to highlight the prohibition of oppressing a convert?

A convert may often yearn for a feeling of belonging because he feels uncomfortable and lonely in his new surroundings. Others may sense his vulnerability and feel less inhibited to take advantage of or verbally abuse him. Therefore, the Torah felt the need to reiterate the general prohibition of verbal abuse as applied to the convert to tell us that Hashem feels a special closeness to those who feel victimized, and He answers their prayers.

Not only were the *Bnei Yisroel* foreigners in Egypt, but also in Shushan, where they were defenseless and cried to Hashem, Who ultimately saved them. It is clear that Hashem assists and avenges those who are weak and vulnerable. Further on, the *parasha* repeats the same command and adds, "for you know the soul of a convert," to emphasize that there are times when a person feels alone and his soul reaches out to and begs Hashem for help. Hashem responds compassionately because this lonely soul has turned to Him and recognized that Hashem is all he has.

Hashem's assurance that He will respond to the plea of a downtrodden soul represents more than a mere response to a request. It is an indication that Hashem feels a special closeness to those who feel victimized. By turning to Hashem and recognizing that He is the sole source, He will respond compassionately and mercifully.

Parashas Teruma

L'zecher Nishmas
Fraida Chava bas Reb Zelig Fried

Rabbi and Mrs.
Yaakov and Chani Fried

I. Infinite Potential

Why do people fall short of their potential? Perhaps it is because they underestimate their true potential. People doubt whether they can accomplish anything of real significance, either for their own community or for *Klal Yisroel*, the Jewish People, as a whole.

We can gain an insight into this matter from an episode in the *Midrash*. Hashem instructed Moshe *Rabbeinu* regarding the details of the construction of the

Mishkon. The *Midrash* relates that Moshe asked Hashem, "Can the *Bnei Yisroel* really build a *Mishkon* that would be fitting for the *Shechina* to dwell in?" Hashem answered that even a single Jew has the ability to make a *Mishkon* that would be sufficiently holy for the Divine Presence. This is borne out by the *posuk* (25:2), *"Mai'ais kol ish asher yidvenu libbo* – From every man whose heart will motivate him." The Torah uses the singular form *"ish –* man" even though earlier in the *posuk* a plural verb had been used.

Moshe *Rabbeinu* was the greatest prophet who ever lived. With his unparalleled wisdom and insight, he knew better than anyone the true greatness of the holy *neshoma* that Hashem implanted in each Jew. Yet, he could not fathom that all of *Klal Yisroel*, included amongst them the greatest *chachomim* and *tzadikim*, could together construct a *Mishkon* with the sanctity required for the *Shechina*. Hashem's response to Moshe demonstrates the infinite potential of each person. One person alone can accomplish that which Moshe *Rabbeinu* thought all of the *Bnei Yisroel* could not. One person with a sincere commitment can himself effectuate the *kedusha* in the *Mishkon* necessary for the *Shechina*. We have seen from our own history the difference one person can make. The *Beis Yaakov* movement that was started in Poland by one righteous individual, Sarah Schenirer, saved untold thousands of Jewish girls and today we are reaping the fruits of that individual's labors.

The realization of what one individual can achieve can give us an entirely new perspective on life, but carries with it an awesome responsibility. We will be taken to task by Hashem for all that we could have achieved but did not. Fortunately, Hashem gave us a head start. The *Ralbag* says that the power to keep the entire Torah, in spite of all difficulties, stems from the *mitzvah* of dying *al kiddush*

Hashem. A Jew must allow himself to be killed rather than transgressing one of the three cardinal sins. A Jew can harness this dedication to Hashem to help him overcome trials and tribulations in relation to other *mitzvos.*

Some may wonder, "Is this really applicable to me? Am I really ready to give my life *al kiddush* Hashem? Where will I harness my power from?" Rav Dovid Leibowitz, *zt"l,* answers that every Jew has the innate ability to sacrifice his life for Hashem. He may not feel it currently, but if a situation necessitates it, that power will come to the forefront. There was a "Christian" mayor in Poland who "converted" from Judaism to enable himself to hold such a high position. He traded the Torah for wealth and honor. When the Nazis, *yemach shemom vezichrom,* invaded his town and ordered him to throw a *Sefer* Torah on the ground, he refused and died a torturous death rather than disgracing a *Sefer* Torah. A Jew who was seemingly so distant still had the power to give up his life *al kiddush* Hashem.

We see that each individual by himself has the potential to build a *Mishkon.* We further see that even the most estranged Jew has the fortitude to be *mosser nefesh.* May Hashem help us internalize this message so that we may understand our potential and bring it to fruition?

II. Limiting Laziness

Laziness is a trait that plagues many of us at one time or another and is an inherent part of man's basic nature. How pervasive is this characteristic? Can laziness distract a person from achieving success or can the drive to succeed and the excitement of the ultimate goal motivate us enough to overcome our laziness without any additional effort?

Parashas Teruma tells of the construction of the *Mishkon* – Sanctuary – and its vessels. In the beginning of the *parasha*, Hashem commands Moshe to collect from the *Bnei Yisroel* the materials that would be necessary for the construction of the *Mishkon*: precious metals and stones, fabrics, skins, oil and spices. Hashem then says (25:8-9), "They shall make for Me a Sanctuary – so that I may dwell among them – in conformance with all that I show you, the form of the Tabernacle and the form of all its vessels; and so you shall do." The end of the *posuk*, "*vechain ta'asu* – and so you shall do," seems redundant. Hashem had already commanded Moshe to build a *Mishkon* at the beginning of the previous *posuk*. The *Ramban* explains that Hashem commanded "to do as He said" a second time in order to motivate the *Bnei Yisroel* to do the job with *zerizus* – zeal.

The people who were building the *Mishkon* knew that they were building the place where Hashem's Presence would rest – a unique and awesome event in history. This in itself was a tremendous honor and privilege, and the awareness of this significance should have served to motivate the builders to perform their mission with much enthusiasm. Why did Hashem add the extra phrase of "and so you shall do?" Why would the Jews have needed extra motivation?

Apparently, the drive and excitement that the Jews had for building the *Mishkon* was not enough. It was very possible that without the extra encouragement from Hashem, laziness would have overtaken them, to some degree, causing distraction and impeding them from working with their full potential. The *Ramban* is teaching us that laziness is a "constant companion" of all our efforts and that it can surprise us at any time – even when we are involved in the most important and honorable of projects.

Since Hashem added "and so you shall do," we see that the *Bnei Yisroel* needed further motivation.

The *Mesilas Yesharim* teaches us that the nature of a human being is to be relaxed and lazy. Being lazy may cause a person to procrastinate with rationalizations or excuses that can blur his motivation and prevent him from doing his utmost to fulfill his goal. Therefore, we must be cognizant of the ever-present danger of laziness, even when we think we are immune, as it can overcome us even when our motivation to succeed seems strong.

III. Ever Present Emotions

Parashas Teruma describes the instructions for the building of the *Mishkon*. The first step was collecting the necessary materials such as gold, silver, and precious stones. The *posuk* (25:2) states, "Speak to the Children of Israel and they shall take for Me a donation." Every single person was to be involved in some way with a donation and thereby share in its construction.

The *Yalkut Shimoni* notes that since Hashem needs nothing for Himself, His intention in asking the Jews to build Him a *Mishkon* was to benefit them. The Divine Presence resting in it would bring great honor to the Jewish nation. The *Mishkon* would also serve as atonement for the sin with the golden calf.

This *Midrash* derives from the words in the *posuk* that Hashem instructed Moshe to beseech the people to donate money – as if they were doing Him a favor. Surprisingly, Hashem felt that the people needed additional urging and cajoling to motivate them to donate to a cause that was exclusively for their benefit. Didn't they realize that all their money had been obtained through the miraculous events in Egypt, as a direct gift from

Hashem? Yet, Hashem still had to speak in a manner of one asking for a handout.

Rabbi Yehuda Leib Chasman, author of the *Ohr Yahel*, explains that even though the Jews should have generously donated "their" money, certain emotional forces might have led them to be slow in responding. Hashem, recognizing the power of self-interest, felt it was necessary to provide additional encouragement for them to override the natural desire to keep the money.

A person is inherently programmed with many emotional attitudes that are all necessary at certain times. Nonetheless, we must discern when these emotions begin to impact our decisions. One may erroneously believe that he can dissociate personal interest from objectivity and arrive at a logical conclusion. This is never true. Emotions alter a person's work, thought, concentration, and even judgment, and usually we are not even aware of it.

IV. Worth the Struggle

We have all heard many times, "You gave it your best try, and that's what counts." Sometimes, that is hard to believe. We live in a world that rewards results more than effort. A player on a winning team is given a championship ring, even if he didn't spend a minute on the field, while the losing quarterback, even if he scored many touchdowns, walks away with nothing. Should our accomplishments be the yardstick of our success in life? The Torah tells us otherwise.

In *Parashas* Teruma, the Torah enumerates all the materials that were collected for the *Mishkon*. The order they listed is: gold, silver, brass, blue-dyed wool, purple-dyed wool, red dye, linen, goat hair, ram's skin dyed red, *tachash* skin, acacia wood, oil for lighting, oil spices for for anointing, *ketores* spices, and finally, the precious stones for the *Ephod* and *Choshen*. The *Ohr HaChaim HaKadosh* asks why the precious stones for the *Ephod* and *Choshen* were mentioned last. Pound for pound, precious stones are the most valuable item on the list and should have been written first. The remainder of the list seems to be in an evaluative order, with gold and silver on the top and oil and spices on the bottom. Why were exceptionally valuable precious stones mentioned last?

To answer this, the *Ohr HaChaim* quotes a *Midrash* stating that every morning, the Clouds of Glory delivered precious stones to *Bnei Yisroel* along with the *mon*. Due to the fact that these stones came to the Jews with no effort on their behalf, parting with them was not considered as great an act as parting with the other items necessary for the *Mishkon*.

We see from here the Torah's accounting system. By virtue of the fact that one had to expend resources and effort to acquire the oil for donation to the *Mishkon, that* oil became more valuable in the Torah's eyes than diamonds and rubies that had been acquired without effort. Effort is not merely one factor taken into account when evaluating one's deeds; it is the central, defining currency by which all things are judged.

Let us take this lesson to heart, and not become discouraged when, despite our best efforts, a *mitzvah* or *chesed* in which we are involved does not yield the drastic results we were hoping for. We must realize that in *Shomayim*, our actions are judged based on the struggles we went through to accomplish them. Not only is our toil considered in evaluating our deeds, but it is the token definition of our actions.

Parashas Tetzaveh

I. Knock Before Entering

Derech eretz kadma laTorah – derech eretz, proper behavior and conduct is of such monumental importance that it precedes even the Torah itself. Its *halachos* teach us how to behave appropriately in all of our relationships and in all situations. How far does the Torah's concept of *derech eretz* extend? How much does the Torah expect of us?

Parashas Tetzaveh describes the intricate details of the vestments of the *Kohen Godol*. In its discussion of the *me'il ho'ephod*, the Robe of the *Ephod*, the Torah instructs us to attach golden bells to the hem of the *me'il*. The *posuk* then states (28:35), "It must be on Aharon in order to serve. Its sound shall be heard when he enters the Sanctuary before Hashem and when he leaves, so that he will not die." *Rashi* interprets the phrase "so that he will not die" in reference to all of the *Kohen Godol*'s garments, teaching us that entering the *Mishkon* without any one of the garments is a capital offense punishable by death.

The *Ramban* understands the *posuk* to be dealing specifically with the *me'il*. The golden bells adorning the *me'il* were meant as a "sounding device" to announce the entrance and exit of the *Kohen Godol*. It was incumbent upon the *Kohen Godol*, as per the *halachos* of proper *derech eretz*, to announce his arrival to the palatial residence of Hashem.

Hashem would certainly not be caught unaware by the sudden appearance of the *Kohen Godol* – He is keenly aware of the movements and whereabouts of every man. In addition, the *Kohen Godol* was coming to the *Mishkon* to perform the service of Hashem – Who was eagerly awaiting and expecting his arrival. What was the purpose of this announcement?

It seems that the Torah views "the sounding of the bells" as a requesting of permission to enter, and is necessary even in this situation. The *posuk* is revealing how lofty and far-reaching are the implications of the Torah standards of proper *derech eretz*. Modes of behavior that may seem superfluous to us are considered standard by the Torah. Not only Hashem, but also every individual who is a *tzelem Elokim*, created in the image of Hashem, deserves the highest level of our respect and consideration.

Parashas Ki Sisa

Dedicated by

Dr. and Mrs. Zvi Naierman

I. Love and Harmony

The social barriers to endless slandering and tale bearing have disappeared. Even if the information being spread is of questionable veracity, the general public no longer regards this behavior as negative. It is justified by the need to satisfy "the public's right to know." This is the very antithesis of the Torah's perspective that views the sin of *loshon horah* as a grave transgression in the eyes of the Torah. We can be inspired to uphold the Torah standard by examining the conduct of our greatest leader.

The Torah relates that the *Bnei Yisroel* expected Moshe *Rabbeinu* to return forty days after ascending Mount Sinai. A segment of *Klal Yisroel*, having miscalculated and concluded that the time had already passed for Moshe's return, decided to create an *eigel hazahav* to replace Moshe as a conduit between the people and Hashem. Following Aharon's instructions, the people waited until the following day to actually celebrate and offer sacrifices before the *eigel*.

When Moshe *Rabbeinu* descended the mountain, he encountered his *talmid* Yehoshua who had been waiting for him. Upon hearing sounds of a commotion emanating from the *Bnei Yisroel*'s encampment, Yehoshua exclaimed, "There is a sound of war in the camp." Moshe *Rabbeinu* responded, "It is a sound of merry-making." Moshe *Rabbeinu* knew that the cause of the merry-making was the worshipping of the *eigel*; Hashem had already told him. Why didn't Moshe *Rabbeinu*, in correcting Yehoshua, tell him precisely what was causing the commotion? The *Ramban* answers that Moshe *Rabbeinu* did not want to speak disparagingly about the *Bnei Yisroel* by telling Yehoshua that the *Bnei Yisroel* had sinned.

Moshe *Rabbeinu*'s reluctance to speak negatively about *Klal Yisroel* is nothing short of amazing. Yehoshua was moments away from personally discovering the sad truth, and it would therefore not have been *halachically* forbidden for Moshe to tell Yehoshua. Furthermore, had Moshe *Rabbeinu* divulged the news to Yehoshua, it would not have been a purposeless affront to *Klal Yisroel*. Rather, it would have served as a practical lesson in understanding the *Bnei Yisroel* that would be beneficial for Yehoshua, a leader-in-training. We must also take into account the state to which the *Bnei Yisroel* had descended by creating the *eigel hazahav* and betraying Hashem and Moshe *Rabbeinu*. Notwithstanding all three mitigating factors,

Moshe *Rabbeinu* would not speak negatively about the Jewish people.

Moshe *Rabbeinu* had great love for *Klal Yisroel* and this love generated an acute sensitivity within him that did not allow him to utter even a few disparaging words about them. Although furious with them for performing a grave sin, he would not speak negatively about them.

Moshe *Rabbeinu*'s conduct is in stark contrast to the values of secular society. Though furious, Moshe *Rabbeinu* could not bring himself to speak against the *Bnei Yisroel*. We should strive to emulate this trait by refraining from disparaging another individual in a way which engenders strife and discord, thereby sanctifying the gift of speech – a gift endowed by the Creator – to foster love and harmony between members of *Klal Yisroel*.

II. The Antidote

In this week's *parasha*, Ki Sisa, Hashem tells Moshe to descend Mount Sinai because *Bnei Yisroel* had erected a golden calf and had begun to serve it as God. In the next *posuk*, Hashem criticizes *Bnei Yisroel* as stubborn people, and the fact that *Bnei Yisroel* had descended into paganism is only mentioned as an afterthought. What is so significant about them being a stiff-necked stubborn people?

The *Alter* of Slobodka, Rabbi Nosson Tzvi Finkel, explains that the *Bnei Yisroel*'s trait of stubbornness was viewed as a sin more deserving of punishment than idol worship. Even though idol worship is a cardinal sin and deserving of grave consequences, it might not merit national destruction. *Bnei Yisroel*, created in the image of Hashem, had a choice between right and wrong. A single impulsive act based on poor judgment would not be sufficient reason for Hashem to destroy *Bnei Yisroel*.

However, the character trait of defiance and unwillingness to wait until Moshe returned from Mount Sinai indicated a fundamental problem within *Bnei Yisroel*; a flaw that would severely limit their free will and was, therefore, serious enough to justify destroying *Bnei Yisroel*.

Any single sin may be viewed as a brief lapse, but one who is stubborn and is not willing to heed to Hashem's commands has a fault within himself that will ultimately drive him away from Hashem. Such a flaw will ultimately remove his clarity of judgment and ability to make choices. Only a deeply ingrained character trait could have been a valid reason to destroy *Bnei Yisroel*.

One must always keep in mind the need to identify and change one's less-than-perfect character traits. Even a single bad trait makes it difficult to choose the proper course of action. Immersing oneself in the study of Torah and *mussar* is the antidote to poor character and restores our ability to think clearly and choose a proper course of action.

III. The Leadership Lifestyle

From this week's *parasha,* we can learn an important lesson in leadership. Hashem told Moshe that the Jews deserved to be destroyed due to the sin of the golden calf. Moshe beseeches Hashem to spare the Jews, concluding his prayers by saying (*Shemos* 32:32), *"V'im ayin mcheini na misifrecha asher kosavta* – If you do not forgive them, wipe me out from the book that you have written." The *Sforno* explains that Moshe was telling Hashem that he should take the merits from all of Moshe's *mitzvos* and transfer them to the Jews, in order that they should be worthy of being saved.

Moshe was the greatest *tzadik* who ever lived – one who deserved a reward way beyond anything we can imagine. In order for Moshe to reach this amazing level, he must have worked tirelessly, year after year, to perfect himself and to perform the *mitzvos*. Yet, Moshe was willing to sacrifice the efforts of his entire life, and the tremendous reward that he deserved, in order to save his fellow Jews. This was the degree of dedication that Moshe had for the Jewish people.

The *parasha* continues that Hashem accepted Moshe's prayers and spared the Jews. At the same time, Moshe is commanded to move his tent outside the Jewish camp. The Torah tells us that when Moshe walked to his tent, the *Bnei Yisroel*, "*Hibitu acharei Moshe* – they stared at Moshe." The *Gemorah* in *Kiddushin* (33b) relays different opinions as to what they were thinking when they stared at Moshe. One opinion is that they were thinking, "Look how fat he is from eating our wealth."

This seems very strange. Moshe just saved them from total destruction, he offered his entire life work and his portion to in the World to Come to save them, yet they viewed him disparagingly, believing that he was getting fat from stealing their wealth.

The Torah is teaching us that no matter how sincere and dedicated a leader is, there will always be people who will criticize him and view him disparagingly. This is true of all leaders: a leader of a nation, a leader of a school, a leader of a classroom, and even a leader of a family. True leaders do not become leaders in order to gain popularity. Rather, they do so only to help the people they are leading, and are totally dedicated, regardless of whether or not they are appreciated.

Parashas Vayakhel

I. Tapping Into Talent

Every individual possesses certain unique talents and abilities. These talents, given to us by Hashem, allow us to develop our full potential for serving Him in our own individual manner. Many times an extremely talented individual, whose abilities would otherwise have gone undetected, finds himself during a moment of inspiration rising to new heights with his special gifts. On the other hand, someone could possess qualities that could impact the entire world but might decide not to use his talents. Is this improper? To what extent must a person utilize his God given skills?

Parashas Vayakhel describes the building of the *Mishkon*. A tremendous amount of wisdom and skill was required for constructing the *Mishkon*, and the work demanded working knowledge of science, engineering, tapestry, etc. The *Bnei Yisroel* had been slaves in Egypt and had never attended any classes on the various skills needed in the *Mishkon*'s construction. Yet the *posuk* states (35:21), "Every man whose heart inspired him came…and brought the portion of Hashem for the work of the Tent of Meeting." The people simply felt inspired to step forward to volunteer their skills. The workers from the *Bnei Yisroel* must have already possessed the amazing talents that they used in building the *Mishkon*. From where did they acquire these abilities?

The *Ramban* says that the people discovered that inherent in their nature were the skills necessary to build the *Mishkon*. They simply felt a yearning to perform with these suddenly discovered talents. They knew that Hashem granted them these talents. This realization caused them to channel their abilities towards the service of Hashem – building the *Mishkon*. The Torah praises this as *"nasa'o libo."* Is it not normal for someone who possesses certain skills to use them in a proper way? What was so special about the *Bnei Yisroel* using their talents to help in the building of the *Mishkon*?

It seems that there is a contrary force in our hearts that can cause us to neglect using our talents for the service of Hashem. This force can cause a person to lack the drive for accomplishment and cause his talents to remain dormant. The *Bnei Yisroel* had to lift their hearts for inspiration in order to involve themselves in the construction of the *Mishkon*. Their nature would have been to dismiss the opportunity of using their talents by saying that they were not fit for the job. To overcome this nature, they inspired themselves to use their knowledge and build the *Mishkon.* They required the additional motivation of knowing and feeling that they were fulfilling the will of Hashem.

It is important for us to recognize the talents that we possess. However, this alone is not enough. We must also inspire ourselves to tap into our vast resource of abilities with which Hashem has endowed us. Only then can we hope to reach the ultimate fulfillment of our potential.

II. Hidden Motives

In this week's *parasha,* the Jews commence the building of the *Mishkon. Chazal* point out that when funds and supplies were needed, the *Nesi'im* – princes – were the last to give, and their contributions were limited to the precious stones placed on the *Kohen Godol*'s garments, the olive oil, the anointing oil, and the incense. In contrast, we find that during the dedication ceremony after its construction, the *Nesi'im* were the first to bring sacrifices.

The *Midrash* explains that when Moshe first asked for contributions, the *Nesi'im* announced that after everyone would give their donation, they would provide the rest of the needed materials or monies. They underestimated the generosity of the Jewish people as the Jews immediately over-filled the quota and there was hardly a deficit for the *Nesi'im* to cover. Only a few items were left to donate. At the dedication, they did not allow themselves to make the same mistake and they therefore arrived first.

In the *posuk* (35:27), "The *Nesi'im* brought the precious stones for the apron and the breast-plate," the word *Nesi'im* is spelled without the letter "*yud.*" *Rashi* explains that the absence of the letter indicates that when the *Nesi'im* came up with their "great" idea to give last, they were in fact motivated by a slight degree of laziness. They didn't live up to the title of *"Nasi"* – from whom we expect leadership. Since they didn't accomplish that which was expected of them, part of their title was left out.

At first glance, the offer of the *Nesi'im* to cover any shortfall could hardly be considered an act of laziness. Yet, the Torah teaches us that they were lacking to some degree in their eagerness to participate and this lack emanated from a slight feeling of "laziness." What seemed to be a terrific idea was really an excuse. Although these *Nesi'im* were the heads of their respective *shevatim* – tribes – and they were great individuals, they were not sufficiently energized because of slight feelings of laziness. Even more instructive is that they didn't even realize that they were being so influenced.

If the *Nesi'im* could not detect this subtle emotion of laziness, we, who are not as great as they, must be especially diligent. Many times we are confronted with situations in which we think we make decisions to act or not to act for seemingly valid reasons, yet possibly we are being prompted by another motivation such as laziness. We must therefore, reevaluate every decision, searching for such a hidden motive, and sometimes ask an objective individual his opinion.

III. Taking the High Road

From early childhood through our teenage years and even into adulthood, we are constantly being told stories and *Midrashim* about our *Gedolim*. On a simplistic level, this is done to inspire us to emulate their ways and follow in their footsteps.

Chazal tell us we should constantly ask ourselves, *"Masai yigu ma'asai l'ma'asei avosai* – When will my

actions reach the level of the actions of my fathers?"
Recognition of our forebears' tremendous holiness and
perfection will not just inspire us, but will enable us to
more closely emulate their ways. Realizing the
tremendous capacity that is imbued within the human
being will open up new vistas of spiritual perfection.

This week's *parasha* provides us with a keener
insight into the greatness of our *Gedolim*. Moshe says,
"*Re'u koreh Hashem b'shem Betzalel* – Look, Hashem has
called him by the name Betzalel." Hashem chose Betzalel
to build the *Mishkon*. The *Da'as Zekeinim* explains that
even Moshe was surprised when learning that Betzalel,
and not Moshe himself, was chosen for this very special
task. Hashem explained that the reason for this was that
the *Mishkon* was being built as a *kaparah* – atonement –
for the sin of the golden calf. Since Betzalel's grandfather,
Chur, was killed as a result of the incident of the golden
calf, it was appropriate to give his grandson the *zchus* to
build it.

If the *Mishkon* was being built to atone for the *eigel*
– calf – Betzalel would be the one most likely to have
some reluctance to help atone for their actions! Any
human being would have deeply ingrained feelings of
hatred for the individuals who killed his grandfather.
Those feelings would naturally hinder the *simcha* and
excitement needed to build the *Mishkon* with the proper
kavanah and emotions!

It must be that Hashem knew that Betzalel did not
harbor any resentment towards his grandfather's killers,
and that he would be able to rise above the normal
emotions that we would expect him to feel at such a time.
Betzalel is a model of human perfection with an enduring
lesson for all future generations.

May we be *zocheh* to be motivated and inspired to utilize the almost limitless capacity for greatness and perfection that each and every one of us has embedded within us.

Parashas Pekudei

Dedicated by

Mr. and Mrs. Roy and Orli Sasson
and Family

I. All That Glitters

In *Parashas* Pekudei, after the Torah tells us the measurements of the *Mishkon* and details of its construction, it then lists the total amounts of gold, silver, copper, and other materials used in the construction of the *Mishkon* and its contents. Many *pesukim* are written just to tell us the exact quantities of the materials that went into the *Mishkon* and its contents. Why is it so important for us to know how many ounces of gold and other materials were used to build the *Mishkon*?

The *Sforno* explains that the Torah tells us the exact quantities not to impress us with how much gold and silver were used, but to show us that the *Mishkon* was actually much smaller and less expensive to build than the first and second *Batei Mikdosh* – holy Temples. The *Beis HaMikdosh* had much more gold, silver, and other treasures than the *Mishkon*. The material value of the *Mishkon* paled in comparison to that of the *Beis HaMikdosh*, yet the *Mishkon* was considered much holier than the *Beis HaMikdosh*. The *Shechina* – Hashem's presence – in the *Mishkon* was constant and directly apparent to all.

In contrast, the *Shechina* was less evident in the first *Beis HaMikdosh* and not even present in the second *Beis HaMikdosh*. The *Shechina* resided amongst the Jews in the desert for forty years because there was a high level of fear of Hashem, and good deeds were being constantly performed. The *Shechina* was evident in the *Mishkon* even though the *Mishkon* was not as beautiful as the first *Beis HaMikdosh*, which itself was less beautiful than the second *Beis HaMikdosh*. The *Shechina* was not attracted by the more expensive edifice and lavish contents of the *Batei Mikdosh*. Although the laws of *kovod* demanded that a proper, respectful abode be constructed, there was no advantage gained by investing more because that investment did not bring down the *Shechina*.

The *Sforno* implies that without this detailed accounting in the *parasha*, one could have mistakenly concluded that the more beautiful the edifice, the more attractive it is to Hashem. After learning about Hashem's relationship with Avrohom, Yitzchok, Yaakov, Moshe, and Aharon, how could anyone think that fancy buildings bring down the *Shechina*? Certainly, the Torah has made clear that good deeds and fear of Hashem attract His presence! How could anybody possibly think that fancy *shuls* and lavish contents could substitute for fear of Hashem and good deeds?

People are attracted to and impressed by wealth and beautiful appearances. It is plausible for a person to erroneously conclude that even though *mitzvos* and good deeds are needed to attract the *Shechina*, an expensive and lavish edifice can enhance the attraction and further ensure the dwelling of the *Shechina*. A beautiful *Beis HaMikdosh* might be considered to have more holiness than the less lavish and simpler *Mishkon*, so the Torah details the rather limited amount of gold, silver, and other materials that went into the *Mishkon* in order to highlight the fact that despite this limited financial investment, the presence of the *Shechina* was greater in the *Mishkon* than in the first or second *Batei Mikdosh*. The enhanced value and cost of these later structures, while dictated by the requirements of proper *kovod* to Hashem, in no way attracted the Divine Presence.

We must constantly be aware that we can fall into the trap of applying a *gashmiyus* – material – value system to matters of *ruchniyus* – spirituality. We must realize that even though people are attracted by wealth, it is the beauty of the *yiras* Hashem taking place and the *mitzvos* that are being done that attract Hashem to us. We must constantly be sensitive to our natural attraction to wealth and worldly displays of beauty. In doing so, we may mistakenly assign an inappropriate degree of importance to these attractions. If we train ourselves to minimize this tendency and focus on developing our commitment to *yiras* Hashem and good deeds, then our value system will become aligned with Hashem's value system.

II. Sensitivity Training

In anticipation of the approaching holiday of Pesach, *Parashas Hachodesh* is read. Moshe and Aharon were taught the *mitzvah* of *Korbon* Pesach by Hashem when they were standing outside the city limits because the cities were full of idolatry, and it would be improper for Hashem's presence to descend into such a place. In contrast, the prophecy of *Makas B'choros*, the killing of the first born, was given to Moshe while he was standing inside Pharaoh's palace, a place of great idolatry. Why didn't Hashem trouble Moshe and Aharon once again to leave the city?

The *Baalei Tosafos* answer that *Makas B'choros*, the last plague, demonstrated Hashem's love for us by completing the plagues and preparing us to leave Egypt. Therefore, Hashem made an exception from the normal procedure as an expression of His great love for us. The command of the *Korbon* Pesach was only to inform us of a *mitzvah* and, therefore, the usual protocol of meeting outside the city was followed.

Isn't every *mitzvah* from Hashem an expression of His love for us because through their performance we earn *Olam Habbah* – the World to Come? The entire purpose of leaving Egypt was to receive the *mitzvos* from Hashem, so why should the *chesed* of *Makas B'choros* be treated as a greater expression of Hashem's love for us than the *Mitzvah* of *Korbon* Pesach? Objectively, the command to fulfill the *Mitzvah* of *Korbon* Pesach is a far greater display of Hashem's love for us than the prophecy of *Makas B'choros*. However, we are only human and perceive our experiences in a physical, not spiritual sense. We more easily appreciated the prophecy of *Makas B'choros* than the command of *Korbon* Pesach because we benefited physically from *Makas B'choros*. Our nature leads us to a greater awareness and appreciation of the physical *chesed* than the spiritual *chesed*, even though the spiritual *chesed* is actually more important.

We can learn an important lesson about *chasodim*. When performing a *chesed* for someone, we must realize that even though this *chesed* may be in their best interest spiritually, they may not fully appreciate what we are doing. Therefore, we should do our best to help them appreciate it. Conversely, we should sensitize ourselves to appreciate *chasodim* done to us that may "only" benefit us spiritually more than those that are materially beneficial.

III. It's Contagious

We all know that displaying negative *middos* is to be avoided. However, sometimes we rationalize and tell ourselves that it's acceptable to get a little angry or haughty. We may even permit ourselves to indulge in slander by convincing ourselves that this specific information isn't really prohibited at all. In this week's *parasha*, we see how dangerous this line of reasoning can be.

In *Parashas* Pekudei, we are told that Moshe *Rabbeinu* gave an accounting for all the donations given to the *Mishkon*. The *Midrash Tanchuma* explains that Moshe needed to give this accounting because there were members of *Klal Yisroel* who were speaking *loshon horah* about Moshe, claiming he had embezzled money from the collection for the *Mishkon*.

The *Midrash* asks how anyone could dare suspect Moshe of such a sin. It quotes Rabbi Yehoshua ben Levi, who explains this to be the meaning of the *posuk* in *Tehillim* (50:20), "You sit and speak about your brother from your father, and slander your brother from your mother." As a result of *Klal Yisroel*'s having spoken *loshon horah* about Eisov *HaRasha*, who is considered like a brother from the father, they eventually spoke about Moshe the *tzadik*, who is considered a closer relative. Although at the outset, *Bnei Yisroel* would not have spoken ill of Moshe, since the *Bnei Yisroel* had gotten into the habit of speaking *loshon horah* about Eisov, this unscrupulous behavior eventually snowballed into their speaking *loshon horah* against Moshe as well.

We see from here how contagious negative *middos* are. One may think he has a *middoh* "under control," but really, it may be the negative *middoh* that has him under its control. It is indeed very difficult to mitigate the negative impact that exercising a poor *middoh* has on our psyche. Let us take this to heart and redouble our efforts to be extremely cautious; inculcating or allowing negative *middos* into our behavior in any way is truly playing with fire.

IV. Under the Microscope

The last number of *parashiyos* detailed the enormous effort of gathering donations, building the *keilim*, and constructing the *Mishkon*. In addition to the self-sacrifice of the donations and the exquisite skill of the physical labor, *Klal Yisroel* invested a purity of cause that was able to turn a physical structure into a spiritual home for Hashem. With the work now finished, *Parashas* Pekudei relates that Moshe made a meticulous accounting of all the donated money and how it was used for the *Mishkon*.

The *Baal Haturim* comments that the word "*pekudei*" is written *malei* with the "*vav*" to teach us that Moshe made sure that the donations of each and every member of *Klal Yisroel*, all 600,000, were used for the *Mishkon*. Moshe exerted this effort to make sure that no one suspected him of taking any of the money.

The entire construction of the *Mishkon* was undertaken with such pure intentions and such amazing dedication, solely for the sake of Hashem. Certainly the great Moshe, with all of his dedication to *Klal Yisroel,* would be above suspicion! Could anyone possibly suspect Moshe of diverting money from this great and holy cause?

It seems that if there were even the most unlikely and small amount of suspicion of impropriety, it would be worthwhile for Moshe to spend his valuable time dispelling that suspicion. Can you imagine the effort involved in accounting for every single donation for all of *Klal Yisroel*? There were vast amounts of gold, silver, *techeiles*, and many other materials. Yet, Moshe took the time and invested the effort to make sure that there wasn't even the slightest sliver of suspicion attached to him.

Moshe *Rabbeinu*'s extreme care should remind us that often, our own actions are under the microscope. At times, others may have a tendency to see even the smallest of our indiscretions. We should therefore, always be careful that all of our dealings are able to withstand this intense scrutiny.

V. Good Intentions, Bad Actions

In this week's *parasha*, Moshe, after gathering *Bnei Yisroel*, first commands them to observe Shabbos and then instructs them in the building of the *Mishkon* and its vessels. The juxtaposition of the *halachos* of Shabbos and the *halachos* of building the *Mishkon* teaches us that the *mitzvah* of erecting the *Mishkon* did not supersede the prohibition of *melacha* – constructive activity – on Shabbos. Even if one, out of zeal to perform the *mitzvah*, knowingly chooses to do *melacha* on Shabbos for the construction of the *Mishkon*, he will have committed a sin deserving of death – the violation of Shabbos.

Why should a person who is sincere and enthusiastic about fulfilling the *mitzvah* of building the *Mishkon* be deserving of death just because he erroneously thought that building the *Mishkon* was more important than observing Shabbos? Shouldn't his good intentions lessen his guilt?

The Torah answers that although this person is trying to fulfill a *mitzvah*, he is nevertheless transgressing the word of God. Even though he will not be found culpable in our courts, because he merely violated the will of God by mistake, in the Heavenly Court he will be held responsible for his ignorance. He should have studied the Torah to understand how to fulfill Hashem's will and avoid committing any well-intended sin due to ignorance of the *halacha*.

Rabbi Akiva, while walking along a road, happened upon an unclaimed corpse, a *meis mitzvah*. He struggled to carry the body a great distance to a Jewish cemetery to give the body a proper burial. When Rabbi Akiva told Rabbi Elazar and Rabbi Yehoshua of how he had performed this heroic deed, they informed him that every step he had taken while moving the body was as if he had committed murder. The *halacha* dictates that a *meis mitzvah* must be buried where it is found; Rabbi Akiva's "heroic" deed was actually a violation of Hashem's will. Rabbi Akiva then concluded that if one can come to err when he has proper intentions, certainly he will sin when he does not have any intention at all. Based on this, Rabbi Akiva concluded that it is necessary for one to learn Torah so that one will not commit sins due to lack of knowledge.

It is very easy for one to sin based on mistaken reasoning when one is uninformed of Hashem's will and the *halachic* ramifications. It is therefore imperative that we study Torah to know what Hashem considers right and wrong, rather than apply our own value system.

SEFER VAYIKRA

Dedicated by the Sobol Family
in memory of our beloved mother and bubby,

Ruth Sobol,
Rus bas Tzvi Noach, a"h,

who personified the posuk
"Kol kevuda bas melech penima"

Parashas Vayikra

In honor of our children

Danielle, Gabriella,
Boaz & Yocheved,

who give us great nachas and joy every day
of our lives and whom we hope and pray
will embody Torah like this sefer does.

Ephraim and Yael Sobol

I. Sins of the Soul

Slobodka, a small town in Lithuania, is synonymous with *Mussar*. In Slobodka there was a *Mussar* Yeshiva geared to enhance a person's awareness of *godlus ho'odom*, the great potential every person has within him as a direct consequence of his being a *tzelem Elokim* – created in the image of Hashem. This goal was accomplished by a constant focus on *rommemus* Hashem – the greatness of Hashem – and *godlus ho'odom*. This enhanced and constant awareness will sensitize a person enabling him to internalize these concepts.

It says in this week's *parasha*, *Parashas* Vayikra (Vayikra 4:2), "*Nefesh ki sechetoh vishgoggo* – a soul that sins unintentionally must bring a *korbon chatos* – a sin-offering." Many *meforshim* question why the term used to describe this person is called nefesh – soul – rather than the typical term *odom* – man?

The *Ramban* answers that the *nefesh* is the pure soul that Hashem gave us and it must remain pure. Sins are the impurities of the soul. Therefore, in order to regain its purity, the Torah directs the commandment to the soul, which needs this offering.

The *Da'as Zekeinim* offers a different answer. He says that the main part of the sin is dependent on the soul, and therefore it is the preferred term. He gives a *moshol* – a parable. Two people, one of them a foreigner and the other a member of the royal court, committed crimes against a king. The king put both of them on trial. He "threw the book" at the royal person, but he excused the foreigner. The other members of the court asked the king why he ruled in this manner. The king replied, "The member of the royal court lives in my palace and recognizes the kindness I bestow upon him, yet he still committed a crime against me. Therefore, he was punished, but the foreigner, who does not know of me and does not recognize my kindness was not punished." Similarly, the soul that is from the celestial heights is pure and should remain that way. When it sins, it is treated more severely than the body that is from the lower and earthly world.

According to the *Da'as Zekeinim*, the soul is punished because it is more responsible than the body. We can understand why the king would treat his royal member more harshly if the sin were deliberately done, but the *posuk* is talking about an unintentional sin, a *shogeig*! Why should the royal member's close relationship to the king be a factor in an unintentional sin? There was no intent to sin!

We must answer that since a person is so close to Hashem, having been created in his image, he is responsible for all his actions and should not have made a mistake. If he does, he must bring an atonement for not having felt the great and awesome love that Hashem has for him and how much greatness Hashem has bestowed upon him. Being so close to the King, he is held accountable even for not anticipating and avoiding unintentional sins. This recognition and understanding of the innate greatness of man and his special relationship with Hashem is *godlus ho'odom* as defined by the original Slobodka Yeshiva. Awareness of *godlus ho'odom* propels a person to achieve an even greater level of *zehirus* – conscientiousness – in *avodas* Hashem. It helps a person anticipate and avoid even inadvertent sins and makes his service to Hashem more complete and free from unintentional errors.

II. Believe It, Achieve It

When one considers making a commitment, he sometimes is plagued by doubts of "I can't" or "it's too hard." In *Parashas* Vayikra the Torah gives us an insight into the makeup of a person and how one can avoid succumbing to these negative thoughts.

This week's *parasha* discusses the different animal sacrifices one can offer to Hashem. When one experiences a moment of inspiration and feelings of spiritual loftiness, he is motivated to make a commitment to bring a *korbon olah* – burnt offering. As time passes, these feelings may diminish and he feels less motivated to fulfill his promise. Regarding the *korbon olah*, the *posuk* (1:3) states, "To the entrance of the Tent of Testimony he will bring it, of his own free will, before Hashem." Why did the Torah add in the extra words, "of his own free will?" The *Gemorah* (*Arachin* 21a) teaches that the Torah is telling us that even when he has lost his initial enthusiasm and seems not to want to bring the *korbon*, the *Beis Din* should force him to bring it by seizing his assets until he proclaims, "I want to bring this *korbon*" and offers the sacrifice.

How does forcing him to say, "I am doing this of my own free will" convert an involuntary act into one of free will? Hasn't he still been coerced? Aren't his statement and subsequent offering done to recover assets from *Beis Din*? The *Rambam* (*Gerushin* 2:20) answers that, in fact, his actions are voluntary. We are only forcing his *yetzer horah* to remove itself from involvement in the matter. The *Gemorah* is teaching that each person really wants to fulfill what the Torah says and perform the *mitzvos*. However, the *yetzer horah* causes a person to lapse. In order to force the *yetzer horah* out of the picture, we make him declare, "I am doing this willingly" in the hope that saying the words will convince him of its truth.

Within a person lies his true self-struggling with the *yetzer horah*. As long as the *yetzer horah* is present, that which he does or says may not reflect how he truly feels. Deep within the reaches of his subconscious he may know what is correct, but the *yetzer horah* tries to sway him from allowing his true feelings to surface. We sometimes feel that it is too difficult for us to overcome obstacles we confront, but these feelings may only be an expression of the *yetzer horah*. We all have the potential to deal with and overcome the challenges Hashem places before us. Therefore, we must believe that we can overcome these obstacles and reach our potential. To achieve this level of belief, we should take certain steps to counter the *yetzer horah*, such as the regular learning of Torah and *Mussar*.

III. Honoring Dignity

When we are under stress, we may lash out at the proximate cause of our frustrations, sometimes even criticizing another individual for his incompetence. We may even embarrass someone publicly when we feel wronged by that individual. When we focus on our actions, we may try to rationalize our behavior by saying, "They deserved it! That's what they get for causing me this pain and grief!" The Torah tells us this is not the proper *hashkafa*.

When one brings a *Korbon Chatos*, a sacrifice brought to atone for transgressions, it is slaughtered on the northern side of the *mizbayach* – altar – the same side used for many other *Korbanos*. *Chazal* tell us that the Torah required the *Korbon Chatos* to be slaughtered in the same place as other *korbanos* to avoid embarrassing the sinner. It seems that there was a more appropriate place to slaughter the *Korbon Chatos*, but, because of the potential embarrassment to the sinner who is bringing the *korbon*, the location was altered.

Why is the Torah so concerned about the *kovod* – honor – of someone bringing a *Korbon Chatos*? Doesn't he deserve a little embarrassment? Maybe we shouldn't go out of our way to embarrass him, but one would certainly think the *halacha* shouldn't have to be altered to protect his pride.

We see from here the tremendous lengths we must go to protect the dignity of a fellow human being. Even if he has brought the disgrace upon himself due to his inappropriate actions, the Torah is telling us that we must appreciate his Godliness and inherent lofty nature. Just as one would never use a masterful work of art as a doormat to wipe one's feet, one must go to great effort to avoid shaming one's neighbor. Let us keep this in mind next time we are tempted to berate our fellow man. He is *tzelem Elokim* – made in the image of God – and no matter what he may have done, he must be treated with great respect.

IV. If At First You Don't Succeed

When we read the first word of *Sefer Vayikra*, the small *aleph* reminds us of the humility of Moshe *Rabbeinu*. *Rabbeinu* Yonah in the beginning of *Sefer Vayikra* writes, "Moshe *Rabbeinu* was *shalem bakol hamiddos* – he was perfect." When we think of a *tzadik*, this is what comes to mind. Moshe *Rabbeinu*, a holy person, the *gadol hador*. This is true. Is that truly a *tzadik*, however? One who has accumulated an impressive resume? What really makes someone a *tzadik*?

Rambam in *Hilchos Teshuva* writes in the fifth *perek*: "*Kol adam ra'ui lo lihiyos tzadik k'Moshe Rabbeinu* – Everyone has the ability to be a *tzadik* just like Moshe *Rabbeinu*." Can we really be like Moshe *Rabbeinu*? He reached the highest gates of Torah wisdom!

The answer is that we can never reach Moshe *Rabbeinu*'s level of Torah understanding. However, we can reach his level of *tzidkus*. *Tzidkus* is not dependent on how much one reached in the level of Torah. Rather, it is a function of one's ability to fulfill his potential. If that individual, through circumstances beyond his control, could not learn so much, or at all, he could still reach great heights.

Unfortunately, in our superficial efforts to define greatness, we tend to assign numbers to everything. Who has the highest average? Who has the most field goals? We do this even in areas of *ruchniyus* – spirituality. How many *blatt Gemorah* did you cover? How many *mitzvos* did you do today? It is true that to *paskin shailos*, one needs to know and understand a vast amount of Torah. However, that is *not* the criteria needed to be a *tzadik*.

Most of the struggles that we deal with on a daily basis are hidden from view. No one knows the challenges we face. One person's easy *"mitzvah"* could be another's worst nightmare of a *nisayon ruchanee* – spiritual challenge. All one needs to do to be called a *tzadik* is to put forth his best effort to fulfill the will of Hashem.

It's interesting to note that the word *tzadik* shares the same root as *tzad*, which means side or trap. In order to trap something, you need to come down on the open side of the trap with force to trap the animal inside. A *tzadik* is the same. When faced with a challenge, the *tzadik* chooses to come down on the correct side with force. If a person does that often enough, he is truly a *tzadik*, whom the *Rambam* testifies is of the caliber of Moshe *Rabbeinu*.

Parashas Tzav

In honor of

Rabbi Astkotzky
Rabbi Baumann
Rabbi Bernstein

Mr. and Mrs. Rafael Harrel

I. Made for You and Me

Hashem gave a magnificent gift to the Jewish nation – the Torah. The Torah is much more than a collection of laws and stories. It represents the entire scope of knowledge available to man, and is the blueprint for the world and its contents, events, and outlook. This level of understanding is achieved through hard work and commitment to our *Mesorah* with success ultimately bestowed upon an individual as a gift from Hashem. For whom was this Torah meant? Is the learning of the Torah restricted to the great scholars of each generation or is it an opportunity available to all?

The *Midrash* in *Parashas* Tzav relates an incident with Rav Yanai. While walking, Rav Yanai saw someone who appeared to be a distinguished *talmid chochom* strolling in the street. Rav Yanai, seeing this as an opportunity to discuss words of Torah with another scholar, invited him to his house. During the meal, it became apparent that the man knew absolutely nothing about *Chumash, Mishnah, Midrash,* or *Gemorah.* Rav Yanai discovered that this man was actually an *am ho'oretz,* an ignoramus. When he requested of his guest to lead the *benching,* the ignoramus refused because he did not know how. This man, who had appeared to be a distinguished *talmid chochom,* was not even able to lead the *Bircas Hamozon.* Rav Yanai, in apparent disgust, uttered, "A dog ate from the bread of Yanai." Rav Yanai meant that this ignoramus was like a dog, in that the ignoramus has no knowledge of Torah. The man reacted by grabbing Rav Yanai and accusing him of holding back his inheritance. The ignoramus had interpreted Rav Yanai's statement to mean that he had no right to the vast knowledge of Torah. The man objected to Rav Yanai's attitude because he felt that every Jew has an inherent right to the Torah. He explained, that once he was walking by a yeshiva and heard the students calling out, "*Torah tzivoh lonu Moshe morasha kehilas Yaakov* – The Torah that Moshe commanded us is the heritage of the Congregation of Yaakov." The ignoramus pointed out that the verse states, "the inheritance of Yaakov" and not "the inheritance of Yanai," meaning that the Torah is bequeathed to each and every Jew equally. The verse clearly reads that the Torah is the inheritance of Yaakov – meaning all Jews. He was angered that Rav Yanai implied that he had no right to Torah learning.

Every Jew has his rightful portion in the Torah and an equal right to even the loftiest levels of Torah knowledge. Torah was not intended for an elite few. Despite the fact that the ignoramus had almost no knowledge of Torah, he was deeply hurt by the remark of Rav Yanai and reacted as if someone were taking away a valuable possession. If each person felt that the Torah is his rightful inheritance, then this would act as a powerful force to motivate him to spend more time and effort learning about what belongs to him. This attitude of "ownership" is enough to create a sense of loss when one does not know Torah and to bring a person to commit himself to *morasha kehilas Yaakov*.

II. Show Me the Money

One of the concepts frequently discussed in *Sifrei Mussar* is the idea of a *negiyah* – a vested interest. In this week's *parasha*, we find a startling example of the profound effect a *negiyah* can have on us.

In the beginning of the *parasha*, Hashem commands the *kohanim* regarding the laws of *korbonos*. In explaining *Rashi*, the *Sifsei Chachomim* say the word "*tzar*" is intentionally used to increase the level of *zerizus* of Aharon and future generations of *kohanim* in bringing the *Korbon Oleh*. There is a concern that they may not have the same level of enthusiasm towards the *Korbon Oleh* as they have for other *korbonos* since they would feel a monetary loss because a *Korbon Oleh*, unlike other *korbonos*, only allows for the *kohanim* to keep the hide of the animal while the rest is consumed.

This seems very strange. First of all, we are discussing *tzadikim* of the caliber of Aharon and his sons; how could they possibly be affected by a little bit of money? Second of all, as the *Sifsei Chachomim* point out, there really isn't any loss of money in this situation, but simply less of a gain than if this had been a different kind of a *korbon*. Finally, as *Rabbeinu Bechaya* says, out of the thirteen different kinds of *korbonos* that exist, the *Oleh* is the one that brings about the greatest level of *kaparah* – atonement. Wouldn't the merit of being the one to bring such a *korbon* sufficiently outweigh the small monetary loss involved?

We see from here the effect that a vested interest can have on a human being. Despite the many reasons that the judgment of the *kohanim* should not have been affected by the vested interest, Hashem, in His infinite wisdom and understanding of human nature, felt it necessary to write the word "*tzar*" to raise their level of *zerizus*.

Let us remember, when we find ourselves in a situation of performing a *mitzvah* and may incur a monetary loss, we must be cognizant of the magnitude of the challenge we are facing and realize the extent to which our judgment can be clouded. Through sincere introspection, seeking advice, and *siyata diShmiya* – heavenly help – may we be *zocheh* to overcome all our obstacles.

Parashas Shemini

I. The Wheel of Life

The *Midrash Tanchuma* on *Parashas* Shemini offers an important insight into the nature of our feelings. Our lives are like a wheel that is constantly turning – the *gilgal hachozer* – the cycle of life. Sometimes we are on the top and sometimes we find ourselves at the bottom.

The *Midrash* presents two examples to demonstrate the principle of the "turning wheel." Hashem was extremely "excited" at the completion of the world, since it was the perfect environment for Adam to do *mitzvos* and to serve Him. However, Adam committed a sin that forced Hashem to punish him with mortality. The feeling of Hashem's excitement had been deflated almost as fast as it had appeared. If Hashem, who is not subject to emotions, expresses that His "feeling" of happiness does not remain, then certainly man can be assured that his feelings do not remain forever.

The second example in *Parashas* Shemini is where the Torah discusses the eighth and final day of the inauguration period of the *Mishkon* and the *kohanim*, when Aharon *Hakohen* and his sons officially began their service in the *Mishkon*. After sacrifices were brought in honor of the occasion, a fire descended from Heaven to consume the sacrifices. The event culminated in Hashem's Presence descending into our midst and Moshe and Aharon blessing the Jewish People. The *Midrash* tells us that among all the people involved in this great event, the greatest *simcha* was experienced by Elisheva bas Aminodov, Aharon *Hakohen*'s wife, who was related to five people or groups of people who were closely involved with the dedication of the *Mishkon*. Her husband, Aharon, had been anointed as the *Kohen Godol*, her brother-in-law Moshe had arranged and performed some of the ceremonies, her four sons began their positions as *Kohanim* along with their father, her brother Nachshon ben Aminodov had been elevated to serve as the *Nasi* – prince – for the tribe of Yehuda, and her grandson Pinchas had been promoted that day to a sergeant. Tragically, this state of perfect joy was suddenly shattered on that very day by the death of her sons, Nodov and Avihu. This woman had been experiencing the joy of five *simchas* at one moment. Yet, at the next moment she had lost two of her precious children. Even during her time of greatest joy and happiness, she was subjected to the impact of the tragic events that followed.

The "wheel of life" can also turn sadness into happiness. When a person is encountering difficult times and feeling sad, he may be inclined to believe that all future joy will be dimmed by the sadness he is presently feeling. However, it is only a matter of time before the wheel will come around; his sadness will dissipate and he will feel complete joy at moments of *simcha*.

The feelings of a human being are short lived and easily changed during different stages in life. Even though one may have experienced pain and suffering, he must believe that he will be able to feel a full amount of *simcha* when the occasion arises. We must understand that life has its uplifting experiences as well as its downfalls. If one realizes that his emotions are subject to change, he will be able to deal with each situation with a new perspective – a perspective which will allow him to deal successfully with happiness as well as tragedy and pain.

II. The Same as a *Tzadik*

Immediately after the tragic death of Aharon *Hakohen*'s two sons, Nodov and Avihu, and even before their burial, Aharon and his remaining sons were commanded to continue the inauguration service of the *Mishkon*. In contrast to the general *halacha* that exempts the immediate relatives of the deceased from certain commandments until burial, the unique circumstance of the inauguration of the *Mishkon* mandated an exception. After they had slaughtered the *korbon chatos*, Aharon and his sons burnt it completely on the Altar, but nevertheless did not eat from it because of their status as mourners. Their refraining from eating was atypical, as the *kohen* usually ate from the sacrifice he brought. When Moshe found out that they did not eat, he got angry at them because he felt that they were required to eat from the sacrifice just as they had been required to offer it on the altar. Aharon then explained to Moshe that according to the law in this unique situation, they were not supposed to eat the sacrifice, even if they offered it. The *posuk* (10:20) says, "When Moshe heard this, he approved."

The *Gemorah* (*Zevachim* 101a) explains that Moshe's approval consisted of his saying, "I made a mistake, and I forgot the *halacha*." Moshe could have saved himself the embarrassment by saying that he never knew the *halacha*, but he admitted his mistake. The *posuk* is praising Moshe for overcoming this inclination to cover up a shortcoming.

Many commentators ask why Moshe was praised for this act. Since Moshe was a great *tzadik*, why would it be considered remarkable for him to overcome this urge to justify his actions? Yet, the Torah tells us that he was inclined and that this was a powerful force to possibly seduce Moshe. When Moshe resisted it, he was acting in a most noble manner and is therefore praised. Apparently, the *yetzer horah* of a *tzadik* is a most formidable antagonist.

Many people think that *tzadikim* are different, that they are superhuman, and their inner struggles are minor. The Torah's praising of Moshe teaches us that *tzadikim* also undergo the same struggles as average people. They also battle the same urges that we recognize within ourselves. People at every level of devotion to Hashem have these struggles and must work to overcome them. Furthermore, when we see *tzadikim* acting correctly, we cannot dismiss their behavior as "natural." Rather, we must view it as an example of how to successfully battle the *yetzer horah*.

III. Under the Influence

Hashem commands Aharon to bring an *eigel* – calf – as a *Korbon Chatos* (*Vayikra* 9:2). *Rabbeinu Bechaya* explains that it served as atonement for his sin of the golden calf. He then cites a *Midrash* which states that because of Aharon's involvement with the calf, he was in danger of losing the *kehunah*. In verse seven, Hashem then commands *Bnei Yisroel* to bring a calf as a *Korbon Oleh* also as a *kaparah* – atonement – for the sin of the golden calf.

Rabbeinu Bechaya asks, "Why did Aharon need to bring a calf as a *Chatos*, while *Bnei Yisroel* brought a calf as an *Oleh*?" He answers that an *Oleh* is brought for a sin that is done willingly, whereas a *Chatos* is brought for an unintentional *aveirah*. Aharon's involvement in the sin of the golden calf was totally *leshem Shomayim*, as he only participated to protect *Bnei Yisroel* from sinning further. His thoughts were pure; therefore, he only required a *Chatos*. *Bnei Yisroel*, on the other hand, willingly wanted the golden calf and required an *Oleh* to achieve forgiveness.

We can understand that despite the fact that Aharon had no sinful thoughts, he still needed to bring a *Korbon Chatos*, similar to one who does a sin *b'shogeg* – by accident. But how could the *Midrash* state that he was in danger of losing the *kehunah* for such a sin? That appears to be extreme.

Rabbeinu Bechaya adds that through the bringing of the *korbon*, the purity of Aharon's intentions would become clear. Apparently, there were some skeptics who doubted the sincerity and real motivation of Aharon in his involvement with the calf. When *Bnei Yisroel* would see that Aharon only needed to bring a *Chatos*, it would indicate to everyone that his intentions were pure. Had he not brought this *korbon* to gain the firm respect of the entire nation, he would have needed to relinquish his rights to the *kehunah*, having lost the basis of leadership.

Aharon was a great *tzadik*, most worthy of the lofty position of *Kohen Godol*. Together with Moshe, he led the *Bnei Yisroel* to freedom and the receiving of the Torah. Yet, retaining his position of *Kohen Godol* was placed in doubt due to the false perception of others. We see the awesome responsibility of a leader. In order to influence others, we must first gain their respect. We need to act properly and our actions must not be misunderstood. This is true of all leaders – a leader of a nation, a school, a classroom, a family, and even one's own peers. If we are not careful, we may lose their respect and place ourselves in danger of forfeiting the great *zchus* of bringing others closer to Hashem.

Parashas Tazria

In honor of our son

Yitzchak Yisrael Gutt

on the occasion of his Bar Mitzvah.

Mr. and Mrs. Alex and Sandra Gutt

I. Objective Living

Parashas Tazria discusses *negah tzoraas* — a spiritual affliction that manifests itself as a colored spot on one's skin, clothing, or house. Only a *kohen* is authorized to determine whether or not a colored spot meets the *halachic* requirements of a *negah,* thereby rendering the individual impure. A *mishnah* in the second *perek* of *Negaim* rules that a *kohen* is prohibited from passing judgment on a spot on himself. He must go to another *kohen* to render a decision that may proclaim him impure because he would be biased on his own *negah* and judge it inaccurately. His judgment would be impaired because of his personal involvement.

There is a *Gemorah* that delivers the same message. In ancient times, the *Beis Din* – Jewish legal court – convened to decide whether to make the current year a leap year by adding a second month of Adar. The *Gemorah* rules that the *Kohen Godol* serving in the *Beis HaMikdosh* could not be part of this *Beis Din* because he had a good reason why he would not want to add a month to the year. During the service in the *Beis HaMikdosh* on Yom Kippur, the *Kohen Godol* must immerse himself in the *mikvah* five times. The addition of an extra month to the calendar would push the next Yom Kippur farther into the colder months and would cause discomfort to the *Kohen Godol* because the *mikvah* would be colder. As the *Kohen Godol*'s vote might be slightly biased due to his personal involvement, he was not permitted to participate in the *Beis Din.*

A *posuk* in Acharei Mos (*Vayikra* 18:6) states that a person is prohibited from "coming close" (*lo sikrevu*) to someone with whom relations are forbidden (*erva*). The *Sha'arei Teshuva* explains that the Torah is telling us that one is not allowed to have even minimal physical contact with an *erva* because it might potentially lead to forbidden relations. We know that many times when the Torah forbids something, *Chazal* made decrees to prevent a person from transgressing that prohibition. This time, however, the Torah itself is prohibiting an action because it may lead to another sin.

The *Sha'arei Teshuva* cites another example of the Torah creating a safeguard for another Torah law. A *nazir* is forbidden to drink wine. Furthermore, the Torah also forbids the *nazir* from drinking anything that contains even a small amount of grape product. The reason is that it might cause the *nazir* to have a desire for wine and lead him to drinking real wine.

Some people may feel that these types of preventive restrictions do not apply to them because they can control themselves. The Torah, however, knows our nature far better than we do. The Torah prohibits even casual contact or private seclusion with a forbidden person because it knows that the individual is unable to decide what will lead to sin and what will not when he is personally involved.

One is inclined to rationalize a decision when he is involved in its outcome, and may even be unaware of his bias. Therefore, when he finds himself in such a situation, he should go to the Rabbis of his generation to ask advice. Since they carry the wisdom of the Torah and are not personally affected by the consequences in that specific situation, they have a true and unbiased perspective. When we realize that we cannot fully trust our own judgment regarding personal matters, our decisions will become more objective, and the outcomes will enhance our lives.

II. Personal Responsibilities

In *Parashas* Tazria, the Torah explains the laws of one who has *tzoraas*, an affliction of the skin, scalp, clothing, and buildings that comes directly from Hashem for certain sins. He must show the affected area to the *Kohen*, who alone has the authority to decide which *halachic* actions should be taken. Several times, the Torah states (13:3-8), that the *Kohen* alone must be shown the *tzoraas*, and only he decides what measures to take. Why is so much emphasis placed on the *Kohen* and his exclusive role? Why must the Torah repeat, "The *Kohen* sees it" or, "The *Kohen* secludes him?" Why wouldn't any Torah scholar or even dermatologist be qualified to diagnose and deal with the affliction?

The *Sforno* answers that the *Kohen*, having been charged exclusively with this responsibility, will acquire special insight to discern which lesions are *tzoraas*, which are questionable, and which are pure. He will develop great skill and accuracy to distinguish between the different types of *tzoraas*. However, the *Sforno*'s answer appears to leave a more basic question unanswered. How does the placing of this responsibility on the *Kohen* lead to accuracy? How will the *Kohen* be given this great insight and skill?

A deeper analysis of the *Sforno* will lead us to conclude that since the *Kohen* alone is charged with the responsibility to look at the affliction, he will exert every effort to perform his task skillfully. Only when the *Kohen* is cognizant that it is his responsibility will his analysis be precise. The Torah repeated that the *Kohen* is the one who is responsible so that his awareness will be heightened and he will train himself to become an expert in examining *tzoraas*.

This principle can be extended to all of us. A person who understands and accepts that he is responsible to perform a task is more likely to perform it successfully than someone who does not feel a personal responsibility. Every Jew must recognize that it is his personal responsibility to follow the Torah because if he does not feel this, he will ultimately find himself lacking in areas that he should have improved. However, if one feels that it

is his duty to do the *mitzvos* and perfect his *middos*, he is
assured of a more successful outcome.

III. The Weight of the World

Parashas Tazria deals with sources of impurity that
emanate from within people and their possessions, such as
the state of impurity that occurs after childbirth or when
one is afflicted with *tzoraas*. The previous *parasha*,
Parashas Shmini, taught about both those animals that are
pure and kosher and those that are impure and non-kosher.
Why did Hashem describe the laws pertaining to animals
first and those relating to people next?

The first *Rashi* in *Parashas* Tazria uses a *Gemorah*
and a *Midrash* to answer our question. The *Gemorah* in
Maseches Sanhedrin (38a) tells us that one of the reasons
man was created on the sixth day was so that if he should
become haughty, Hashem would be able to say to him:
"You think you are so important? Look at this flea; even it
was created before you!" The *Midrash* adds, "Rabbi
Simlai said, 'Just as the creation of man came after the
creation of all the animals, so too, his laws of impurity
were taught after the laws of animals, beasts, and birds.'"
What is the connection between the order of creation and
the order of teaching the laws of impurity? Although the
Gemorah explained a logical reason for the order of
creation, why is that same order relevant to the specific
laws?

The Maharal, in his commentary on *Rashi*, *Gur
Aryeh*, explains the relationship between creation and
laws. Although both animal and man were created long
before their *halachos* were introduced, they remained
purely physical creatures. Their creation was complete
only when their *halachos* were taught. This is why the
Torah in the description of creation said, "*yom hashishi –*

on the sixth day," and not simply "*yom shishi*." According to the *Midrash*, Hashem was hinting to a different "sixth" – the sixth day of Sivan, the day *Bnei Yisroel* received the Torah. All of creation was dependent upon the Jews accepting the Torah at Mount Sinai, and had they not accepted it, the entire world would have returned to a state of "nothingness." When *Bnei Yisroel* accepted the Torah, the creation of the world was finalized. Therefore, the Maharal explains, the giving of the Torah with the *halachos* pertaining to the purity and impurity of animals and man, are all included in the act of creation. Just as during creation, animals came before man, so too, the *halachos* of animals were explained before those of man.

Many objects in this world seem to exist solely as physical entities without any relationship to spirituality. Yet, the existence of all material objects depends on the Torah and its laws. As we approach the holiday of Shavuos, commemorating our acceptance of the Torah, we must realize that learning Torah helps sustain the entire world.

Parashas Metzora

I. Speaker of the House

Hashem has granted us the gift of speech – a gift that makes man unique. In order for us to show our appreciation to Hashem, we must demonstrate how much we value this gift by using it properly. Optimally, it must be used for the service of Hashem by talking about Torah or applying speech to acts of *chesed*. At the very least, we must never pervert this gift by lying or speaking deceptively. There are many degrees of falsehood, ranging from an outright lie to usage of a term that may convey a misleading message. The Torah warns us to distance ourselves from all of these scenarios.

An example of the level of extreme caution the Torah expects of us in choosing our words can be found in *Parashas* Metzora, where the Torah speaks about the affliction of *tzoraas*. When a person's skin, hair, clothing, or a wall of his house becomes characteristically discolored and meets the specifications set forth by the Torah, the afflicted person or object becomes *tomei* – ritually impure. This discoloration is called a *negah*. We are told that if a person sees a potential *negah* on the wall of his house, he must go to the *Kohen* and say to him (*Vayikra* 14:35), "I found something similar to a *negah*." The *Kohen* will inspect the area and decide if it is really a *negah*. The *Mishnah* in *Maseches Negaim* (12:5) tells us that even if the owner of the house is a *talmid chochom* – scholar – who is an expert in these matters, and knows whether or not the spot will be deemed a *negah*, he must still say to the *Kohen* that he saw something "similar" to a *negah* and cannot say that he saw a *negah*. Several commentators ask that if the owner of the house is a *talmid chochom* and an expert in these laws and knows that this is a *negah*, why does he have to say to the *Kohen* that it is something "similar" to a *negah*? Why can't he just say that it is a *negah*?

Tosafos Yom Tov answers that a discolored patch is considered a true *negah* only after a *Kohen* pronounces it as such. If the *Kohen* does not declare it to be a *negah*, it is not really a *negah*. If the *talmid chochom* were to come to the *Kohen* and say to him that he has a *negah* on his house, it would not be true since the *Kohen* had never pronounced it as such! Therefore, the *talmid chochom* would be using an inaccurate term and would not be telling the absolute truth.

Doesn't this seem a bit extreme? The *talmid chochom* was clearly using the generic term *negah* to describe the spot on his wall. This spot on the wall did meet the physical description of a *negah*! He also knows that only the *Kohen* can announce it to be impure and he never intended to supersede the *Kohen*'s authority. He was only saying that the physical status of this spot was a *negah*; not that the house was impure! Why does the Torah require him to avoid even a generic usage of *negah* and say that it is "similar to a *negah*?"

The answer is that the word *negah* implies that the spot is *tomei* and the term therefore sounds untrue. Even though the *talmid chochom* is only discussing the physical status of the *negah*, the Torah does not permit him to use the generic term because it gives the impression that he is also declaring it impure and this is not fully consistent with the truth.

The Torah's expectation that we choose our terms carefully goes even further. Should the *Kohen* be unfamiliar with the details of a *negah*, he is required to ask a *talmid chochom* for advice that will serve as the basis for the *Kohen*'s proclamation. If the *talmid chochom* suggests it is not a *negah*, the *Kohen* will pronounce it as such, allowing the homeowner to return to his house. What could be considered a greater act of honesty than a *talmid chochom* owner proclaiming his own home as a *negah* at great personal expense? Surely this demonstrates his intentions are pure, yet the *talmid chochom* may not use the term *negah* because it is not totally true. He still must say "like a *negah*." Not only must we be honest, but we must be careful to choose our words honestly.

II. Heeding a Warning

What is our approach to financial setbacks? How do we react to a parking ticket on our windshield or flashing lights in our rear view mirror? We tend to bemoan our "bad luck," and make a feeble and short-lived commitment to use more caution in the future. The Torah tells us that there is another reaction we should have to adversity, and if we take this lesson to heart, we may never look at loss quite the same way.

In *Parashas* Metzora, the Torah tells us that the plague of *tzoraas* cannot only afflict one's body, but one's clothes and home as well. The *Da'as Zekeinim* asks why this plague should affect a house; surely the stones and beams of the house have done nothing wrong!

The *Da'as Zekeinim* explains that it is a tremendous benefit for *Klal Yisroel* to have this Divine retribution upset one's home, because in doing so, Hashem is sending a warning sign to the homeowner: "You have sinned; do *teshuva* and save yourself!" Hashem sends the plague on the sinner's belongings as a message to improve his ways, even though this individual committed sins which should have resulted in direct negative results for the sinner. Hashem is only sending the plague on the sinner's possessions when it is the sinner who truly deserves it!

We see from here the tremendous love Hashem has for us. Even though we may be deserving of direct harm and a strict consequence, Hashem waits patiently for our *teshuva*. He sends us warnings by way of afflicting our belongings, when in truth, it is we who deserve the affliction. It is our task to heed the warning signs and improve ourselves.

This is the proper response to many of life's adversities. Let us view that unexpected roof leak, auto repair, or tax bill as a sign that all is not right with our *mitzvos bein adam laMakom* or *bein adam lachaveiro*. Let us use these misfortunes to galvanize our efforts and effect a *teshuva gemura*.

Parashas Acharei Mos

In memory of
Malka bas Tzvi Brafman

Rabbi and Mrs. Avrohom Anton

I. Self-Esteemers

Towards the end of *Parashas* Acharei Mos, the Torah discusses the incestuous relationships that are forbidden to *Klal Yisroel*. The last *posuk* in the *parasha* states, "You shall safeguard My charge that these abominable traditions not be done, and not make yourselves impure through them; *'Ani Hashem Elokeichem,'* I am Hashem, your God." The *posuk* is warning us not to participate in the acts of immorality that were then being committed among the nations of the world. "*Ani Hashem*" – the final words in the *posuk* – is the deterrent that prevents us from acting immorally.

Rashi addresses how "I am Hashem your God" serves as a deterrent and why it is needed. If we defile ourselves, Hashem will no longer be our God because we will have cut ourselves off from Him. As Hashem no longer has any use for us, we deserve annihilation. The *Sifsei Chachomim* explains *Rashi*. He says that "*Ani Hashem*" is a statement that the *Bnei Yisroel* have accepted Hashem's decrees, and had we not agreed to the stipulations that Hashem put on us, we would not have been deserving of Hashem's taking us out of Egypt. By not keeping Hashem's commandments, we are defiling ourselves and thereby severing our relationship. What benefit and purpose could the world possibly have from the Jews if they do not follow what they previously agreed to do? Our unique purpose and position in the world disappears. The world will say that if we cannot accept Hashem, the Creator of the universe, as our King, we lose our integrity and cannot possibly accept a regular king to lead us. Consequently, we will end up getting destroyed by outside nations because the world will recognize that we are of no value.

The standard understanding throughout the Torah of "*Ani Hashem*" is that good will be rewarded and evil will be punished. The *Sifsei Chachomim* explains that *Rashi* deviates from this typical meaning because "*Ani Hashem*" is already used at the beginning of this *perek*. To deter people who are not already deterred by the first "*Ani Hashem*," Hashem now gives a second admonishment. How is this second warning capable of deterring someone from such acts if he was unfazed by the first deterrent of "*Ani Hashem?*"

The answer is that the first deterrent of punishment may be ineffective in the presence of such great temptation. The second deterrent is a direct challenge to our self-esteem. No person can easily tolerate hearing that his status will be greatly reduced and that the world will see him as useless. A person needs to feel that his life has a purpose. Warning him of what will happen should he choose the wrong path may stop him, but pointing out his loss of status and personal importance will serve to deter him much more powerfully.

We see how strong the drive to maintain self-esteem can be. By building up a person's self-esteem, it is possible to stop a person who has lost his self-control from sinning, even to a greater degree than just awareness of the consequences he will face in the World to Come.

Self-esteem is a prerequisite to developing a sincere respect for another person. When one has a proper attitude towards oneself, he can then show proper respect to his friends. During this tragic time of year, when we mourn the loss of 24,000 of Rabbi Akiva's students, we should reinforce our self-respect, which will help us gain respect for others and improve our relations with those around us.

II. Within Reach

As one learns more about Hashem's commandments, he may feel that the level of observance Hashem expects in the area of character and morality is far beyond the standards of our society. Some conclude that achieving such high levels may be impossible and, in despair, do not try to observe them. *Chazal* tell us that our special relationship to Hashem gives us the ability to perform every *mitzvah* that we have been commanded.

In *Parashas* Acharei Mos, Hashem tells Moshe to tell *Bnei Yisroel*, "I am Hashem your God. Do not follow the ways of the Egyptians or Canaanites where I am bringing you. Do not follow their customs." The Torah then explicitly defines the forbidden carnal relationships.

The *Ohr HaChaim HaKadosh* explains why Hashem introduced the *parasha* of the forbidden relationships with, "I am Hashem your God," and mentioned our having lived in Egypt and traveling to Canaan. *Bnei Yisroel* might question their ability to follow commandments that demand such a high standard of morality, especially after coming from Egypt and going to Canaan, whose societies were saturated with immorality.

How could Hashem expect *Bnei Yisroel* to refrain from acts of immorality after such an intense exposure? Hashem answered them by introducing the laws pertaining to immorality with a special statement. Hashem was implying that only a non-Jew isn't expected to adhere to such a level of purity, as the corrupt influences of society weaken him. However, says Hashem, "I am Hashem – I, Hashem, have a very close relationship with you."

Even though we had been exposed to such corruption, our special relationship with Hashem allows us to follow the Torah and abstain from immorality. That relationship actually enhances our ability to achieve spiritually. We must realize that none of Hashem's *mitzvos* are beyond our capacity, as we are the beneficiaries of a spiritual closeness to Hashem.

Parashas Kedoshim

I. Live and Love

Parashas Kedoshim teaches us the *mitzvah* of *veahavta lereiacha camocha* – to love your neighbor as yourself – which is deemed by Rabbi Akiva to be the cardinal principle of the Torah. The *Gemorah* relates a story about a non-Jew who approached the sage Hillel to be taught the entire Torah while standing on one foot. Rather than off-handedly rejecting the request, Hillel responded, "What one does not want done to himself he should not do to others; this is the main part of the Torah. The rest is commentary." This was the abridged version of the Torah according to Hillel. The pivotal role of this *mitzvah* deems its proper fulfillment most important. How can we enhance our love for our fellow man?

The *Ramban* comments that to fulfill this *mitzvah,* one must remove from his heart any feelings of jealousy or resentment he may have towards another. If one sees his neighbor experiencing financial or personal success, he should be just as joyful as if he were the recipient of such good fortune. A good example of rejoicing over another's success is the love of Yonason, Shaul's son, for King David. Shaul *HaMelech* was the king of the Jewish People in *Eretz Yisroel.* His son Yonason should have succeeded him as the next king, but Hashem punished Shaul for not completely eradicating Amalek. Hashem announced, through the prophet Shmuel, that Shaul's dynasty would be terminated, and Dovid, from the tribe of Yehuda, would be the new king at a future time. One might think that Yonason would feel some resentment towards Dovid during the remaining years of Shaul's rule. This was not the case, as the love between him and Dovid was the deepest relationship possible. The *Ramban* explains that Yonason was able to be very close to Dovid because Yonason had conquered his jealousy and resentment toward Dovid and was therefore happy when Dovid was anointed.

At first glance, the *Ramban*'s explanation seems incomplete, as it seems that the *Ramban* is equating the removal of jealousy with the love of fellow man. One would think that we should focus on the positive aspect of loving our fellow man, but the *Ramban* seems to imply that removing jealousy alone causes us to love our fellow man. Does removing jealousy mean that we will have love or respect for another person?

The *Ramban* is telling us that Hashem created every single person with an *inherent* capacity to love his fellow man. Every Jew was designed to love, appreciate, and respect his fellow Jew. However, there are many obstacles that prevent us from loving our neighbors, such as jealousy, hatred, and resentment. Once we remove the jealousy and other negative feelings that cause us to view our neighbors in an unfavorable light, then the original feeling of love and respect that Hashem has placed in us will emerge.

II. Indirect Love

Many times people justify their actions and remarks toward their neighbor because of prior incidents with that neighbor. Our bias impairs our ability to make good decisions.

In *Parashas* Kedoshim, the Torah explains the prohibition against revenge. The *posuk* (19:18) says, "Do not take revenge nor bear a grudge against your fellow Jew. You must love your neighbor as yourself. I am Hashem." *Rashi* brings a classic example of revenge. A man, Reuven, asks his neighbor, Shimon, to lend him a sickle and Shimon refuses. The next day, Shimon tries to borrow Reuven's axe and Reuven refuses, claiming, "I won't lend to you just like you didn't lend to me." The *posuk* teaches us that in this case, it is Reuven's refusal that constitutes revenge.

The *Baalei Tosafos* ask why the Torah didn't criticize Shimon for not initially lending his sickle. One would assume that Shimon should be more culpable for starting the entire cycle. Reuven was provoked and his anger caused him to react selfishly, so why should he be the one who is singled out as the sinner?

The *Baalei Tosafos* answer that the Torah understands human nature: no person is perfect, and some people are very nervous and protective of their possessions. Perhaps, Shimon had a fear that his sickle would be damaged or lost. Therefore, the Torah does not label him as the sinner. While there is room for improvement in his character traits and generosity, the Torah recognizes that the fallacies of human nature prevent him from making the proper decisions. However, Reuven's refusal was because his feelings of hatred overpowered his natural generosity. He wasn't able to control his hatred and instead sought revenge. The Torah says this is inexcusable and in violation of the law. We clearly see the Torah's perspective of the dangers inherent in a person whose emotions aren't properly guided and controlled by *halacha*.

How does one learn to control and avoid responding with hatred to such provocations? The *Baalei Tosafos* provide us with guidance from the end of the *posuk*, which says, "I am Hashem" – the Hashem that provides for all our needs and that we love "with all our heart." If we understand these concepts, gradually our hatred toward another person will dissipate because we will view our neighbors as images, creations, and children of Hashem. As we direct our love towards Hashem, our neighbors will necessarily become an object of that love as "images of Hashem." Therefore, by directing our love to Hashem, we will find it easier to love all of our fellow Jews, even those individuals who interact with us in a way that would normally give us ample reasons to dislike them.

III. Love Thy Neighbor

The *mitzvos* in the Torah can be divided into two categories: those involving our interaction with other people, the interpersonal *mitzvos*, and those involving our relationship with Hashem. To follow the Torah properly, one must keep both types of *mitzvos*. A Jew is incomplete if he follows the *mitzvos* pertaining to Hashem but treats his companions improperly, or if he treats his companions properly but does not follow the other *mitzvos*.

These two types of *mitzvos* seem to be two distinct ways to serve Hashem, and although one must keep both types, it would appear that the interpersonal *mitzvos* have nothing to do with the *mitzvos* between man and Hashem. The *Gemorah* recounts the story of a man who came to Hillel the Elder and asked to be converted to Judaism on the condition that he be told the entire Torah while standing on one foot. Hillel replied that the entire Torah is based on one concept: Don't do to another what you wouldn't want done to yourself. The rest of the Torah is just an explanation of that principle.

Although Hillel's response is a great lesson in ethics, it seems that he omitted all the *mitzvos* between man and Hashem. The *mitzvah* that Hillel told this convert may be an important lesson in the Torah, and perhaps it even encompasses all the interpersonal *mitzvos*, but it fails to address the *mitzvos* between man and Hashem! This man converted on condition that he be told the entire Torah, yet Hillel only told him about some of the *mitzvos*. Why didn't Hillel tell the convert anything about *mitzvos* between man and Hashem?

By telling the convert to care for others as much as he cared for himself, Hillel was saying that the Torah is based on selflessness. When one cares more about others, he becomes less self-centered. The reason a man sins against his fellow is because he is selfish and he cares only for himself, not his friend. The reason people sin against Hashem is because they place a primary emphasis on their own lusts and desires. A person who is commanded to follow the Torah's commandments would not eat *treif*, work on Shabbos or avoid putting on *tefillin* unless he was giving priority to his own needs before Hashem's needs. To observe the entire Torah, one must exercise selflessness.

There is even a greater lesson in Hillel's answer. The two seemingly different ways of serving Hashem are, in fact, completely interdependent. One must also develop an attitude of selflessness to keep the *mitzvos* between man and Hashem. Conversely, if one learns fear and respect of Hashem, he will learn to behave properly towards his friend as well. Since every man is created in Hashem's image, a man who fears and respects Hashem will also treat others who are created in His image properly.

IV. Not-So-Sweet Revenge

"*Lo sikom, velo sitor* – One may not take revenge" (*Vayikra* 19:18). This sounds like an ideal platitude, but when we are wronged by our fellow man, it is difficult to squash those feelings of ill will directed towards those who have done us harm. How are we to overcome this human sentiment?

Yosef held no grudge against his brothers, who came within a hairsbreadth of killing him. He certainly took no revenge. Yosef personified the dictum of *lo tikom, velo sitor*. How was he able to forgive those who had so egregiously wronged him?

We are told that upon returning from their father's burial, the brothers sensed a need to mollify Yosef, fearing that, with their father gone, he may now retaliate for their sins against him. Yosef responds with the words, *"Atem chashvtem alai raah."* According to the *Sforno*, this is to be understood as, "You thought me to be evil." Yosef was saying that their devastating actions against him were the result of a mistaken impression. The brothers truly believed that Yosef was trying to kill them, and as such, had a right to retaliate with deadly force. Yosef was telling his brothers, "I do not hold you responsible for selling me into slavery. You carefully analyzed the situation and arrived at a conclusion that left you no other choice. Had your impression been correct, your course of action would have been justified. I cannot retaliate against a mistaken impression!"

Yosef was able to overcome his natural feelings of revenge by viewing the scenario from the perspective of his aggressors. When we are wronged, it would benefit us to think carefully as to what prompted these offensive actions and to look at the situation through the eyes of our antagonist. Perhaps we would arrive at the same conclusion that Yosef did and possibly remove our temptation for revenge.

Parashas Emor

In honor of the Bar Mitzvah Parsha
of our son, Shmuel Dov, n"y.
Rabbi and Mrs. Mordechai Palgon

I. A Learned Leader

Moshe *Rabbeinu* was the leader of the *Bnei Yisroel* for over 40 years. The commandments of Hashem were transmitted through him to the people and it was essential that the people listen to and totally accept his instructions, so that Hashem's word would be fulfilled. Which specific quality enabled Moshe to have such a powerful and lasting influence on the *Bnei Yisroel*?

Perhaps the trait of humility was the outstanding quality that motivated *Klal Yisroel* to unquestioningly accept the *mitzvos*. Because Moshe was a humble person, the people respected him and listened to his words. Or perhaps one would suggest that since Moshe spoke *"Peh el peh* – mouth to mouth" to Hashem, the *Bnei Yisroel* listened to him. Moshe's credibility was most certainly enhanced by this direct contact with Hashem.

However, the following *Midrash* suggests that another trait was the primary cause of Moshe's ultimate success. The *Midrash Rabbah* (31:5) quotes the *posuk* in *Mishlei* (21:22) which says, "a wise man scales the city of the mighty and casts down the stronghold in which it trusts." *Chazal* explain that *chochom* – wise man – refers to Moshe, *oz* – stronghold – refers to Torah, and *mivtacha* – it trusts – means that when a person toils in Torah, people will listen to him. What the *posuk* now means is "Moshe scales the city of the mighty, and since he exerted much effort into learning Torah, people listened to him." The *Midrash* is telling us that the *Bnei Yisroel* listened to Moshe because Moshe toiled with much effort to learn and understand Torah. Humility and credibility, although necessary, were not sufficient to ensure that the people would be influenced by Moshe. The listener might have thought of a logical argument or reason to question Moshe's commandment. Did Moshe get the details correctly from Hashem? Maybe his applications are vague? Perhaps other factors mitigate the law in certain situations? Even though Moshe has done much for *Bnei Yisroel*, there is still room for us to interpret what Hashem said. An intelligent and committed *Bnei Yisroel* could have made all these arguments in the absence of complete submission to Moshe's word. The people knew that Moshe had considered all the other options, objections, and questions and still came out with the truth. His profound toiling in Torah was the primary reason the people listened to Moshe.

The more effort a person puts into his Torah learning, the more people will respect, consider, and adopt his advice and perspective. When we need to influence others, the amount of toil that we will have put into Torah study can determine the degree to which we will be listened to, if at all. As leaders of our families or a group of friends, we will need people to respect and accept our opinions.

One who does not exert effort in his learning will lack true leadership. This is the quality that people recognize when they accept and adopt a person's advice, perspective, or attitude. The people listen and are influenced by his words even if they originally felt otherwise. The leader has the qualities to convince them that they should do as he says because it is correct and in their best interests. Only diligence in Torah study allows one to achieve a perspective that rings true to those who seek his advice.

II. Impure Influences

Kohanim are prohibited from becoming ritually impure through contact with any *meis* – dead body – other than their seven close relatives: father, mother, son, daughter, brother, unmarried sister, and wife. After the Torah lists the relatives for which a *kohen* may become impure, the *posuk* says about the *kohen* (*Vayikra* 21:4), "A leader among his people – *baal beamov* – shall not make himself impure to defile him."

The *Sforno* explains that the Torah is telling us that the reason a *kohen* is not allowed to become impure through contact with a *meis* is that he is a *baal beamov*. The *kohen* is the one who teaches the people Torah and demonstrates to them a spiritual lifestyle. Since the people look to him as a role model, he has the constant responsibility of showing others the proper path in life and it is demanded of him to act as a nobleman. Since the *kohen* is perceived to be on a very high level, it would not be within his stature to defile himself through contact with a *meis*.

At first glance, one would think that the exact opposite should be true. By being involved with a *meis*, he would be demonstrating kindness to the *meis* – a *chesed* – and showing a sense of caring and sensitivity towards the family members. The *kohen* should be obligated to become involved in such activities, as they would heighten his reputation as one who cares and is concerned with peoples' problems, thereby enhancing his role as a teacher. Why does the Torah's claim that such activities will lessen the respect of others for the *kohen*?

The *kohen*'s holy obligation and privilege to serve in the *Beis HaMikdosh* confers upon him a unique status. This status alone is special enough to elevate him to a position of authority, enabling him to influence people to act properly. Once the *kohen* becomes impure by coming in proximity to a *meis*, he is temporarily forbidden to serve in the *Beis HaMikdosh* and this "demotion" diminishes his influence on the community, as he is now perceived as being impure and imbued with a lower, more common status. People *may not even realize* that they are assigning less significance to the advice of the *kohen*, yet there is a subconscious awareness that is powerful enough to diminish the *kohen*'s influence. The Torah prohibited the *kohen* from becoming ritually impure, as this will disqualify him from serving in the *Beis HaMikdosh*, thus reducing his status and ultimately diminishing his influence on the people.

The *kohen*'s role as a teacher and mentor for the *Bnei Yisroel* demands that he remain in a special "status" of being fit for Temple service. All of us are role models in one way or another. Parents, teachers, siblings, friends, and leaders of the community all have an influence on others, and that influence depends on how others perceive our status. For our advice and influence to be accepted, we must be extremely careful not to act in a way that "disqualifies" us. Our study of Torah requires us to behave in accordance with its laws. By acting improperly, even for a brief moment, we become like the *kohen* who, by entering the cemetery, loses his power to influence others to live in accordance with the Torah.

III. Commitment to Commandment

In this week's *parasha*, Emor, we are taught a very important lesson regarding each person's responsibility to properly serve Hashem. *Parashas* Emor deals with laws relevant to *Kohanim* and the proper procedure for offering *korbonos* – sacrifices. In the midst of the laws about *korbonos*, the *posuk* says, "Watch My *mitzvos*, and do them, I am Hashem. Do not profane My holy name amongst your fellow Jews, I am Hashem who made you holy. I took you out of Egypt, I am Hashem." Why is this general warning about making a *chillul* Hashem – profaning Hashem, located in the middle of the instructions to the Kohanim on performing the temple service? Furthermore, the Kohanim were the holiest of Jews and hardly needed a warning to perform *mitzvos* and not rebel against Hashem. Should not this message have been placed in a different section and addressed to all of *Bnei Yisroel*?

The *Sforno* explains that Hashem gave this message to the *Kohanim* not because they needed it more than the other Jews, but because he expected more from them. They witness the miracles Hashem performs daily inside the *Beis HaMikdosh* and therefore are on a higher level than the rest of *Bnei Yisroel,* and must be even more careful to not disgrace Hashem. The *Sforno* further points out that the *posuk* is not just warning the *Kohanim* about heeding to the commands of Hashem, but it is also warning them against failing to fulfill Hashem's commands completely and in a precise manner. The *Kohen*'s appreciation of Hashem's greatness obligates him to act in an elevated manner. They have a higher "ranking" than other Jews and, therefore, need to act in accordance with this rank. If a *Kohen* does not fulfill Hashem's command with precision, it is deemed a more serious transgression. The *Kohen* may be doing the same action as the non-*Kohen*, but for him it is a desecration of Hashem because only the *Kohanim* witnessed the miracles of Hashem on a daily basis.

As Torah Jews, we recognize Hashem's presence in this world and understand the role Hashem plays in our lives. This awareness creates a heightened responsibility to serve Hashem. Just as the *Kohanim* had to raise their performance of *mitzvos* to a higher level, Torah Jews must also share this responsibility. Included in this responsibility must be a commitment to not only avoid doing what is wrong but also to fulfill Hashem's commands as completely and properly as possible.

IV. Remembering Our Mesorah

Torah Judaism requires a commitment to study and uphold our oral tradition – the *Mesorah* – tradition that has been passed on to us from previous generations. We place great emphasis on how our ancestors lived and recognize the importance of feeling a personal connection to them. From the episode of the Blasphemer in *Parashas* Emor, we learn the importance of following our *Mesorah,* and how it can help us overcome life's challenges.

During the *Bnei Yisroel*'s travels through the desert after leaving Egypt, a man whose father was Egyptian and mother was Jewish wanted to pitch his tent among the members of his mother's tribe, the tribe of Dan. When his neighbors challenged his right to dwell amongst their tribe, he defended his actions by telling them that his mother was from Dan. His neighbors objected because they felt that the father, not the mother, determined the privilege of tribal membership. When Moshe ruled against him, he became enraged and cursed Hashem. Since such an act had no precedent, Moshe did not know whether the sinner deserved to be killed or spared. The man was incarcerated until Moshe consulted with Hashem, Who told him that cursing Hashem was a capital offense. Why does the Torah relate all the details of this unpleasant story? It could simply state the necessary *halachic* rulings and omit the details of the actual case, thereby sparing the disgracing of Hashem's name being recorded for posterity!

Rabbeinu Bechaya answers that the Torah wanted to emphasize that he was the only person who had committed such a horrible crime and that he had flawed ancestry – his father was an Egyptian. The Torah recorded this incident to make us aware that the knowledge that one's ancestors are virtuous people is an immense psychological boost to help a person properly respond to life's challenges. If one feels pride in his heritage and mission, he can resist the *yetzer horah*'s attempts to convince him that he and his actions are irrelevant. In order to teach this important lesson, Hashem was willing to record this event, even at the risk of making a *chillul* Hashem.

The *Chizkuni* adds a further dimension to our understanding of this episode. Although Moshe's ruling was in accordance with the law that the encampment was to be arranged according to paternal lineage, this law had not yet been taught by Hashem to Moshe! Only later, in the second year after leaving Egypt, was Moshe officially ordered to arrange the camp. Since the story of the Blasphemer occurred in the first year, how could Moshe have known this rule?

The *Chizkuni* answers that more than a century earlier, Yaakov had instructed his family to travel in a certain formation when carrying his coffin from Egypt to *Eretz Yisroel*. This formation was later applied when the descendants of Yaakov's children again travelled through the desert to *Eretz Yisroel*. Moshe ruled against the Blasphemer solely because of the tradition inherited from

Yaakov and refused to deviate even if it only affected a single Jew. We see from here the immense importance of upholding the tradition that has been handed down to us. Though the significance of some of these traditions may not be readily apparent, we must safeguard them and pass them on to future generations.

In a similar vein, the *Midrash Rabbah* quotes a *posuk* from *Shir Hashirim*, "*Gan naul achosi chalah; gal naul maiyan chasum* – As chaste as a locked garden, my sister, o bride; a spring locked up, a fountain sealed." One explanation of this verse is that the "locked garden" refers to Sarah who was able to withstand Avimelech's pursuits, and a "spring locked" refers to Yosef, who was able to resist the wife of Potifar. The *Yefes Toar* says that by remembering Sarah and Yosef the *Bnei Yisroel* in Egypt were able to resist capitulation to the Egyptians, who were constantly looking for ways to take advantage of the Jews. They told themselves that if these two people were able to withstand kings and powerful people then surely we can resist a lowly Egyptian.

How did recalling the actions of Sarah and Yosef help the Jews in Egypt oppose temptation? What comparison were they making? How could the actions of Yosef and Sarah, who were amongst the most righteous people ever, affect the actions of the Jews in Egypt? We must conclude that the Jews in Egypt were not relying on a logical argument to avoid submission; rather they viewed their ancestors as role models to inspire them. When they thought about their ancestors, people who had faced temptation and had overcome it, they were motivated to resist their personal temptations. As participants in the chain of Jewish tradition we can learn an important message from this *Yefes Toar*. When we need inspiration to help us resist a temptation, we should remember the actions of previous generations. Seeing the accomplishments and achievements of our ancestors and realizing that we are their descendants should motivate us to defy all wrongdoing.

These words of the Torah and our Sages highlight several very meaningful insights about following our *Mesorah*. If we appreciate our lineage, and treasure the righteous people we follow, it will aid us in overcoming our *yetzer horah*'s attempts to convince us to sin by minimizing our self-image. From Moshe's ruling against the Blasphemer we see how vital it is to abide by the *Mesorah*. When faced with a specific challenge in life, if we connect to our *Mesorah,* we will be motivated to conquer this test and overcome our own battles. If we keep these lessons in mind, then we can better overcome life's challenges and properly continue the chain of our great tradition.

Parashas Behar

I. Cause and Effect

Parashas Behar teaches (25:17), "Do not oppress one another and you shall have fear of your God; for I am Hashem your God." The *Talmud* in *Bava Metziah* (58b) explains that the *posuk* is not referring to financial abuse, such as overcharging a customer (which was prohibited by an earlier verse), but to cases of *ona'as devarim* – verbal abuse. One example that the *Gemorah* cites is that one may not remind a *baal Teshuva* – one who previously had not kept the *mitzvos* but then began to observe them – of his earlier improper actions. Other types of *ona'as devarim* include giving bad advice intentionally *(eitza she'eina hogenes)* and giving someone a misleading impression *(geneivas da'as)*.

Rav Yochanan, the great Talmudic sage, highlights the seriousness of this sin by contrasting verbal abuse with financial abuse. If one steals money and later wishes to repent and be forgiven, he need only return the money. However, if one is guilty of verbal abuse, he can never *completely* repay the hurt feelings he has caused, making total forgiveness nearly impossible. The *Talmud* metaphorically illustrates the gravity of transgressing this *mitzvah*. When the *Beis HaMikdosh* was still standing, Hashem accepted many types of prayers in the merit of the *Beis HaMikdosh*. After its destruction, the gates through which prayers pass into Heaven shut, with the exception of the gate opened by the tears of the victim who has no recourse. Hashem accepts the *tefillos* of this type of victim more so than others because of the extreme pain and suffering he is experiencing – a pain that cannot be assuaged.

The *Talmud* in *Yevamos* tells us that during the period of *Sefiras HaOmer*, between Pesach and Shavuos, 24,000 students of the great Rabbi Akiva died tragically because "they did not treat each other respectfully." Many commentators note that this criticism does not reflect the type of disrespect with which we are familiar. These students were on a very high spiritual level and therefore were held accountable to a higher standard. Their actions were scrutinized through the "magnifying lens" of greater expectation. Hashem took into account slight acts of disrespect that may not have been noticed by us.

We should take to heart the lesson of the *Sefira* by enhancing our awareness of and sensitivity to the serious nature of verbal abuse, particularly in a situation where we may be tempted to rationalize such actions for "just cause." If we consider the potential harm that may come about, we will prevent ourselves from succumbing to this grievous sin. With a split-second of reflection, we can prevent a lifetime of consequences.

II. Leveling Up

The Torah says that there is an obligation to help another Jew who is in financial distress. The basis for this is a *posuk* in this week's *parasha*. The *posuk* states, "*vechi yamuch achicha imach* – If your friend is needy, go ahead and help him out." The *Ohr HaChaim* says that this *posuk* is not only talking about money, but also refers to Torah. If there is someone who is poor in Torah knowledge, the Torah obligates you to teach them. This even applies to someone who is a complete *am ha'aretz*.

This obligation to share Torah is further illustrated in the *Midrash Rabbah*. The *Midrash* quotes the *posuk* in *Mishlei*, "*Rash v'ish tochichim nifgasho* – A poor person and an average person met." The *Midrash* explains the *posuk* as talking about the poor person's lack of Torah knowledge. The poor person asks the average person to teach him a *perek* of *Mishnayos*, which he gladly does. As a result, they both merit *olam hazeh* and *olam habbah*. The *Midrash* then quotes a second *posuk* in *Mishlei*, "*Ashir v'rash nifgasho* – A poor person and a *talmid chochom* met." The poor person asks the *talmid chochom* to teach him a *perek* of *Mishnayos*. This *talmid chochom* says it's beneath him to teach him *Mishnayos* and suggests that he seek out somebody on his own level. According to *Rashi* in *Temurah*, as a result of his stinginess, this *talmid chochom* slowly loses his Torah and the poor person becomes a *talmid chochom*.

We see from the *Midrash* the great reward that awaits one who teaches his friend Torah! Even one who is not a *talmid chochom* can reap bountiful rewards for himself and elevate his fellow Jew by being involved in Torah learning. In these weeks leading up to Shavous, we need to work together to prepare *all* of *Klal Yisroel* for a *kabalas HaTorah*.

Parshas Bechukosai

In honor of the talmidim of
Yeshiva Toras Chaim.
May you be zoche to continue your growth
in ameilus baTorah and shmiras vikiyum
hamitzvos and enjoy the bracha that
Hashem promises to bestow on those who
do.

Rabbi & Mrs. Yehuda Bergida

I. A Slippery Slope

In *Parashas* Bechukosai, the Torah describes a sequence of increasingly horrible punishments known as the *tochocho*. *Rashi* explains that these retributions result from a seven-step deterioration in how *Klal Yisroel* serves Hashem (26:14-15). The process first begins when one (1) fails to apply his full mental capacity while studying Torah – *ameilus beTorah* – toiling in Torah. As a result of not learning deeply enough, (2) he will ultimately begin to flounder in his observance of the *mitzvos*. This will lead him to (3) despise others who are more observant, and to (4) despise the *chachomim* – sages. He will then (5) resort to actually preventing others from fulfilling the *mitzvos*. After this, (6) he will begin denying that the *mitzvos* exist, and, finally, (7) he will deny the existence of Hashem altogether.

The first step in this sequence that converts a God fearing Jew to a hater of anyone who observes or learns Hashem's Torah, is not some terrible and traumatic event but a lack of *ameilus beTorah*. A person may be a diligent *masmid* who studies Torah many hours a day, but if he does not totally apply himself while learning, he will slip downward. Not everyone reaches the stage of denying Hashem, nor is this descent achieved in one generation. We must all realize that although it is a tremendous accomplishment to learn *Gemorah* for several hours or to listen to a Torah lecture, the ultimate goal should be to concentrate fully and learn with all of our energy.

A psychological analysis of this person's orderly deterioration suggests symptoms of one who is struggling to live with a guilty conscience. This person knows what is correct and is troubled that he is not living up to his own standard. However, the final step, denying Hashem, does not fit into this theory. He should stop after step six – the denial of the existence of *mitzvos*. Why does he deny Hashem? We must conclude that his conscience is not totally assuaged and he remains in turmoil. On the surface, this man has taken steps toward soothing his tortured soul, but deep down he knows the truth. One cannot simply deny the existence of that which he knows to be true. He is driven to slip even further in his search to calm himself and escape from his pangs of guilt.

There was a renowned *maskil* (one who has been "enlightened" and has left the way of the Torah), who had previously learned in the Yeshiva of the *Alter* of Slobodka – Rav Nosson Tzvi Finkel, *zt"l*. A man approached the *Alter* and tried to argue that this *maskil* was proof that the *Alter*'s method of teaching was not effective. The *Alter* responded by bringing this man into his office and showing him a letter the *maskil* had sent him. In the letter, the *maskil* liberally cursed the *Alter* for instilling within him a guilty conscience that was haunting him every time he sinned. Even this *maskil*, who had surely sunk to such a low level, could not eradicate his soul's recognition of the truth, as presented to him by the *Alter* of Slobodka.

The power of this innate awareness and recognition of truth is evident in another way. A subconscious knowledge of the real truth can also lead even the worst sinner back to the correct path and cause him to become a *baal teshuva*. Let us hope that we can absorb the lessons of the *tochocho* and be *zocheh* to all the *brochos* that are promised to those who follow the ways of the Torah.

II. Strength in Numbers

In *Parashas* Bechukosai, we are told that if we follow the Torah, five of us will chase one hundred of our enemies, and one hundred of us will chase ten thousand of our foes. *Rashi* points out the seeming mathematical inconsistency. If five of us can chase one hundred, then one hundred of us should be able to chase only two thousand of our enemies. Why does the Torah say that the group that is one hundred strong can chase ten thousand, five times our expected strength?

Rashi explains, "You cannot compare a small group involved in Torah to a large group following Torah." When five are dedicated to Torah, their power is great;

when a group of a hundred is committed to Torah advancement, their might increases exponentially. This is what gives the larger group their extra vigor.

Upon further analysis, this *Rashi* contains an additional lesson. When one sees the words, "You cannot compare a small group involved in Torah to a large group following Torah," one may think of comparing a lone individual to a thriving metropolis of thousands of Jews.

This is not the case. In order for a group to have that status of "a large group following Torah" and to be the beneficiary of the special *brocha* of exponential strength, one need only be in a group of one hundred. One hundred people joined together, involved in the study and practice of Torah, is deserving of this significant bequest of *siyata diShemaya* – Heavenly help.

On Shavous night, the custom for generations has been to learn Torah the entire night. This year, let us achieve our *Tikkun Leil Shavous* together with others who are doing the same. When we combine our Torah learning with that of others, the result can be one of astonishing growth for ourselves, and all those around us.

SEFER BAMIDBAR

Dedicated in memory of
Reb Alan Grodko z"tl
(Avraham Yosef ben Shraga Feivel)

Reb Alan (Avraham Yosef) Grodko *z"tl* was truly a living *Kiddush* Hashem. Although his physical eyesight was impaired, his spiritual vision was crystal clear. As a man who valued *Ruchnius* and understood the *sheker* of *gashmius*, Alan was constantly involved in working to get closer to Hashem. He was strongly committed to selflessly helping others. Whether it was the *rebbe* or taxi driver, everyone knew they could turn to Alan for *chizuk,* advice, or just a listening ear. Alan connected to people from all walks of life.

Despite his physical ailment, Alan was always a positive and proactive person; always yearning to learn and grow. Driven by the words of his dear *rebbe*, Rav Avigdor Miller *z"tl*, Alan always strived to see the *Hasgacha Pratis* (Divine Providence) in life, while constantly expressing his utmost appreciation to *HaKadosh Baruch Hu.*

His overflowing *Bitachon* and *Simchas Hachaim* will forever resonate in those fortunate enough to have known him.

He was a loving husband and father, and continues to be our inspiration.

Parashas Bamidbar

Dedicated by

Rabbi & Mrs. Harayl Askotzky

I. The Complexity of Human Emotions

In *Parashas* Bamidbar, the Torah says, (3:12) "And I have taken the *Levi'im* from among the children of Israel in place of all the firstborn men...and the *Levi'im* shall be mine." Hashem had originally chosen the firstborn men to perform the roles of *Kohanim* and *Levi'im* in the *Beis HaMikdosh*. After the firstborn men failed to demonstrate their loyalty by participating in the sin of the golden calf, Hashem assigned the mission to those *Levi'im* who had not sinned (*Rashi*). The very next *posuk* explains Hashem's original choice of the firstborn: "On the day that I smote every firstborn in the land of Egypt, I made the firstborn of Israel holy to Me."

Rav Nosson Tzvi Finkel, the *Alter* of Slobodka, elaborates on the explanation provided by the *posuk*. When Moshe announced the impending arrival of the last of the ten plagues, the killing of the firstborn, both the Egyptians and the Jewish firstborn anticipated this plague with great trepidation. The Jewish firstborn were anxious, fearing that the plague would kill them as well. And in fact, during the actual plague, the Jews could not help but fear that at any moment, death would come. Because the Jewish firstborn had felt this fear, a fear that Hashem had never intended them to feel, Hashem compensated by elevating them to serve in the *Beis HaMikdosh*.

Why did the Jewish firstborn feel this anxiety in the first place? Hadn't Hashem promised the Jews that He would not harm them throughout all ten plagues? Didn't they see that Hashem had selectively turned Egyptian water into blood, but not the Jews' water? This pattern repeated itself throughout the first nine plagues. Hadn't Hashem told them before the plague of the firstborn to put blood on their doorposts so that the Angel of Death would spare them? Furthermore, wouldn't the unbounded joy felt by the Jewish people at the anticipated exodus overshadow any anxiety?

The *posuk* is teaching us that man is a sensitive and complex being comprising many very delicate feelings – sometimes in diametric opposition to each other. Even though they had every reason to feel secure, and they realized intellectually that they had nothing to fear, there was a small but definite sense of fear within the Jewish firstborn. Although it was irrational to feel afraid, the reality of the impending plague caused them fear. This fear, albeit minimal, was considered by Hashem to be significant, and therefore warranted compensation. Therefore, the Jewish firstborn were appointed to serve in the *Beis HaMikdosh*.

This explanation by the *Alter* highlights our exquisite sensitivity and the responsibility to go to extreme lengths to avoid hurting another person's feelings. Even in an emotional environment of great joy, a person can still react with anxiety to a remote and unlikely cause. The person may not display a negative reaction outwardly, but still feels the hurt within. He may not even be consciously aware of this hurt, but it has an adverse impact.

This seemingly minor feeling of fear came about as an unintended and unexpected result of the plague on the Egyptians. Nonetheless, Hashem felt the need to compensate the Jewish firstborn greatly for the inadvertent outcome. So too, we must realize that any negative feeling, however small, is important, and if we cause such a feeling, even unintentionally and even if we had no alternative, we must assume full responsibility for its impact. On the other hand, we can take personal comfort in knowing that even the small, seemingly insignificant hardships that we endure to learn Torah cause Hashem to shower great rewards upon us.

II. *Zerizus* 101

This week's *parasha* opens with Hashem instructing Moshe on the first day of the second month to take a census of the entire assembly of the Children of Israel (*Bamidbar* 1:1). Several *pesukim* later (ibid 1:18), the Torah relates that Moshe began taking the census on that very same day. The *Ramban* comments that the reason the *posuk* mentions the actual day Moshe began the census is to emphasize the *zerizus* – alacrity – of Moshe *Rabbeinu*. Even though counting all of *Klal Yisroel* wasn't a one day job, Moshe *Rabbeinu* took immediate action, starting on the same day that Hashem issued the command.

If we were talking about any ordinary person, then it makes sense to emphasize that he did it with zeal. However, Moshe *Rabbeinu* was appointed by Hashem to be the leader of the Jewish People. He was among the holiest people who ever lived; the Torah tells us that there will never be a *Navi* – prophet – as great as Moshe. Why *wouldn't* Moshe take the census right away? This is an instruction he's receiving directly from Hashem. Why would he even consider delaying it?

People, by nature, have a strong tendency to procrastinate. Even when a person you respect and love gives you instructions, there is a small – but natural – desire to resist. Laziness is an emotional and biological component of human nature. The only way to battle this tendency is with constant effort, vigilance, and training.

Moshe was comprised of the same human tendencies and emotions as everyone else. It was only because of his constant work and focus that he attained his lofty status. The *Ramban* is telling us that if Moshe *Rabbeinu* had not expended such great effort in developing this special trait of alacrity, he would surely have pushed off the task of counting the Jewish people. In fact, he actually had a good excuse: he was taking care of the entire nation. It was only because of his strong effort over the years that he had the ability to be a truly zealous person, and for this, the *posuk* emphasizes his speed.

This teaches us an invaluable lesson. Often, an opportunity to do a *mitzvah* or a *chesed* comes our way, but we procrastinate. We may say to ourselves, "Maybe I'll catch the next one right way." The *Ramban* is teaching us that *now* is the time. If a person does not work on overcoming this negative attribute at an early age, it will be most difficult to do so as a person becomes older. If an individual of Moshe's stature needed constant effort to avoid procrastination, then surely we do. With proper focus and diligence, we can conquer our natural tendency of laziness.

III. Honoring Each Talent

The beginning of *Parashas* Bamidbar deals with the census that Moshe *Rabbeinu* took of *Bnei Yisroel*. Moshe is told to, "Establish their genealogy according to their families and fathers' house." The *Ramban* learns that everyone came to Moshe with his half-shekel and said, "I am Ploni the son of Ploni from the house of Ploni which is from *Sheivet* Reuvein." The *Ramban* comments further that Moshe was commanded to count the *Bnei Yisroel* in a manner that would bring great respect and honor to each and every Jew. Moshe was not to ask the head of the household how many children he has or how many people live in his house; rather, everyone should come in front of Moshe to be counted individually.

We know that Moshe was very busy leading *Klal Yisroel*. He was involved in teaching Torah and spreading Torah to the masses from morning until night. Counting 600,000 Jews individually would take Moshe an enormous amount of time. Why was Hashem instructing Moshe to count them individually when he could simply ask the head of each family for the total amount of people in each household? Moshe would then have had more time to continue in his more important task of teaching Torah!

We see from here a great lesson in the importance of being *mechabeid* – giving honor to another Jew. We see that it was worthwhile for Moshe to invest a great amount of time in counting *Bnei Yisroel* separately. This brought great respect and honor to every Jew. Through this exercise, every person counted realized they were special as an individual and that they had unique abilities. As a result, they would then be better suited to use these *kochos*

– strengths – to best serve Hashem. This was the greatest influence Moshe *Rabbeinu* could have had on the *Bnei Yisroel*, even more so than teaching them Torah at that time.

The lesson from this *Chazal* is that we should each realize how, as individuals, we each have great God-given talents and abilities that are unique to us. We all have the ability to use these talents to serve Hashem in our own special way.

Parashas Naso

I. Accountability

One of the topics discussed in *Parashas* Naso is that of the *sotah* – the suspected adulteress. The *posuk* describes the gruesome punishment that befell the *sotah* if she sinned and then drank the potion prepared by the *kohanim*. The very next *posuk* reiterates the method through which the *sotah* dies. The *Midrash* (*Bamidbar Rabbah* 9:35) infers that the reason for the apparent repetition is to teach us that not only does the *sotah* receive the punishment described in the Torah, but the man (the *bo'el*), with whom she sinned, receives the same punishment as well. The *Midrash* elucidates, based on the explanation of the *Maharz*, that since the *bo'el* was an active participant in bringing the *sotah* to sin, the man is therefore punished in a similar manner.

Two questions arise on this *Midrash*: (1) It is clear that the *sotah* was a willing participant in the sin. It is possible that she even instigated the behavior (see the *Gemorah* in *Sotah* 8b). Why then should the *bo'el* be considered as though he caused her to sin? (2) The *sotah*'s gory demise occurs only after she refuses to heed the warnings of the *beis din*. If the *sotah* admitted and confessed, she would not be punished in the gruesome fashion set forth in the Torah. Her decision to drink the *mayim ha'meoririm* – the bitter waters – despite knowing she was guilty and hearing all of the warnings issued by the *beis din*, was a choice made by her alone without any encouragement by the *bo'el*. He appears to have no active role in her decision to refuse admission. Why should he die in the same way?

Based on the words of *Chazal*, it's clear that the definition of one who brings another to sin is much broader than one might have originally thought. It appears that if a person helps another transgress a sin, the enabler is equally responsible for the sin itself *and* any subsequent sin that is a manifestation from the original act. Therefore, in the case of the *sotah*, since without the *bo'el*'s participation, the *sotah* would neither have transgressed the initial sin or the subsequent sin of drinking the water, the *bo'el* is held responsible to the same degree as the woman in the performance of both sins.

The *Midrash* continues that the converse is true as well. A person who causes another to do a *mitzvah* receives reward like the actual performer.

We can take two practical lessons from this remarkable *Midrash*: (1) We must evaluate our actions to ensure that what we say or do does not enable another to transgress, thus avoiding accountability for that sin and any subsequent transgressions. (2) We should seek opportunities to aid others in the performance of *mitzvos*, so that we too can inherit a treasure trove of resulting rewards.

Parashas Behaloscha

I. Sensitivity for Other's Feelings

A story is told about Rav Meir Chodosh (1898-1989), the late *Mashgiach* of Yeshivas Chevron in Israel, who was once hospitalized in Hadassah Hospital. One day, a young intern came to draw blood from Rav Chodosh. The Rav asked if all his guests and relatives could please leave the room while his blood was being drawn. After the blood was drawn, his relatives asked him why he wanted them out of the room. Rav Chodosh explained, "I'm an older man and I know that for older people, it's hard to find the right vein. When I saw this young intern come into my room, I realized that it will probably be hard for him to find the right vein and he will probably be embarrassed to continue sticking me until he finds the right vein. Thus, I sent you all out of the room in order to save him from embarrassment."

In this week's *parasha*, Hashem tells Moshe to make trumpets. These trumpets will be used to call the Jewish people together, inform them when to travel, and to call all the *Nessi'im* – princes – together. The *Ralbag* says that we see an important lesson from the trumpets. It's possible that if Moshe had sent a messenger to go around and call all the *Nessi'im* to a meeting, one *Nasi* might have felt insulted that he was called for the meeting later than another fellow colleague. However, the trumpets solved the problem because all the *Nessi'im* heard it simultaneously and no one's feelings were slighted.

The concept of sensitivity is extraordinary, especially considering about whom the Torah is speaking. These *Nessi'im* were appointed to be the leaders of the Tribes; they were humble and secure individuals. Surely, one would think that a leader wouldn't have to be concerned about a *Nasi* feeling insulted that he was summoned shortly after others. However, the *Ralbag* is showing us the extent to which the Torah demands being sensitive to the feelings of even the great *Nessi'im*. By heeding the words of the *Ralbag*, we will be sensitive to the feelings of others on the level that the Torah warrants from us.

II. Emotional Stability

In this week's *parasha*, Behaloscha, Moshe complained that *Bnei Yisroel* are too much of a burden for him and asked permission from Hashem to resign as their leader. Although Hashem rejected his resignation, He did provide Moshe with seventy *Zekeinim* – elders – to assist him. Each tribe was to submit six names of its greatest leaders, and of these seventy-two candidates, seventy would be chosen. There were two great Jews, Eldad and Meidad, who were selected by their tribe as candidates to be *Zekeinim,* but withdrew their name out of humility. As a reward for their humility, Hashem granted them a higher level of prophecy than that received by the seventy *Zekeinim.* One of the prophecies they foretold was that Moshe would die and Yehoshua would take over. When Yehoshua heard this, he was so upset that he summoned them to *beis din* – court – before Moshe, and said, "My master, Moshe, lock them up." The *Gemorah* tells us that because of Yehoshua's statement, he was punished and did not merit having any sons. What error had Yehoshua committed by recommending that Eldad and Meidad be locked up?

The simple answer is that Yehoshua was instructing Moshe how to react and he was punished for this breach of respect. But why would Yehoshua allow himself to violate this basic rule of a *Rebbe*-student relationship. It is true that Yehoshua was upset at Eldad and Meidad's demonstrating a lack of respect for Moshe by announcing his premature death. Yet, Yehoshua also acted disrespectfully to Moshe by telling him what to do, thereby doing to Moshe exactly what he was upset at Eldad and Meidad for doing. Although he was trying to show more respect for his *Rebbe*, he instead disgraced him. How did Yehoshua come to do this?

The reason Yehoshua inadvertently displayed a lack of respect for Moshe was that he was under the influence of his emotions, albeit driven by good intentions. He was emotionally hurt that someone had shown disrespect for his *Rebbe*. Yet, if Yehoshua had hesitated a second and analyzed his emotions, he would surely have realized that they were in conflict with what was right and he would have approached Moshe with a different tone. He was punished only because he acted exclusively on his emotions.

When we are faced with a situation in which our emotions are telling us to act, we must analyze whether what we are about to do is correct or if we are just reacting on our emotional urges. If emotions take control and are unchecked by a Torah perspective, we will make wrong and even harmful decisions. We should strive to serve Hashem based on His command, notwithstanding our emotional preferences.

III. The Magnitude of a Mitzvah

The *Mesilas Yesharim* tells us, "The only path whereby we can achieve [the World to Come] is in this world through the *mitzvos*." It is truly mind-boggling to think that though our actions in this ephemeral world, we can merit the ultimate reward – everlasting closeness to Hashem Himself. We see in this week's *parasha* an example of how far reaching the effect of a *mitzvah* can be.

Miriam spoke about her brother Moshe in a way that could have been perceived to be pejorative. As a consequence, she was stricken with *tzoraas* – a skin affliction. One of the restrictions on a *metzora* was that they were unable to enter the camp of *Klal Yisroel*, so Miriam was obligated to move outside the Clouds of Glory. The Torah tells us that throughout her seven day ailment, *Klal Yisroel* did not travel. *Rashi* explains that Miriam merited having all of *Bnei Yisroel* wait for her for seven days as a reward for the hour she spent watching and waiting for Moshe when he was a baby set upon the Nile River.

Miriam waited but one hour, and merited to have all of *Klal Yisroel*, over 600,000 adult men alone, wait for 168 hours (seven days). That tabulates to more than 100,000,000 combined hours spent waiting for Miriam in the merit of her single hour of *chesed*!

We see from here the true nature of the *mitzvos*. We cannot fathom the fantastic significance every word of Torah, every *chesed,* and every *mitzvah* has on ourselves and the world around us. The magnitude of its impact is certainly far beyond what we could possibly imagine.

Parashas Shlach

I. Slowly but Surely, You'll Get There

If a person has learned *mussar* and applied it to everyday life, yet does not see the obvious results, one might erroneously believe that obtaining lofty spiritual heights is beyond reach. The *Sforno*, in this week's *parasha*, teaches us an important lesson to the contrary.

The *posuk* says, "And these shall be your *tzitzis*, and when you see them, you shall remember all of God's commandments so as to keep them. You will then not stray after your heart and eyes which [in the past] have led you to immorality. You will thus remember and keep all My commandments, and be holy to your God." The *Sforno* says that when one looks at the *tzitzis*, he will remember that he is a servant of Hashem and that he has accepted His *mitzvos*, similar to a master's signet on his servants, indicating that they are his slaves. A person will fear straying after his heart's desires which are against Hashem's will. Absent of his involvement in those physical activities, he will be able to think about the greatness of Hashem and His kindness. As a result, he will do all the *mitzvos* out of love and reverence of Hashem – and with that, he will be holy to his God.

The *Sforno* is imparting a most important lesson. He didn't say that because of the holiness one gets from looking at the *tzitzis*, a person will automatically reach incredible spiritual heights. Rather, the *Sforno* indicates that it is a *process* that starts with internalizing you are a servant of Hashem and ultimately results in significant spiritual achievements. This progression takes time and substantial character development, a process that isn't instantly attained.

Chazal allude to this concept in *Avos D'Rebbi Nosson*, where we read (chapter six), "What was the beginning of Rabbi Akiva? It is told that at the age of forty, he had learned no Torah whatsoever. Once, while standing next to a well, he queried, 'Who chiseled this stone?' He received a response, 'The water that continuously falls on it every day.' Immediately, Rabbi Akiva applied the following logic to himself: 'If that which is soft carves into that which is hard, then all the more so, the words of Torah, which are as hard as iron, will penetrate into my heart, which is flesh and blood!' Immediately, he returned to study Torah."

Holiness does not come through inheritance. It is not automatic, nor is it reserved for a select few. All Jews have the ability to reach high levels as long as they recognize it is a process and are willing to invest the necessary time and effort.

II. Wrapping Yourself in Mitzvos

One of the main tenets of *mussar* is the difference between knowing something intellectually and feeling it with one's heart. Just being aware of a fact may not be enough for it to influence our behavior; one must take extra steps to heighten one's awareness and increase his consciousness in regard to *mitzvos* and *middos*. We see an example of this principle in this week's *parasha*.

The Torah tells us that on the second Shabbos *Bnei Yisroel* spent in the wilderness, a man violated the Shabbos and was subsequently put to death. This episode is followed immediately in the Torah by the commandment to wear *tzitzis*. The *Da'as Zekeinim* explains that this juxtaposition was not happpenstance. Rather, Moshe approached Hashem claiming that it is written in the *tefillin* we wear, *"Lema'an tihye Toras Hashem beficho* – In order that the Torah should be on your lips."* The wearing of *tefillin* keeps one aware of the *mitzvos*. However, we don't wear *tefillin* on Shabbos. Had the *mekoshesh* been wearing his *tefillin,* he would have remembered and not desecrated the Shabbos. The *Da'as Zekeinim* continues that Hashem responded by informing Moshe of the *mitzvah* of *tzitzis*, which reminds one of all the *mitzvos* of the Torah, even on Shabbos.

The *mekoshesh* wore his *tefillin* six days a week, and apparently they protected him from sin as long as he was wearing them. One would think that if he took them off for only one day a week, the effect would not be so severe. It was only a short respite; he was due to put his *tefillin* back on the next day. Can even such a short interruption in this *mitzvah* cause him to lose his sensitivity to the *mitzvos*?

Even a short gap in the heightened awareness of the *mitzvos* that the *tefillin* provided had disastrous consequences for the *mekoshesh*. We see from here that in order to be constantly and completely conscious of the *mitzvos*, it takes more than just being intellectually aware of them. One needs to surround himself with Torah and *mitzvos*, and never – even for a short time – lose focus of the ultimate purpose of this world.

Parashas Korach

In the zechus of a continued
refuah shelaima for

Eliyahu Moshe ben Nathalie

**Mr. and Mrs.
Mickey and Arin Taillard**

I. The Dangers of Jealousy

At first glance, it appears that Korach was an inherently evil individual. Looking at his actions, it would be easy to conclude that he acted in a rash manner without forethought. Closer examination, however, reveals some surprising elements of Korach and the story of his rebellion.

The *Midrash* tells us that Korach was one of the carriers of the *Aron HaKodesh*, a position which only the greatest members of the Jewish nation merited. Moreover, *Rashi* tells us that Korach was a *pikei'ach* – an astute man

– a description reserved for those who are on a high spiritual level. *Rashi* also teaches us that Korach was on such a lofty level that he had attained *Ruach HaKodesh* – special Divine insight.

If Korach was a spiritually astute individual, steeped in Torah learning and spirituality, how then, could he reject the authority of Moshe *Rabbeinu*?

Rashi (16:1) teaches us that the cause of Korach's downfall was his jealousy of Moshe's appointment of Elitzafan ben Uziel – a *Levi* who was given the position of *Nasi*. Korach felt that *he* was the one deserving of that position, and because Moshe *Rabbeinu* had given it to someone whom Korach felt should not have received it, Korach became jealous and subsequently debated Moshe's authority. *Rashi* clearly attributes the cause of Korach's actions to his jealousy and desire for *kovod* – respect. He could not hold his inner emotions in check, which in turn wreaked havoc with his judgment.

Korach was one of the greatest men of a great generation. Even amongst great men, he shone. He had access to spiritual sights attained by only a select few. How could jealousy affect such a man? How could a person on such a high level fall prey to jealousy?

Korach, through his own personal predisposition towards being the *Nasi*, made the mistake of thinking that Moshe *Rabbeinu* was wrong in his decision to appoint Elitzfan ben Uziel. As a result, he rejected Moshe *Rabbeinu*'s authority. Throughout the entire ordeal, Korach thought that he was doing what the Torah wanted from him; from his perspective, he believed he was correct. However, this was a manifestation of the underlying jealousy that Korach maintained.

There is tremendous harm in even the smallest feeling of jealousy. It may seem like it has no effect, but the Torah teaches us otherwise. If a person of Korach's stature – a man who shone amongst some of the greatest people the planet has ever witnessed – had fallen victim to its clutches, all the more are we susceptible to its dangerous effects and ramifications. We must constantly analyze our decisions and actions, making sure we are not clouded by the dangerous implications of jealousy.

II. The Gift of a Coin

New York Mayor Michael Bloomberg once said, "Every dollar makes a difference. And that's true whether it's Warren Buffett's remarkable $31 billion pledge to the Gates Foundation or my late father's $25 check to the NAACP." Those words are very true. We all appreciate the concept of charity and understand the importance of giving, but do we realize how much influence even a small gift has? We see from this week's *parasha* that charity, even in diminutive amounts, can carry great merit.

In *Parashas* Korach, Dasan and Aviram were punished for creating a schism in *Klal Yisroel*. The earth opened up and swallowed Korach, those in his household, and all his belongings. The *Sforno* explains that the evildoers' property was consumed along with them in order that these *resha'im* should not get any merit from future good deeds done with their property. Hashem wanted to prevent a *tzadik* at some time in the future from receiving assistance from Korach's wealth. The *Sforno* likens this to a situation where one unintentionally dropped a coin from his wallet and a poor man found it and used it for sustenance. The merit of that charity goes to the one who dropped the coin, albeit unknowingly. So to, if a *tzadik* at some future time were to benefit from a portion of Korach's possessions, it would have been a merit for him.

Korach was challenging Moshe *Rabbeinu* and Aharon *HaKohen* in front of all of *Klal Yisroel*. He was ostensibly accusing them of usurping the mantle of leadership and priesthood for themselves and their families. The evil they were perpetrating was great, and was deserving of a unique punishment never seen before or again. Why was it necessary for all of his possessions to be swallowed by the earth? What possible difference could it have made to Korach if a few of his coins were to benefit a *tzadik* at some later date?

We see from here the tremendous power of even a small amount of *tzedaka*. Even a few coins, if spared from the abyss, could have presented a significant merit for Korach and his cohorts. How much more so charity given with pure intentions and a giving heart has the potential to have tremendous impression in Heaven. Let us appreciate the power of *tzedaka* and give what we can. The greatest impact of our gift may even be on ourselves.

Parashas Chukas

I. Honor the Leader

In *Parashas* Chukas, we are told that shortly after Aharon's death, the *Bnei Yisroel* complained that Hashem and Moshe *Rabbeinu* should have left them in Egypt. As a punishment, Hashem sent a plague of poisonous snakes to bite and kill those who were slandering Hashem and Moshe. The *Bnei Yisroel* acknowledged their wrongdoing – in speaking against Hashem and Moshe – and beseeched Moshe to intercede with Hashem on their behalf. Moshe davened for the Jews and Hashem instructed Moshe to construct a copper snake that would ultimately bring atonement.

Rabbeinu Bechaya observes that there is a seemingly unnecessary word in the *posuk*. Instead of commanding Moshe to build a snake, Hashem tells Moshe to "make for yourself" a snake (Bamidbar 21:8). *Rabbeinu Bechaya* explains the meaning behind this seemingly odd language. Hashem already had forgiven *Bnei Yisroel* when Moshe davened on their behalf. However, the affront to Moshe *Rabbeinu's* honor could not be forgiven with just *tefillah* alone. Rather, Hashem told Moshe that he needed to build a special snake that *Bnei Yisroel* could use to attain atonement for speaking badly against Moshe. This construction would serve to inform the Jews of just how strongly Hashem responds to someone who speaks against His leaders.

According to *Rabbeinu Bechaya's* interpretation of the *posuk*, we can learn a powerful message about the seriousness of speaking disparagingly against the leaders of the Jewish people. *Chazal* refer to the generation of *Bnei Yisroel* in the desert as the *"Dor Deah"* – the "generation of wisdom." They were all tremendous scholars, yet they did not realize the severity of their transgression in speaking negatively against Moshe. Without the construction of the copper snake, they would not have realized the gravity of their actions. Certainly we, who are nowhere near the greatness of that generation, cannot comprehend what a horrific transgression it is to speak disparagingly of Hashem's leaders.

Furthermore, *Chazal* teach us that the leaders of *Klal Yisroel*, even if they are not as great as the leaders of *Bnei Yisroel* in previous generations, are still held at the same level of esteem. Therefore, the sin of speaking disparagingly of Hashem's leaders also applies today, to the Jewish leaders of our generation.

Rav Ephraim Greenblatt, *shlit"a*, in his *Sefer Rivevos Ephraim* shares a story that once, a student of Rav Moshe Feinstein, *zt"l*, quoted a Torah passage in the name of Rav Yitzchok Hutner, *zt"l*. The student referred to Rav Hutner without the title of "Rav," and Rav Moshe corrected him that he should refer to Rav Hutner with the prefix *"HaRav HaGaon,"* and sent the student to visit Rav Hutner to personally ask for forgiveness for breaching the level of respect that he should have accorded him.

If we learn the message from *Rabbeinu Bechaya* and Rav Moshe Feinstein, and are keenly aware that insulting the *kovod* of our leaders is a sin beyond our comprehension, we will learn to treat the leaders of our generation with the appropriate level of respect they deserve.

Parashas Balak

I. Don't Brush Off the Dust

The *parasha* teaches that before Billam attempted to curse *Klal Yisroel*, he told Balak to offer several different *korbanos*. Upon completing the *korbanos*, Billam was given a prophecy from Hashem, at which time, Billam returned to Balak and related to him what he had learned. The *posuk* relates Billam's first blessing, which in part, states (*Bamidbar* 23:10), "Who has counted the dust of Yaakov or numbered a quarter of Israel?"

The *Midrash* (*Yalkut Shmoni* #767) explains this blessing to the Jewish people further: "...they wear their *shabbos* and *yom tov* clothing and enter into the dust to go and listen to the elderly who speak words of Torah." It is the same praise that Hashem had given the tribe of Yissochor, saying, "Who caused you (e.g., the tribe of Yissochor) to become Torah scholars? It is because you rolled in the dust..."

It is known that the tribe of Yissochor was the one who merited the "Crown of Torah" – the tremendous level of being praised for their great accomplishments in Torah study. When reading the *Midrash*, it seems that Yissochor merited this title because they "rolled in the dust" of learning Torah.

Without the *Midrash*, one might have thought that such an appointment might have been due to Yissochor's diligence in Torah study or deep analytical skills. Yet the Torah attributes the cause of their great accomplishment to their "rolling in the dust." Surely there were other very commendable things about Yissochor that would merit such great reward. Why is the reward for Yissochor credited to what seems to be a very trivial matter?

The *Midrash* is teaching us a tremendous lesson regarding the greatness of showing admiration and reverence towards Torah. "Rolling in the dust" represented Yissochor's attitude and overall approach. In all of their actions, they personified respect and reverence. While other tribes may have achieved great levels in Torah study, the added component of awe and respect towards the Torah that Yissochor exhibited was the difference that catapulted Yissochor into a league of their own.

Small acts and general attitudes carry far more significance than we can possibly imagine. This tremendously high level in Torah is one to which we should all aspire. We learn from the actions of the tribe of Yissochor that our attitude, approach, and reverence for Torah makes a huge difference. Every measure is counted and every effort is weighed.

The same concept can be applied to our overall outlook on other *mitzvos* as well. Every added measure of *simcha* in a *mitzvah* and every extra added level of desire to learn Torah makes a difference. While small acts may seem to be insignificant, the reality is they have tremendous power. May we develop this heightened appreciation and approach towards Torah and the observance of *mitzvos*, so that we perform them with the utmost of care and love.

Parashas Pinchas

Dedicated by
Rabbi and Mrs. Yehoshua Schloss

I. Emotions – A Swinging Pendulum

Tzlofchod was a Jew who died in the desert and left behind five daughters and no sons. Normally, one's sons would assume his assets when he died. However, since Tzlofchod had no sons, his brothers would have inherited his land and possessions, and Tzlofchod's name would not live on among his tribe. As such, Tzlofchod's five daughters came to Moshe to express their frustration and to determine if there was a possibility of preserving Tzlofchod's legacy. Moshe was unable to answer their question and brought the inquiry to Hashem.

Rabbeinu Bechaya writes that when the daughters of Tzlofchod came to Moshe and explained the story of their father's death, they also clarified that their father was not a part of Korach's rebellion, a fact that Moshe once presumed to be true. When Moshe learned that Tzlofchod did not take part in the rebellion, Moshe's initial hatred towards Tzlofchod evaporated. Furthermore, he even developed a bias in favor of the daughters of Tzlofchod and, as a result, was ineligible to serve as a judge for this case. Unable to render a decision, Moshe, therefore, asked Hashem for guidance.

Although the daughters' explanation served only to remove Moshe's hatred, he nonetheless felt impartiality towards the case. Logically, Moshe should not have developed a bias; he should have only lost his original hatred. Yet, *Rabbeinu Bechaya* is teaching us that emotions are like a pendulum which, when pushed in one direction, can dramatically extend to extremes. Therefore, although Moshe's hatred was appeased, he ultimately felt favoritism toward Tzlofchod's heirs and therefore had to remove himself from the decision process.

By internalizing how a simple push could propel someone's feelings to an opposite extreme, we will realize the importance of weighing our words and actions towards others. Even if what we say or do is intrinsically benign, it could have drastic consequences, both positive and negative.

Parashas Matos-Masai

I. Honor Above All

A story is told of Rav Yitzchok Elchonon Spector
(1817-1896) who was waiting to hear if one of his
precious students, Yaacov, would be drafted into the army.
He hoped he would not, as the army did not allow their
soldiers to learn Torah or keep *mitzvos*. Suddenly, while
Rav Yitzchok Elchonon was involved in another matter, a
boy opened the door and said, "Rabbi, we just found out
that Yaacov does not have to go in the army!" Rav
Yitzchok Elchonon replied, "Such good news. Thank you
for telling me." A few minutes later, another boy opened
the door and said, "Yaacov does not have to go to the
army!" Rav Yitzchok Elchonon did not want to tell him
that he already knew because he didn't want to implode
the boy's enthusiasm, so he responded, "*Boruch* Hashem!
What good news! Thank you for telling me." A few
minutes later it happened again, and yet again. Each time,
Rav Yitzchok Elchonon interrupted himself to show how
happy he was, even though he already heard the news.
Each one of the boys had rushed to be the one to make his

teacher happy and as a result, Rav Yitzchok Elchonon acknowledged each of their efforts with the same level of appreciation.

This tremendous sensitivity to others is portrayed in a fascinating *Midrash*. In last week's *parasha* (Pinchas), the *Midyanim* sent women to seduce the Jews so they would stumble and, therefore, not be worthy of defeating the *Midyanim* in battle. The *Midyanim* succeeded, causing myriads of Jews to have illicit relations with *Midyani* women. In the resultant plague which Hashem sent to punish the Jewish people, over 24,000 people died.

Parashas Matos opens with Hashem commanding Moshe to wage war on the *Midyanim* to avenge the evil plan executed by the *Midyanim*. In the battle, *Klal Yisroel* captured many *Midyani* women. The *Midrash Shir Hashirim Rabbah* relates a brief interaction between *Klal Yisroel* and the *Midyani* women. There were a number of beautiful women among the *Midyanim*. In order to prevent anyone from *Klal Yisroel* from stumbling again, the Jews took precautions. They blackened the *Midyani* women's faces and removed their jewelry, thereby marring their beauty. The *Midyani* women protested, saying, "Are we not made in the image of God? How could you degrade us like this?" *Klal Yisroel* replied that since these women had already seduced countless Jews – which resulted in thousands of deaths – such actions were justified retribution and additional risks could not be taken.

The *Midyani* women were amongst the most wicked women in the entire world. Yet, the *Midrash* implies that if not for the fact that they had already seduced thousands of Jews, they would have had a legitimate claim. Had the women not previously exhibited patterns of behavior warranting such dramatic action, the Jews would have been wrong in blackening their faces and removing their jewelry, thereby resulting in a degradation of their self-worth.

We see from here an astounding message – the degree to which one has to be careful not to hurt, embarrass, or degrade even an evil person. Even for the most noble of causes, one must be careful in not diminishing a person's self-worth and value. If these are the Torah standards for evil individuals, imagine how careful we must be with the honor and dignity of our fellow colleagues. It's only when we respect others with the high Torah standards that we acknowledge they were created in the image of God.

SEFER DEVARIM

In honor of Fradelle and Jeffrey Milrad,
proud parents and grandparents.

In honor of our dear children,
Rabbi Chaim and Malka Milrad and
our darling grandchildren,
Rachel, Chana Rivka, and Simcha Ari.
May Hashem continue to bless you with Torah, good health,
bracha, nachas, and much success.

In loving memory of Ida and Irving Hirsch,
proud parents and grandparents.

In loving memory of Edith and Symcha Milrad,
proud parents, grandparents, and great-grandmother.

In loving memory of Dr. Marvin Hirsch,
devoted son, husband, father, and brother.

They inspired us so much with their love of Torah, *Mitzvot,* and
profound love for family. May their legacy live on forever in
their children, grandchildren, and great-grandchildren.

by Maspero, Inc.

Parashas Devarim

I. They Should Have Complained

Throughout the entire forty year span of Moshe *Rabbeinu's* leadership of *Klal Yisroel*, we find Moshe under a steady fire of complaints from his people. Most of those situations didn't bode well for *Bnei Yisroel* and often the consequences were disastrous. However, we find one situation where *Bnei Yisroel* silently accepted a change and interestingly, Moshe criticized them.

In *Sefer* Devarim (1:13), Moshe *Rabbeinu* complains to *Bnei Yisroel* that they pained him by saying "*tov hadavar* – the thing is good." Rashi explains that this is referring to the procedural change that took place regarding the resolution of *halachic* questions and disputes. Initially, Moshe did it all. Long lines of people stood and waited until Moshe could deal with everyone's problems. When Yisro came, Moshe was advised that the system could not last. It would be more efficient to set up a hierarchy of judges and only the most difficult questions would come to Moshe. When this procedural change took place, *Klal Yisroel* did not object. They took it in stride and felt it was a good idea.

Rashi elucidates Moshe's response to the Jewish people as follows: "You caused me pain; you decided on this matter (the change in the system of judging) for your own benefit. You should have responded, 'Moshe, from whom is it most pleasing to learn – from you or your students? From you – because you suffered for your Torah (referring to the fact that Moshe was on *Har* Sinai for forty days and forty nights without food or sleep). Now we will have many judges appointed over us and if they don't favor us, we can give them a gift and then they will favor us.'"

Rashi is telling us that despite the fact that this new procedural system was necessary, *Bnei Yisroel* should not have accepted this without protesting. Their desire to have Moshe – the ultimate Torah leader – as the judge should have demanded a complaint motivated by the pain of that which was being lost. While we are obligated to recognize that whatever Hashem does is all for the best, nevertheless, when it comes to the possible loss of Torah, we are obligated to express our distress and pain over what we perceive to be losing.

We also see the significance of learning Torah from Moshe compared to others. One would think that his having learned Torah directly from the Creator would transform Moshe into the ultimate teacher. Yet it was specifically because of the sacrifice that went into its acquisition that instilled the sweetness and beauty into his learning, making him the most desirable teacher.

If we combine these thoughts and analyze the words of *Rashi*, an interesting picture of the complexity of the human being emerges. On the one hand, *Bnei Yisroel*'s love and appreciation for Torah was on such a high level that their pain of losing the ultimate Torah teacher should have been so overwhelmingly devastating that it should have caused an irrational outpouring of objection to this new system. However, in the same breath, they saw this as an opportunity to "bribe" the new judges in an effort to sway the decision in their cases. They were on such a high level of appreciation for Torah, yet they could harbor the insidious thoughts of bribing a judge and distorting Torah if it served their self interests.

We see the complexity of the human being and the importance of addressing our true emotions and feelings. It is crucial to recognize and uproot our subconscious flaws that can prevent us from reaching our potential. If we can uncover those psychological obstacles buried in our subconscious, we will open new vistas to reaching spiritual heights and protecting ourselves against future challenges.

Parashas Va'eschanan

I. Preparing for the Challenge

The *yetzer horah* has many tactics and it can be, at times, very difficult to harness the internal strength to conquer our inner struggles and challenges. *Chazal* guide us in this important battle, as evidenced by one powerful strategy learned from the *Gemorah* in *Brachos* 61b.

Three times daily, we say in the *krias Shema* that we should love Hashem "*bechol nafshecha* – with our entire soul." *Rashi* (*Devarim* 6:5) explains that we must be prepared to sanctify Hashem's name even at the expense of giving our lives.

The *Gemorah* relates the torturous death of Rabbi Akiva at the hands of the Romans. As they were peeling off his skin with iron combs, Rabbi Akiva was reciting *krias Shema* with tremendous love for Hashem, as if he didn't feel the pain to which he was being subjected. His students witnessed this horrific event and in amazement, observed their teacher's sincere devotion to Hashem.

The *Eitz Yosef* explains that the students asked their *Rebbi* to instruct them as to how they too can reach such a high level of love for Hashem that would enable them to remain steadfast in their commitment in such extreme circumstances. Rabbi Akiva answered, "My whole life, I was waiting and hoping to fulfill the commandment of loving Hashem with all my soul. Now that the opportunity has finally arrived, I am excited to be able to demonstrate this great love that I worked my entire life to achieve." This great act performed by Rabbi Akiva wasn't an isolated incident, but rather the product of years of growth and preparation that raised him to such a high level of devotion and dedication to Hashem.

This lesson of Rabbi Akiva applies to all of us in a very practical manner. When we anticipate a challenge in our daily lives, we shouldn't wait until the actual moment arrives to start preparing. Instead, with diligent planning, we can organize ourselves with adequate preparation and anticipation. Perhaps we can alter our routine, thereby avoiding the entire situation. We may be able to enlist the help of a *Rebbe* or friend to give us the support we need to do what is expected. Or, like Rabbi Akiva, we can focus our attention on personal growth – all while yearning with anticipation for the moment when we will be able to demonstrate what is really important to us.

Parashas Ekev

I. Heavenly Direction

In *Parashas* Ekev, Moshe tells *Klal Yisroel* (*Devarim* 8:18), "Remember Hashem your God who gave you the strength to do all these mighty deeds." The *Ramban* explains that Moshe was afraid that the Jews would think that everything they had accomplished thus far was due to their own skill and prowess. In order to impress upon them that it was all from Hashem, Moshe relayed the following to them. "Do you think that you are accomplished because of your talents and abilities? Who but Hashem could have fed you in the desert, with nothing to nourish or sustain you for miles around? You have defeated the *Moavi, Midyani,* and *Emori* nations – all three whose strength and numbers far surpass that of yours. But you didn't just defeat them in an open field of battle; you defeated them as they tried to defend themselves from within vast and mighty fortresses, whose battlements and towers soared to the heavens…You see clearly that Hashem and only Hashem brought you to where you are today."

Closer analysis of the *Ramban* seems perplexing. Moshe was addressing an erudite generation that Hashem took out of Egypt – one of the most brilliant generations that ever lived. They were able to comprehend things about which we can only begin to dream. Not only were these brilliant people; they were also on an astoundingly high level of holiness, as evidenced by the fact that they were deemed worthy to receive the Torah. Yet, the *Ramban* is telling us that Moshe was afraid that if not for the rebuke he planned on giving them, the Jewish people would deny the awesome role which Hashem played in bringing them out of Egypt, orchestrating the ten plagues, splitting the sea, making the *mon* fall for forty years, and conquering the mighty nations that occupied Canaan. How could it be that an entire nation – so brilliant and holy – could fall victim to such folly?

The Torah is telling us that implanted within every individual is a powerful natural tendency to attribute all his successes and accomplishments to himself. This dangerous tendency cannot be overcome unless a person diligently and carefully observes the magnitude of what Hashem does for us on a daily basis. The Torah tells us that we have an obligation to love Hashem with all our hearts and all our souls. Imagine the love that would fill our hearts if we appreciated all the Divine Providence in our lives. Imagine the boost it would give to our trust in Hashem. By opening our eyes and seeing the love and kindness that Hashem showers upon us every minute of every day, we will reach new heights of trust, devotion, and love of Hashem.

Parashas Re'eh

Dedicated by

Rabbi and Mrs. David Levine

I. Temporary vs. Long Lasting Happiness

The Torah tells us (*Devarim* 16:14-15), "*Vesamachta bechagecha...vehayisa ach sameach* – And you shall rejoice on your festival...and you will be completely joyous."

The *Rama* writes (O.C. 93:9) that we read *Koheles* on *Shabbos Chol Hamoed* of Succos. The *Mogen Avrohom* explains that the reason *Koheles* is read specifically on Succos is that Succos is a time of *simcha*, and in *Koheles*, King Solomon says in regards to *simcha*, "What does it accomplish?"

This *Mogen Avrohom* seems very difficult to understand. Strangely, King Solomon's words provide us with a reason *not* to read *Koheles* on Succos – the *posuk* is disparaging *simcha*! If we are supposed to be joyous on Succos, why would we read a *posuk* that portrays the triviality of *simcha*?

The *Gemorah* in *Shabbos* (30b) points out an apparent contradiction between two *pesukim* in *Koheles*. First Shlomo *haMelech* says, "And of *simcha*, 'What does it accomplish?'" and then he says, "So I praised *simcha*..." (*Koheles* 8:15). The *Gemorah* explains that the second *posuk* refers to *simcha* from performing a *mitzvah*, whereas the first *posuk* denotes *simcha* which is not derived from the performance of a *mitzvah*. It is clear from the *Gemorah* that when the *posuk* belittles *simcha*, it is referring to the happiness derived from worldly and materialistic pleasures, all of which have no association with *mitzvah*-related *simcha*.

Based on this *Gemorah*, we can now explain why we read King Shlomo's statement on Succos. The public reading of this *posuk* is meant to teach us that while the pursuit of worldly pleasures may provide temporary excitement, they will not make a person ultimately happy. As *Chazal* say, "He who has 100, desires 200 and he who has 200, desires 400." Our Sages, therefore, instituted the reading of *Koheles* on Succos to help us recognize the fruitless pursuit of worldly pleasures, and to help us understand that true happiness can only be achieved from a life dedicated to Torah and *mitzvah* observance.

II. Learning From Your Surroundings

When the Torah discusses the *mitzvah* of bringing *maaser sheni* – second tithe – to Jerusalem to consume, its purpose is stated as (*Devarim* 14:23), "*Lema'an tilmad leyirah es Hashem Elokecha kol hayamim* – In order that you should learn to fear Hashem all of your days." *Tosafos* in *Bava Basra* inquires as to how one's pilgrimage to Jerusalem for *maaser sheni* will impact his *Yiras Shomayim*. *Tosafos* explains that the environment will trigger his spiritual growth. Exposure to a place where *kohanim* are *duchaning*, *Levi'im* are singing, and the *Sanhedrin* are judging will have a direct impact on the person. It is an environment where, "*Kulam oskim b'meleches shamayim* – Everyone he sees is involved in serving Hashem." Observing this alone will be sufficient to influence an individual and indoctrinate him with *Yiras Shomayim*.

It is interesting to note that *Tosafos* makes no mention of any special *shiur* that this individual needs to attend, nor any other specific requirement other than what he will happen to chance upon once he is there! Rather, we see one's environment can have a tremendous effect on his spirituality.

We should always try to surround ourselves with upstanding people who are o*sek b'meleches Shomayim*. In this way, we will always continue to absorb more *Yiras Shomayim*.

Parashas Shoftim

Sponsored in honor of our son

Netanel

and his wonderful Rabbeim and teachers
at Yeshiva Toras Chaim.

Dr. Zev and Dina Raden

I. When Wrong is Right

In this week's *parasha*, *Rashi* explains that even if
our Sages say that right is left and left is right, we still
have an obligation to abide by their instructions. The

Ramban further elucidates *Rashi* and offers two reasons for always following the direction of our Sages. First, even if our Sages appear to be inherently wrong, they are still considered correct because they have the ultimate authority and discretion to interpret the Torah. Second, we should realize that our Sages are intrinsically correct since Hashem protects them from making mistakes and derails them from misinterpreting the Torah. Therefore, it is our obligation to follow their direction.

Upon close analysis of this *Ramban*, the first reason seems superfluous. If the second reason tells us that our Sages are intrinsically correct, why do we need the first reason to tell us that theoretically, if they appear wrong, we would have to follow them anyway?

It is evident from the *Ramban* that if not for the first reason, a person would not be able to accept the second reason. A person would not be able to admit that he is wrong, even when arguing with the greatest Sages who have special Divine Assistance and are protected from making mistakes. If the *Ramban* had not written the first reason, a person would defy all logic and mistakenly conclude that his interpretation is correct, despite the Sages having Divine Assistance. A person's inherent arrogance for being correct would overshadow the acknowledgement that the Sages have special Divine Assistance. However, once the *Ramban* offers the first reason, the problem dissipates and the individual's misconception is nullified. It is only by heeding the advice of the first explanation (knowing that he has to follow the Sages regardless of who is correct) that a person is able to accept the second reason (which reveals that the individual is misguided in his interpretation). The first reason establishes the critical foundation of setting aside one's ego, thereby allowing a person to accept the second reason

– that our Sages have Divine Assistance and are intrinsically correct.

The *Ramban* teaches us a vital lesson – a person's desire to be correct is so powerful that he will think he is right even when the Torah tells him that he is wrong. Only by working on himself to internalize this concept can one hope to overcome the natural human tendency to always assume that he is correct, even when the truth is staring him in the face.

Parashas Ki Seitze

In honor of our children

Mr. and Mrs. Aviel & Atara Raab

I. The Dangers of Anger

In *Parashas* Ki Seitze, we learn that a relative is not permitted to be a witness against another relative. The *Sefer HaChinuch* explains the reason for this. Unfortunately, it is common for conflict and fighting to exist between family members. If the Torah allowed one family member to testify against another, then when an individual gets angry at another family member, he would be able to go to court and falsely testify against him. However, after his anger subsides, he will likely realize what a terrible thing he has done and his remorse and regret will cause great pain and anguish. The Torah has compassion on this person and wants to prevent such a scenario from occurring and therefore disqualifies family members from testifying against each other (*Sefer Hachinuch, Mitzvah* 589).

Falsely testifying against someone is a terrible sin and a person capable of performing such an act would appear to have the hallmarks of a *rasha* – an inherently evil person. Why would the Torah have compassion on such a person with nefarious intentions?

The answer can be found in the second half of the *Sefer Hachinuch*'s explanation. This very same person, the *Sefer HaChinuch* tells us, will later regret what he did, causing tremendous pain and remorse. A truly evil person does not feel bad after he does something wrong. On the contrary, a *rasha* fools himself into believing that he did the right thing. The *Sefer HaChinuch* is teaching us that this person to whom he is referring is not a *rasha*. Rather, the person is an inherently good person who is capable of doing terrible things when getting angry. Therefore, the Torah has compassion on the person and takes precautionary measures to ensure this scenario does not happen.

The *Sefer HaChinuch* teaches us an interesting insight into how anger can transform an average person into doing terrible things he will later regret. People are most likely to make these tragic mistakes when fighting with members of their family. The people whom they love the most are generally the ones they hurt the most. In the end, they suffer terribly and regret what they have done. They wish it had never happened.

We learn from this *Sefer HaChinuch* the dangers of anger. When we are upset, it is hard to control our anger. Nevertheless, we can't afford to let our anger spin out of control, as the consequences can be tragic. Learning to control one's anger is a lifetime project. We can motivate ourselves to control our anger if we appreciate its importance. By working on ourselves when we are not confronted with volatile situations, we will prepare ourselves to handle more sensitive matters calmly.

Parashas Ki Savo

I. Support Your Fellow Jew

The *posuk* states (*Devarim* 26:2), "And you shall take from the first of every fruit of the land…and you shall put it in a basket…" The third chapter in the *Gemorah Bikurim* details the process of this pilgrimage: "The flute played before them until they reached…Yerushalayim… and all of the craftsmen in Yerushalayim would stand up and greet them by saying, 'Our brothers of such-and-such place, come in peace!'"

The *Gemorah* in *Kiddushin* cites this *mishna* as a challenge to a different statement in the *Talmud*. According to our Sages, craftsmen in the middle of their labor are not permitted to stand for Torah scholars because they are working for others. How can it be, questions the *Gemorah*, that a craftsman is not permitted to pause his work and stand up for Torah scholars when the *mishna* in

Bikurim states clearly that the craftsmen would stand for those bringing the first fruits?

The *Gemorah* responds that the situation in *Bikurim* is different because if the craftsmen did not stand for those bringing the first fruits, it could cause them to "stumble in the future." *Rashi* (in *Chulin*, where this exchange also takes place) explains that if those bringing the first fruits were not greeted with a friendly countenance and granted sufficient honor, they would likely not come regularly because of the logistical hassle and monumental effort involved. The people bringing the fruits needed the moral support and encouragement by the craftsmen. Hence, the craftsmen, by not standing, would be causing people to "stumble in the future." Therefore, a special exception was made for the craftsmen to interrupt their work and stand for those bringing the first fruits.

This is a fascinating insight into the human need for encouragement. It is an unequivocal obligation to bring *bikurim*. If people are unable to overcome personal indolence on their own, why should the craftsmen be required to pause their work and encourage them?

The *Gemorah* is teaching us a valuable lesson. A Jew may be obligated to endure the journey to Yerushalayim and bring *bikurim* with or without the craftsmen standing up to greet him, but if this Jew might otherwise neglect that duty – or be discouraged from bringing fruits in the future – the craftsmen must stand. Regardless of obligation, if someone requires moral support to perform *mitzvos*, be it in the form of praise, respect, or just a friendly word of encouragement, our response should be – in the spirit of the craftsmen – one of positive encouragement and unconditional love.

Parashas Nitzavim

I. Components of Effective Tefillah

The *Midrash Rabbah* on *Parashas* Nitzavim opens with a discussion on *tefillah* and reveals one the components of effective prayer.

A *posuk* in *Melachim Beis* (Chapter 22) recounts that during the reign of King Yoshiyahu, a Torah scroll was found in the *Beis HaMikdosh* open to the curses in *Parashas* Ki Savo. A delegation was sent to Chulda (a prophetess) to inquire about the implications. The *Gemorah* in *Megillah* questions King Yoshiyahu's choice of prophet. The prophet Yirmiyahu was a contemporary of Chulda; he was the leader of the generation, surpassing her in Torah knowledge and prophetic ability. Yirmiyahu, a prophet of the very highest order, reached incredible heights of piety and character refinement. His empathy was boundless. It was Yirmiyahu who even composed *Eicha*. Why wasn't the delegation sent to Yirmiyahu instead?

The *Gemorah* answers, "because women are naturally more compassionate." The *Maharsha* clarifies that King Yoshiyahu presumed the prophecy would be negative (and indeed he was correct, as the prophecy ultimately foretold of the impending destruction of the *Beis HaMikdosh* and subsequent exile). He therefore sent the delegation to Chulda, hoping that her compassionate nature would inspire her to pray that the prophecy be changed.

Yirmiyahu would have prayed, but his prayer would have been lacking. It would have been passionate and profound, and issued from a lofty spiritual plane, but it would have been lacking the extra bit of compassion that comes naturally to women. Therefore, King Yoshiyahu sent the delegation to Chulda, knowing that her natural trait of compassion could be the extra emotion that could make the difference in outcome.

Effective *tefillah* requires every bit of concentration, focus, and emotion. Each additional degree of emotion has the potential to make a difference. Imbuing our *tefillah* with the maximum concentration and emotion can catapult our prayers in ways we would have never imagined.

II. An Easy Influence

Parashas Nitzavim begins with Moshe *Rabbeinu* gathering *Bnei Yisroel* together to join them in a covenant with Hashem. The *pesukim* say, "Because you know that we dwelled in the land of Egypt...and you saw their disgusting, putrid idols...maybe there is amongst you a man or a woman or a family or tribe that his heart turned away today from Hashem." The *Ramban* implies that it was possible that all of *Bnei Yisroel* could have subsequently become pagans. *Rashi* explains that Hashem suspected *Bnei Yisroel* of harboring an attraction to idol worship because of the idolatry they saw in Egypt and the other nations they had passed through. This warning implies that if they had not been exposed to idolatry, Hashem would not have suspected them.

During the forty years in the desert, *Bnei Yisroel* were completely involved in Torah study and experienced miracles daily. How is it that they could have been suspected of idolatry after having had such a close relationship with Hashem? Surely *Bnei Yisroel* would never have entertained pagan thoughts!

The Torah is teaching us that there was good reason to suspect *Bnei Yisroel* of paganism because they had been exposed to it in their past. Even though *Bnei Yisroel* were involved only with spiritual matters for forty years, there was a chance that they might yet descend into idolatry because of a prior influence. From the concern that the Torah has about *Bnei Yisroel* deteriorating even after forty years of closeness to Hashem, we see how careful we must be to avoid all negative influences, as sometimes their effects may not manifest for many years.

The exposure to positive influences at a young age can also strongly affect a person years later. In *Pirkei Avos*, the mother of Rabbi Yehoshua was praised for her son's greatness because she put his crib in the *Beis Midrash* so that he would be influenced by the sound of Torah from his youth.

Our surroundings have the ability to influence us greatly, both in a positive or negative manner. We must, therefore, place ourselves in an environment that will only influence us properly and go to great lengths to avoid negatives influences.

Parashas Vayeilech

I. Torah Beyond Value

In this week's *parasha*, Moshe *Rabbeinu* says his parting words to the Jewish people. He says (*Devarim* 31:2), "*Lo uchal od lotzeis v'lovoh* – I can no longer go out and come in." *Rashi* explains that Moshe is referring to *divrei* Torah – that the tradition and depths of learning were taken from him. The *Sifsei Chachomim* explain that Hashem was doing a *chesed* for Moshe by minimizing any internal pain when Yehoshua would take over as the next Jewish leader. Since Moshe lost the ability to learn Torah at the same level he had previously experienced, he no longer felt any purpose in living, and therefore the transition to Yehoshua was easier for Moshe to process.

This concept of having lost the depth of learning Torah, with seemingly no point to continue living, doesn't appear to be logical for Moshe. Consider that Moshe was the Jewish people's greatest teacher and prophet, with an unusually close relationship with Hashem. While he may have lost his ability to learn the depths of Torah familiar to him, he nonetheless remained a glorified prophet, maintained his ability to perform *mitzvos*, and preserved a close relationship to God. Shouldn't these wonderful aspects of his life been reason enough to continue living, even without the ability to learn Torah?

It is hard for us to fully appreciate the ability to learn and teach Torah. Being a prophet, performing *mitzvos*, and having a close relationship with God are all incredible opportunities – but without the Torah, they lose considerable meaning and value. They cannot compare to the greatness of learning and teaching Torah. Moshe, who had seen and experienced this ultimate greatness, felt that without the gift of Torah, there was no purpose to his life. This outlook – that life isn't worth living without the ability to learn Torah – demonstrated the greatness and value of learning and teaching Torah. It's our job to appreciate this amazing gift and be filled with tremendous *simcha* and contentment when immersing ourselves in Torah study.

Parashas Ha'azinu

I. The Power of Hope

In this week's *parasha*, Moshe tells the Jewish people, (*Devarim* 32:7) "Remember the days of old; understand the years of generation after generation." *Rashi* explains that Moshe was telling the nation to learn the lessons from past generations, when people transgressed and Hashem responded with severe punishment. However, continues *Rashi*, Moshe relayed to *Klal Yisroel* that if they don't commit themselves to learning the lessons from past generations, they should recognize that in the future, Hashem will reward those who follow the Torah, during the days of *Moshiach* and in the World to Come.

Implicitly, Moshe was saying that if the memories of the past (e.g., fear of punishment) won't arouse the nations' emotions, knowing that Hashem will reward those who follow His commandments in the future will motivate people to come closer to God.

Wouldn't the knowledge of a proven system and time-tested historical accounts have a stronger influence on a person? Could a person be more inspired from future rewards than from previously documented punishments?

It appears that it is easier to stimulate a person to follow Torah and *mitzvos* due to the hope of reward than to serve Him due to fear of punishment. The human psyche is stirred by positive encouragement, excitement, and anticipation of reward. While the lessons of the past are valuable, important, and should be studied, the value of longing for future rewards cannot be underestimated. Actively stressing the ultimate reward, happiness, and pleasure in learning Torah will encourage greatness.

Parashas Vezos Habracha

I. Unconditional Love

In the opening verse of the final *parasha*, the Torah tells us (*Devarim* 33:1), "And this is the blessing that Moshe, the man of God, blessed the Children of Israel before his death." The *Midrash Tanchuma* (Va'eschanan 6) explains that Moshe was told it was time for him to leave this world, at which point he responded that he first needed to bless the Jewish people. Since Moshe strongly warned and heavily rebuked the Jewish nation in recent addresses, he didn't want anyone to have the mistaken impression that he was leaving with an angry attitude towards them. To remove any possible misconceptions, Moshe felt it was critical to bless the Jewish nation in the final moments of his life, solidifying his unconditional love for the nation.

Had Moshe not blessed them, the *Bnei Yisroel* would have mistakenly inferred that Moshe was, on some level, angry at them. Moshe made a conscious effort to bless each tribe individually, in order to show that he loves them with a whole heart.

Is this the most important task that Moshe had to do in the last moments of his life? Surely the greatest leader of the Jewish nation had more important matters to address before leaving this world. Why did Moshe use his final minutes to teach the Jewish people he harbored no anger?

The purpose of Moshe's life was in teaching the Jewish people the magnificence and beauty of Torah. A student's nature is to listen more attentively and adhere to a mentor's advice when the student knows he is loved. Moshe's top priority was addressing and proving his unconditional love to the entire Jewish nation. It was with this hope that he believed his students would then cling to the Torah with full dedication and unparalleled devotion. We must never underestimate the power and influence our love has on the people around us.

YOMIM TOVIM

Dedicated in memory of
Dr. Abe Chames
Avraham Zev ben Yaakov
(1954 – 2008)

Abe would have "shepped nachas" to see this volume "**Mussar Haskel: Courage to Change.**" The fact that this is a product of the yeshiva boys would have made him so proud. He loved the yeshiva. He loved the boys and most importantly, he loved what the Yeshiva stood for; *yashrus, ehrlichkeit* and *emes.* In fact that is what he stood for and all those who knew him knew this to be so.

The Chames Family wishes the yeshiva much hatzlacha as they continue to grow and may they grow in *yashrus, ehrlichkeit* and *emes* so that we all can continue to be proud of the Yeshiva's endeavors.

Deborah S. Chames
Eric, Melissa, Abie and Allie Shalolashvili
Jonathan, Jennifer and Ava Chames
Jacob Chames

Rosh Hashanah

I. High Expectations

As we approach Rosh Hashanah and Yom Kippur, a sense of awe and respect arises within us, hopefully accompanied by a desire to correct our negative behavior. To succeed in our goal of self-improvement, it is essential for us to recognize that we have the opportunity to reach great levels of spirituality. The Torah reveals the great level Hashem expects us to aspire to.

The *posuk* in *Parashas* Kedoshim states, "*Kedoshim tihyu ki kodosh ani Hashem Elokeichem –* You must be holy since I am Hashem your God and I am holy." The beginning of the *posuk* tells us be holy, but the end of the *posuk* refers to Hashem's holiness. What is the reason we need the latter half of the *posuk*? Isn't it enough for the Torah to tell us to "be holy?"

Chazal answer that without the latter half of the verse, one may think that he can attain a level of holiness equivalent to that of Hashem. To teach us otherwise, the Torah states that although we can achieve tremendous spiritual accomplishments and goals, Hashem's holiness is still greater than our own. It is impossible for us to reach that level.

From the mere fact that *Chazal* thought that we might be able to reach levels of holiness rivaling those of Hashem, we can realize what expectations *Chazal* had of us. *Chazal* understood that man has a tremendous potential that can be developed into true greatness. They knew man's capabilities and the heights to which he can soar. However, we actually are on a much lower level than this, and it is much harder for us to fathom the concept that it may be possible for man to reach a level so close to that of Hashem. If we take *Chazal's* words seriously, this alone can be the greatest motivation to realize that we have a much greater potential than we may think. We may feel that we have accomplished most of what we are capable of doing, but in truth, we may only have fulfilled a small portion of what we can truly achieve.

As the time of *teshuva* and repentance draws near, we should internalize this most important concept. We must believe that we can achieve lofty goals. We ask Hashem that, in the merit of our yearly and lifelong commitments, He grant us happiness, health, long life, and prosperity.

Succos

I. True *Klal Yisroel*

At times, we tend to be insular. We may "circle our wagons" to prevent ourselves from the undue influence of society at large. We may even cut ourselves off emotionally from those whose *mitzvah* observance or Torah scholarship doesn't meet our expectations. We may feel that our service to our Creator can be better fulfilled without the "distraction" of those less pious than ourselves. The Torah shows us that this is far from Hashem's will.

The Torah in *Parshas* Emor tells us that on the first day of Succos, we should take the *arba minim* – four species. The *Da'as Zekeinim* understands each of the *minim* to be referring to a different type of Jew. The *esrog*, with its exceptional aroma and taste, represents the *tzadik*, who possesses the sweet aroma of Torah and the exquisite "taste" of *mitzvos*. The *lulav* grows on a tree, which produces tasty fruit, but has no scent. This symbolizes the

Jews who perform many *mitzvos*, but are not steeped in Torah learning. The *hadas*, with its delightful fragrance but no taste, corresponds to those Jews who are learned, but are lacking in the performance of *mitzvos*. The *arava* – which lacks both taste and smell – characterizes those Jews who lack both Torah and *mitzvos*. The *Da'as Zekeinim* concludes by saying that we take all four together on the holiday to signify that Hashem only desires to be close to *Klal Yisroel* when they are united.

We can readily understand Jews of varied levels of piety joining together in the service of Hashem to be a significant occurrence, but why must we include the *arava*, those who lack both Torah and *mitzvos*? Of what possible advantage could it be to us to band together with those who are so far removed from Torah and *mitzvos*?

We see from here that our *avodas* Hashem is incomplete unless we are uniting all Jews – even those less observant than ourselves. There is a great responsibility to reach out to those who are far from Torah and *mitzvos* and band together with them in the service of Hashem. May we be *zocheh* to help ignite that spark of greatness that resides deep within all of us.

Purim

I. Getting Off the High Horse

The story of Purim includes an episode in which Achashveirosh rewards Mordechai, who had earlier saved his life, by parading him dressed in royal robes around the entire city of Shushan on the royal horse. Why did

Mordechai deserve such a great honor? True, Achashveirosh rewarded Mordechai because he had saved his life, but what did Mordechai do to deserve such honor from Hashem?

The *Midrash* answers that Mordechai received this public display of honor as a reward for davening every day with great intensity and devotion. The *Midrash* continues that even though Mordechai was aware of the great status to which the king had elevated him after the parade, it did not lead to arrogance and a false sense of security from the peril confronting the Jews. He returned to davening with great intensity, as the *posuk* in Esther (6:12) says, "And Mordechai returned to the gate of the palace" – meaning he returned to fasting and praying.

The Jews were in a life and death situation. Haman had a public decree from Achashveirosh giving him full power to kill all the Jews and every single Jewish life was at stake. Surely the imminent danger was evident to Mordechai who was a prophet, a *talmid chochom*, and a leader of the Jews. Yet, even a great man like Mordechai is praised for not succumbing to a false sense of security that might be produced by his moment of fame. He was not fooled by the great honor given to him by the king, as he understood the gravity of the situation.

Mordechai dismounted the horse, removed the royal robes, and returned to his davening, which was the key to our salvation. Even before this episode, Mordechai recognized the peril and had turned to Hashem. He could have relied on his political connections with the palace, as the queen was his own relative! Yet, he knew that all salvation comes from Hashem and he turned to Hashem exclusively. The royal parade, with Haman leading the horse, was a strong signal to Mordechai that success was imminent and his prayers were to be answered. We should expect that Mordechai would continue to pray for salvation, yet the *Midrash* finds this very act most praiseworthy. Such is human nature. When we receive what we pray for, we relax our vigilance and may even ascribe our success to our efforts or contacts in high places. Even the great Mordechai could be susceptible to this self-deception and he is therefore praised for resisting it.

We, who are not as great as Mordechai, can more easily delude ourselves into thinking that success is the product of our labor. While basking in the warmth of our own accomplishments, we must be self-vigilant not to lose track of how they were achieved – as a gift from Hashem. We can achieve this self-vigilance by recognizing that Hashem is the provider of all success and following Mordechai's example of continuing to daven to Him for assistance.

II. Undivided Attention

Prayer is how we ask Hashem to fill our needs and desires. The *tefillos* of the Jews in the time of Mordechai and Esther to be saved from Haman's decree were overwhelmingly successful. What can we learn from their prayers that will allow our *tefillos* to get the results we hope for?

When Achashveirosh decreed that the Jews should be annihilated in eleven months, Mordechai reacted immediately. He told Queen Esther, his niece, to convince King Achashveirosh to revoke the evil decree. Esther decided to make a banquet in which she invited both Achashveirosh and Haman. Why did Esther purposely go out of her way to invite the wicked Haman when Achashveirosh was the one who was issuing the decree?

The *Gemorah* in *Megillah* (15b) quotes Rav Nechemiah who explained that Esther invited Haman because she wanted to avoid overconfidence on the part of the Jews, lest they say, "There is no need for us to repent fully because we have a sister in the palace, and she will surely protect us!" She reasoned that Haman's attendance at the banquet with the King would suggest to the Jews that she did not have a plan, or that she might have given up on saving the nation and was trying to curry Haman's favor so that she could save herself, while neglecting the rest of her nation. This would inspire them to intensify their prayer.

The *Megillah* (4:3) describes the reaction of the Jews upon hearing that Achashveirosh had issued this genocide decree. The verse states, "In every province, wherever the King's command and his decree extended, there was great mourning among the Jews with fasting, weeping, and wailing; many of them lying in sackcloth and ashes." It is clear from this verse that the Jewish people were in a state of extreme anguish and worry. Why then did Esther have to be concerned that the Jews might rely on her and not pray to Hashem? The Jews were already anxious and afraid! Why did Esther deem it necessary to invite Haman to the banquet?

Esther thought that despite their anxiety and fear, they might have placed some of their hopes in her, thereby reducing their reliance on Hashem. Esther knew that the *Bnei Yisroel* would daven to Hashem. However, she was concerned that their reliance on her might reduce the intensity of their *tefillos*. Esther wanted the *Bnei Yisroel* to realize that even though she was doing all that she could do to save them, Hashem was the final arbiter of their fate. There is no substitute or exchange for the trust and faith that we place in Hashem. Esther was worried that if they relied on her, they would not look to Hashem for deliverance. Therefore, Esther invited Haman to the banquet to ensure that the Jews would remain concerned, thus causing them to daven most intensely to Hashem. She knew that this small change in the attitude of the Jewish People might make the critical difference.

We can glean from Esther's actions that we must genuinely feel that Hashem is the one who is in control of all situations. Despite the fact that we may have prominent leaders or armies, Hashem is the ultimate ruler. Therefore, we must concentrate on placing all of our trust in Hashem and hope to have our prayers answered according to our request.

III. Count Your Losses

It is characteristic of the human condition not to take full responsibility for the negative outcomes of our actions. If we were to realize the extent of our responsibility for the negative results of our actions, we would contemplate them more carefully. From the Purim story, we can see how far our level of responsibility reaches.

The *Megillah* relates that once the decree was passed that all Jews were to be killed on the fourteenth of Adar, Mordechai begged Esther to go before Achashveirosh and plead on behalf of the Jews. Initially, Esther refused, but Mordechai told her that if she remained silent, the Jews would be saved by other means and, *"V'at u'beis ovich toavdu* – You and your father's house will perish."* *Chazal* explain this to mean that she would lose her portion in the world to come. The *Maharal* explains that Mordechai felt that Esther's fear for her life caused her to rationalize. She therefore believed that the right thing to do was to delay going before Achashveirosh until summoned. If so, what was the logic Mordechai was trying to convey to Esther? Why would Esther's refusal to go before Achashveirosh result in such a terrible punishment if she had a valid rationalization and was afraid of death? Esther, who was a prophetess, had worked on her personal spiritual perfection for many years and achieved a great status. Why would a single failure outweigh all of her earlier work?

The *Chovos Halvovos* tells us that one's reward is greater for teaching others than the reward for personal growth, even if one personally attains a level that is near perfection. Esther, a very righteous individual, who undoubtedly had performed countless personal *mitzvos*, had been given the opportunity to save all future generations of Jews. Her failure to act would make her responsible for the lost merits of all future generations. Her single failure would have led to catastrophic results that would have been far more impacting than all the good she had previously accomplished. Therefore, she would be punished by losing her portion in the world to come.

Many of our actions can have an effect on future generations, albeit less dramatic. If we fail to perform actions that can positively affect future generations, we will be missing the great opportunity of helping others and be subject to great punishment. Conversely, if we act properly in matters of such importance, we will receive great reward.

A similar lesson can be learned from a *Gemorah* in *Maseches Megillah*. The *Megillah* says, *"Ish Yehudi haya beShushan habira, ush'mo Mordechai ben Yair ben Shimi ben Kish ish Yemini* – There was a Jewish man in Shushan, the capital, whose name was Mordechai son of Yair son of Shimi son of Kish, a Benjamite." Was Mordechai an *"ish Yehudi* – man from the tribe of Yehuda" or was he an *"ish Yemini* – man from the tribe of Binyomin?" The *Gemorah* explains that the *Megillah* is alluding to complaints the Jewish people had against two individuals earlier in history. The first was King Dovid, from the tribe of Yehuda, who had spared Shimi's life after Shimi had cursed him. One of Shimi's descendants was Mordechai, and because Mordechai's refusal to bow down to the idol had angered Haman and caused the trouble for the Jews, they had a complaint against Dovid. The other complaint was directed against King Shaul, who was from the tribe of Binyomin. Although instructed to completely destroy Amalek, he spared Agag for one night, allowing him to produce descendants, one of whom was Haman. Although many generations had passed since the time of Dovid and Shaul, these claims were indeed valid, says Rabbi Yaakov of Lisa. Dovid and Shaul are held responsible for the actions of descendants many generations later, even though they could not have foreseen these outcomes.

In the *Nesivos's* introduction to *Megillas Esther,* he asks why we say on Purim, "Cursed is Haman, blessed is Mordechai" when we don't do this at other holidays. He answers that the Jewish people had a complaint against Mordechai for bringing Haman's wrath upon them by refusing to bow to his idol. Conversely, Haman earned a tremendous merit for his heinous actions. *Chazal* observed that the removal of the ring to seal the decree condemning the Jews, had a greater impact than forty-eight prophets who had constantly rebuked *Bnei Yisroel,* because it catalyzed a mass repentance. *Chazal* felt that this action might be deserving of immense reward, and to therefore counteract any potential blessing, we say for all generations, "cursed is Haman." Haman, even though he triggered a national repentance, is still cursed. Mordechai, despite his role in initiating the decree to destroy the Jews, is still blessed. Haman, who hoped for the opposite of what eventually happened, is credited with such great merit that all future generations are commanded to say "cursed is Haman" to establish who is the cursed one. *Chazal* are highlighting the fact that when the masses are affected by our actions, even an unintended good that is caused by our conduct will result in tremendous merit.

From the Purim story, we learn important lessons about accountability for our actions. If we fail to perform deeds that will affect future generations, we will be held accountable for these losses, even if the effects of our action or inaction are totally unpredictable. We also learn that if our actions cause good, whether intended or not, we will earn tremendous reward. We should therefore evaluate our actions with greater thought and planning, to ensure that what we are doing is correct. In doing so, we will avoid the responsibility of unintended future losses and gain the inestimable merit of the generations to come.

IV. An Angel of Intellect

On Purim, we read from *Megillas Esther*, which describes how the Jewish people were saved from Haman's plans to eradicate them. When Mordechai heard about the decree to destroy the entire Jewish nation, he told Queen Esther to plead before King Achashveirosh on behalf of her people. In preparation for the crucial meeting with Achashveirosh, Esther instructed Mordechai to command the Jews of Shushan to fast for three days. After the three days, Esther went uninvited to meet Achashveirosh and requested permission to host a party for Achashveirosh and Haman. During the party, Esther asked Achashveirosh and Haman to join her for a second party, at which Achashveirosh asked Esther what she desired. Esther responded that she wanted her nation to be saved from the decree of annihilation. When Achashveirosh asked her who was responsible for the decree, she responded (7:6), "A man who is an adversary and an enemy, this wicked Haman."

On this statement, the *Gemorah* in *Maseches Megillah* says in the name of Rav Elazar, that when Esther made the accusation of, "A man who is an adversary and an enemy, this wicked Haman," she was trying to point towards Achashveirosh. However, a *malach* pushed her arm aside so that she pointed towards Haman.

Esther understood that the fate of her people depended on the outcome of her meeting with Achashveirosh. What possessed Esther to point at Achashveirosh and accuse him of being an adversary and an enemy, thereby jeopardizing the lives of the Jewish people and undermining her own plan?

We must conclude that when Achashveirosh asked Esther who was responsible for the decree, she was overcome with shock and disbelief at seeing Achashveirosh acting so innocently that her true feelings surfaced. Everything Haman had been trying to do had the approval of Achashveirosh, and when she heard him ask this question innocently, as if he had not taken part in it, she could no longer maintain control and tried to point at him. Fortunately, Hashem sent a *malach* to move her hand.

What Esther did teaches us an important lesson about human nature. A person can put on a show for a long time – but not forever. Of course Esther knew intellectually what she was supposed to do, but her emotions overpowered her. One can try to veil one's feelings, but under extreme stress, one's actions will be based on emotion rather than intellect.

A person may think he has already overcome his negative traits, but when under pressure, he will realize that he has not. In order to correct negative character traits so that one will not be driven to act in an uncontrolled manner, it is imperative for each individual to learn *mussar* daily. Some people consider perfecting character traits an endeavor that does not require much time. In reality, however, it is a lifelong process.

V. Dress the Part

Chazal tell us, "*Rachmana Leiba Baui* – Hashem cares about what is in our hearts." It would seem that our outward appearance is insignificant, as long as our intentions and convictions are proper. We see from the *Megillah*, however, that that is erroneous thinking.

Mordechai, after learning of the plot to kill the Jews, donned sackcloth and ashes and proceeded to go just outside the courtyard of the king in order to alert Esther to the impending threat. He could not, however, enter the courtyard without proper clothing. Esther heard of Mordechai's mournful state and sent him respectable clothing so that they could meet in person. Mordechai, however, refused the clothing. The *Vilna Gaon* explains, that his refusal was due to the fact that he didn't want to separate himself from his *teshuva* for even a moment.

Why couldn't Mordechai have continued his *teshuva* in his heart, while outwardly wearing respectable clothing? He needn't have removed his mind from *teshuva*; he only needed to temporarily change his clothes to gain access to the kings courtyard. Did Mordechai really need to "dress up?"

Rather, we see that it was impossible for Mordechai to reach the same level of *teshuva* wearing respectable clothes, that he could reach wearing sackcloth and ashes. Even a temporary deviation from his somber dress would have had a significant impact on his ability to have the humility he needed to feel before Hashem. Apparently, clothing has such a drastic effect on a person that even Mordechai the *tzadik* was not immune to its influence.

In our lives as well, we must realize the tremendous effect our clothing has on us. When our garments fail to represent our lofty aspirations, they have the ability to pull us down and stunt our spiritual growth. When we dress in a respectable, honorable way, the way befitting a *ben* Torah, our garments help us feel that elevation and raise us up.

Pesach

I. Converting Our Sensitivities

As we prepare for the Pesach holiday, we realize that there are many important and essential lessons to be learned from the Exodus from Egypt and how the Torah relates these events to us. Yet the simple historical fact of our bondage in Egypt has *halachic* ramifications. In *Parashas* Mishpotim, the *posuk* (22:20) says, "You shall not insult a convert because you were strangers in Egypt." How does the fact that we were strangers in Egypt lead to the commandment not to insult a convert?

Rashi answers, that the second half of the *posuk* is not an explanation for the prohibition, but a motivational tool to help us restrain ourselves from insulting the convert. *Rashi* tells us that if we insult a convert, he will insult us right back by saying that our ancestors were also strangers in a strange land! The chance that he might insult us back should prevent us from insulting him in the first place.

Elsewhere, in two different places, the Torah has already prohibited insulting any Jew. Here we are further commanded not to insult a convert because he is alone, without any family, in a new environment and extremely vulnerable and sensitive to any insult. The Torah is telling us to take special care with the convert. Apparently, to assist us in fulfilling this command, the Torah tells us to remember that our ancestors were strangers, thereby arousing within ourselves a higher level of sensitivity to the convert. However, *Rashi* seems to be offering a different explanation. We ourselves should feel vulnerable to insults, and this will be the motivation to achieve an enhanced sensitivity to the convert. It is not enough to empathize with a convert. We have to feel vulnerable and only then will we become sensitive to the convert.

This *Rashi* requires further explanation. The person who is insulting the convert probably does not even know his own great-great-grandfather! Why should he care if someone insults his ancestors from over 2300 years ago? They have no connection to him! How will this make him feel vulnerable and prevent him from insulting the convert?

When the convert responds by insulting us, even though we do not feel insulted, subconsciously the insult will cause deep emotional pain because our ancestors are a part of us. True, the insult may not bother us as much as an insult directed at a closer relative, but pain is inflicted nonetheless. We may not be aware of this pain because we have become desensitized. However, it does affect us – albeit to a very small degree.

Sometimes, we may poke fun at people and think that they really do not mind. They may even say they do not mind. It still hurts because damage is inflicted. We learn from this *mitzvah* how sensitive a person really is and how sensitive we must be to everyone's feelings. If a person is damaged because of a comment directed at his ancestor, all the more so he will really feel hurt if an insult is directed at him!

Pirkei Avos (6:6) describes the forty-eight different qualities which are required to become a *talmid chochom*. Most of these qualities do not involve education. Rather, they discuss the *middos* and sensitivity a person must have towards other people. When a person has negative *middos* and is insensitive to others, then he cannot be considered a true *talmid chochom*. Even if a person is able to learn the Talmud and its commentaries, he is not a *talmid chochom* if he has poor ethical values. In contrast, if a person has very good *middos*, it will improve his understanding of Torah.

II. Time Value of Money

There is a bank that credits your account every morning with a gift of $86,400 but unfortunately does not carry over the unused balance from day to day. Rather, it cancels the balance you have failed to use. If you had an account in this bank, you certainly would draw out every cent every day! Well, we do have such a bank account, and its name is "Time." Every morning, we are credited with 86,400 seconds. Every night, whatever amount of this currency we have failed to invest properly is lost. It carries over no balances and allows no overdrafts. Each day we are credited with a new deposit, and if we fail to use the day's deposits, the loss is ours. There is no going back, nor is there any drawing against tomorrow. We must live in the present – on today's deposits.

It seems strange that so much focus is placed on the *mitzvah* of *matzoh* considering that this *mitzvah* represents only one aspect of the Exodus from Egypt – that the Jews were rushed out of Egypt so quickly that the bread had no time to rise. Why isn't more attention focused towards the actual event of the Exodus rather than the speed with which this event occurred?

An answer is given by the former *Mashgiach* of the Chevron Yeshiva, in his *sefer Ohr Yahel*. During the final days of the Egyptian exile, the Jews had already sunk to the forty-ninth level of *tumah* – spiritual impurity. The Jews, having been rushed out of Egypt made it "just in time," for had they tarried a few hours longer they would have sunk to the fiftieth level and would never have been redeemed from Egypt. These crucial few moments made the difference between slavery and freedom, between receiving and not receiving the Torah. These few moments were the most important period of time that they had ever encountered. Their entire history would have changed because of a few short moments. They would have remained in Egypt, eventually assimilating. The Jewish nation would have been totally lost from the face of the Earth. This is the message of the *matzoh* – a few extra moments would also have made the dough rise. However, since the *Bnei Yisroel* hurried, the dough did not have a chance to rise and therefore remained *matzoh*. Hence, because the *matzoh* symbolizes the crucial element of salvation from the exile in Egypt, we focus much of our attention and time discussing it.

Time is a commodity that must not be wasted or misused. One should not rationalize when he pushes off important activities to the next day. One never knows what may arise to prevent him from achieving his goals and must therefore be cognizant of the importance of time.

Shavuos

In loving memory of our mother

Jeanette Levine
Chaya Yachet Elka bas R' Yisroel Yitzchak

In her lifetime she taught us valuable Torah lessons that will continue to keep her memory alive through her children grandchildren and imy'h great-grandchildren.

Mr. and Mrs. Ari Sipper

I. A Living Entity

As we move closer to Shavuos, each day is like a precious coin needed in order to acquire the Torah. This is why we count *up* to Shavuos instead of counting down.

One of the most central *middos* needed to acquire the Torah is found in the beginning of *Parashas* Bechukosai.

Parshas Bechukosai begins, *"Im b'chukosai teileichu* – If you will go in the ways of my laws." *Rashi* explains that it cannot be referring to doing the *mitzvos*, as that is the next part of the *posuk*. Rather, *Rashi* says, it means, *"Shetihiyu ameilim b'Torah* – You should toil in Torah."

One has to realize that Torah knowledge is unlike any other knowledge in the world. It is not a law book or blueprint to holiness; it is a *metziyus* – a living entity. That is why the *Gemorah* in *Megillah* says, *"Yagati v'matzasi* – I worked and I found." Even after hard work, it is like something you have found. True understanding is a gift from Hashem.

Part of the explanation for this is the statement, *"Yisroel v'Oraisa v'Kudsha B'rich Hu chad hu."* On a deep level, *Yisroel*, the Torah, and Hashem are one. This is how the *Ovos* and *Imahos* were able to know the Torah even without having anyone to teach it to them.

This was not just a phenomenon in the "old days." Rather, this was seen in the *baal teshuva* movement in Russia during the 1980s. The underground Yeshivas were in need of *Rabbeim* and a rotation of *Magidei Shiur* would go to Russia for two-week periods to teach, almost nonstop.

Rabbi Ezra Hartman related upon returning from one of his trips how amazed he was at the high level of understanding these *baalei teshuva* had. They were constantly being *mechavin* to the *svaros* and *peshatim* of Rabbi Akiva Eiger, Rav Elchonon Wasserman, Rav Shimon Shkop and other *Gedolim*. It was a mystery to him until the following episode occurred.

One of the *baalei teshuva* asked him the following *halachic* question. In order to learn his regular session, which was eight hours straight, he would do certain exercises first. One of those exercises was to stand on his head for five minutes. He was afraid to waste all that time, so he wanted to know if it was appropriate to learn *Mishnayos* by heart, or if it was not the proper *kovod haTorah* to do so.

Rav Hartman said that at that point, he finally understood. It was their great *ameilus baTorah* which caused Hashem to reveal to them so much of His Torah.

Silver Donors

Dr. & Mrs. Moishe Jeger

In memory of Yehoshua ben Avraham, Avraham
Yehudah ben Ezriel, Breindel bas Yisroel Aryeh

Rabbi and Mrs.
Naftali and Carol Kalter

In memory of our dear son
R' Yosef z"l ben R' Naftoli Shimon Hakohen

Leah and Avi Reichman

In honor of Chaim and Samantha who are true
role models of what it means to be a good friend.

Mr. and Mrs. David Korros

In honor of our children and grandchildren.

Silver Donors

Dr. and Mrs. Ira Krumholtz
Dedicated to all the rebbeim of YTC on behalf of our son Shimmy.

Ari Zeltzer
Dedicated as an ilui neshama, for my great aunts Hannah Spiro (Hannah bas Avraham) and Flora Kaplan (Flora bas Avraham)
May their memory be for a blessing.

In honor of Dr. Allan Jacob.
Your brilliant editing, critical thinking, and depth of Torah knowledge made you an irreplaceable mentor throughout the Mussar Haskel project.
~The Inaugural Mussar Haskel Team

Bronze Donors

Rabbi & Mrs. Yitzchak Berkowitz

Rafi Fertig

Yaakov Goldenberg

Tzvi Hertzberg

Ahron Levy

Chanan Mayerhoff

Moshe Leib and Atara Miller

Avrohom Eliezer Niman

Yehuda Palgon

Meir Peikes

Jonathan Rosenblum

Roy Sasson

Moshe Vatch

Simcha Vatch